Ideal
and
Actual
in
The
Story
of
the
Stone

Ideal
and
Actual
in
The
Story
of
the
Stone

Dore J. Levy

NEW YORK
COLUMBIA UNIVERSITY PRESS

Columbia University Press
Publishers Since 1893
New York   Chichester, West Sussex
Copyright © 1999 Columbia University Press
All rights reserved

Library of Congress Cataloging-in-Publication Data
Levy, Dore Jesse.
   Ideal and actual in the story of the stone / Dore J. Levy.
      p.   cm.
   Includes bibliographical references and index.
   ISBN 0-221-11406-0. — ISBN 0-231-11407-9 (pbk.)
   1. Ts'ao, Hsüeh-ch'in, ca. 1717-1763.—Hung lou meng. 2. China—
Social life and customs—1644-1912. I. Title.
PL2727.S2L47   1999
895.1'348—dc21   98-44246

∞

Casebound editions of Columbia University Press books are printed on
permanent and durable acid-free paper.
Designed by Chang Jae Lee
Printed in the United States of America
c 10 9 8 7 6 5 4 3 2 1
p 10 9 8 7 6 5 4 3 2 1

For Hsiao-lan and Fritz, with love

CONTENTS

ACKNOWLEDGMENTS
IX

INTRODUCTION
I

1. IDEAL AND ACTUAL, REAL AND NOT-REAL
7

2. "FAMILY TOGETHERNESS"
Patterns of Authority and the Subversion of Family Structure
27

3. PREEXISTING CONDITIONS
Retributory Illness and the Limits of Medicine
67

4. A WORLD APART
Poetry and Society in the Garden of Total Vision
103

5. THE CHIMING OF THE VOID
Poetry as a Vehicle to Enlightenment
139

NOTES
157

GLOSSARY
183

BIBLIOGRAPHY
191

INDEX
207

ACKNOWLEDGMENTS

At every stage of research and writing of this book, I have enjoyed the enthusiastic support of students, colleagues, friends, and family. Without them I could not have imagined, let alone completed, this study.

The manuscript was written at The Institute for Advanced Study, where I was a Member of the School of Historical Studies in 1996–1997. I am happy to express my gratitude to the Director and the Faculty of the Institute for this unique opportunity for study and intellectual exchange, in the publication of the project completed in their company. I thank Robert Fagles and Andrew H. Plaks for their confidence in my project proposal. Giles Constable and Patricia Wolf reassured me as to the accessibility and interest of my analysis. I was also encouraged by Oleg Grabar, Irving and Marilyn Lavin, and Joan Scott at crucial points of my research. Many of my fellow members also supported me with their frank enthusiasm, especially Deborah Klimberg-Salter, Harry Liebersohn, David Nirenberg, and Charlotte Schoell-Glass. Marian Zelazny and Dorothy David made all the practical aspects of my stay seem effortless.

As early as 1990–1991, a grant for independent research from the National Endowment for the Humanities allowed me to turn to Chinese fiction and begin forming the interpretative model for this study. Professor Kathryn Spoehr, Dean of the Faculty at Brown University, encouraged me throughout and arranged for a generous subvention for the publication of this book.

Many offered their suggestions, guidance, and much patient listening. A conversation with Yu-kung Kao is always a source of enlightenment, with or without poetry. Perry Link offered a voice of reason and a vote of absolute confidence. Nicola di Cosmo, Wai-yee Li, Hsien-hao Liao, Earl Miner, Susan Naquin, and Fusheng Wu confirmed the need for a multidisciplinary study of *The Story of the Stone*, and seemed certain I could write one. The friendship and confidence of Charles Hartman have been an inspiration to me throughout my career, and his keen suggestions at all stages have been invaluable. I also wish to thank Maxine

Weinstein, a colleague and friend whose warmth and intellectual breadth embraced all the issues of my study.

At Brown University, many friends read my manuscript and agreed that *The Story of the Stone* should be part of *any* literary education, East or West: Edward Ahearn, Nancy Armstrong, Michel-André Bossy, Jerome Grieder, Laura Hess, David Lattimore, Karen Newman, Hal Roth, Newell Stultz, and Ann and Arnold Weinstein. Maggie Bickford cut through layers of vagueness whenever she caught me waffling, and directed the hunt for a cover illustration. Siu-leung Li offered penetrating observations on matters of literary theory and helped me with many details on Chinese drama. Chieh-fang Ou Lee was a fountain of information on so many of the details that give *The Story of the Stone* its resonance, but that we are now in danger of losing forever.

My students inspired me to write a general study, and many of them assisted me in aspects of the research and by reading the manuscript to offer suggestions and note essential gaps: Jonathan Ansfield, Gary Brichkov, Luying Chen, Jack Chiueh, Neil Hausmann, Gary Lazarus, Johanna Massé, Jubin Meraj, Andrew Schonebaum, and Emily Wages. At Harvard University, Jack Chen chased references for me just for the fun of it.

Special thanks are due to Ann Hudson Jones, Robert Nelsen, Jeffrey Perl, Suzanne Poirer, and Richard Selzer for their interest and encouragement.

Jill Martin of Penguin Books Ltd. arranged for permission to quote extensively from *The Story of the Stone*.

I am grateful to two anonymous readers for Columbia University Press for their deep engagement with the novel, which has so benefited my understanding of it. Jennifer Crewe, Publisher for the Humanities, more than matched my enthusiasm for the project in every aspect. At the Press, I have been privileged to work with Anne McCoy, Leslie Kriesel, Debra Soled, and Chang Jae Lee, who have made the preparations for publication a pleasure. These people have done their best to educate and to correct me; the errors that remain are mine alone.

The Story of the Stone has been a household presence for quite some time now. My husband, James Trilling, read and edited every version and endured endless harangues on arcane points of interpretation. He insisted on the cohesiveness of the analysis and profoundly influenced my sense of the text's deep humanity. My daughters Gabriel and Julian met the upheavals brought into their lives with great patience and good cheer. My mother and father have also been constant companions in understanding, reading the manuscript, arguing the analysis, and coming up with the *mot juste*.

From my earliest studies of China, indeed, from nearly my earliest childhood, F. W. Mote and Ch'en Hsiao-lan have filled my life with the love of China and inspired my faith in the transcendent power of the humanities. Their wisdom and sense of life have shaped my imagination of art and its power. Without them, I could never have conceived this study, let alone achieved the sense of China preserved, living, in *The Story of the Stone*. This book is only a small token of my gratitude.

D.J.L.
Providence, Rhode Island

Ideal
and
Actual
in
The
Story
of
the
Stone

The Story of the Stone, by Cao Xueqin (1715?–1763), is the most highly esteemed work of prose fiction in the Chinese tradition.[1] A mammoth narrative of 120 chapters, it is admired both for its realistic depiction of the life of the Chinese nobility during the Qing dynasty (1644–1911) and for its thoroughly romantic vision of personal relations. Furthermore, *The Story of the Stone* is widely regarded as a roman à clef, weaving elements and individuals of the author's personal history into his larger vision of the world.

There are as many readings of *The Story of the Stone* as there are readers. The novel, which is regarded as an embodiment not only of the Qing dynasty at its zenith but of Chinese culture as a whole, is now finding its place in cultures distant from China. With one book, the genius of Cao Xueqin proves to have the universality of Shakespeare. Its combination of intellectual scope and immediate human drama has no counterpart in Western fiction. To appreciate its position in Chinese culture, we must imagine a work with the critical cachet of James Joyce's *Ulysses* and the popular appeal of Margaret Mitchell's *Gone with the Wind*—and twice as long as the two combined.

Part of the appeal of *The Story of the Stone* is its magical beginning and the variety and opulence of the world the reader enters through the gateway of the Land of Illusion in the first chapter. Another part of its appeal is a cast of characters so varied, vital, and engaging that the reader is moved by the least of them. Yet another part of its appeal is that the tale itself holds out a brilliant hope of spiritual transcendence, while vibrating with pity for those caught in the coil of mortal existence.

On one level, the author's genius is so encompassing that the readers' full participation seems inevitable: No analytical explanation is needed, and none will serve. On another level, the analysis of style and technique can bring us closer to an understanding of how he achieved his goals. *The Story of the Stone* combines two modes of expression in Chinese poetics—the vicarious mode of narrative experience and the integrative mode of lyrical experience—with unique success.[2] Since the Chinese literary tradition is primarily lyric, narrative in poetry and prose has distinct characteristics derived from the principles of lyric aesthetics.[3] *The Story of the Stone* presents a poetic view of life, written so that the reader experiences the narrative in the way that one experiences lyric poetry. The plot is organized not as a unified, dynamic temporal sequence but as a sequence of lyric vignettes, each potentially a complete moment of insight beyond *self*-awareness, when the self is laid aside and integrated with the moment in a state of lyric transcendence. In sequence, these vignettes further integrate the reader into the fictional world, in all its emotion and intelligence.[4]

In reductive terms, the novel follows the career of the Stone in his quest for enlightenment through the experience of a human life. In this task, the text ranges over all human experience. The overriding frame of the story favors transcendence and provides reader and characters with two *genii loci*, the lame Taoist Mysterioso (*Mangmang dashi*) and the scabby-headed Buddhist monk Impervioso (*Miaomiao zhenren*), who arrange for souls in need of awakening to be incarnated and act as protecting godfathers when the path to liberation bogs down. While Taoist vitalism and Buddhist nihilism are analytically incompatible notions, the partnership of this eccentric pair points to the irony that, in the world of *The Story of the Stone,* they are mutually reinforcing. In Cao Xueqin's day, distinctions between these schools of thought were recognized, but notions of transcendence and escape from the bonds of material existence originally associated with Buddhism had passed into popular culture. Even Confucian thinkers accepted some Buddhist notions of transcendence through intellectual means, though not the practice of retiring from society to seek individual liberation.

The presence of the Taoist, the Buddhist, and several others of their mysterious colleagues—not to mention the exemplary wisdom expressed by certain ordinary human characters—emphasize that in *The Story of the Stone* hard distinctions among the three sectarian teachings are not so much unimportant as beside the point. This does not mean that the teachings were not profound or distinctive; doctrine and scholasticism were always available for those who sought them, but popular notions of vehicles to enlightenment were inclusive. The devout and spiritually aware practitioner could apprehend the Buddha or the nature of the Void through the least object, as a devout Christian might have insight into the encompassing nature of God through the last piece of tinsel on a spent Christmas tree.

The protagonist of *The Story of the Stone*, the boy Jia Bao-yu, ultimately takes a Buddhist path to liberation. In the world of his incarnation, however, Buddhist or Taoist transcendence is not privileged over Confucian ethics. In the novel, Buddhism may seem spiritually superior by virtue of its professed detachment from the mundane world, but those who rigorously disdain their social, and, especially, their familial obligations are targets of severe criticism. Confucianism in principle emphasizes social and familial responsibility and support but, in practice, can stifle spirituality with empty forms and over-whelming obligations. A good deal of the intellectual and emotional complexity of the text derives from the sense of conflict between the ideals held out by *any* mode of belief and the actual vicissitudes of try-ing to conduct a life in accordance with those ideals. *The Story of the Stone* is not Buddhist, Taoist, or Confucian: It is all, simultaneously and all the time, and as such is an authentic embodiment of eighteenth-century Chinese culture.

Because *The Story of the Stone* ranges over all human experience, there is something for everyone in the text. Yet it is underread, certain-ly outside China, probably in China too. Why? The text is long, but that in itself should not be a barrier. The first chapter, glittering with magi-cal beings and mystical pronouncements, can daunt a reader who ex-pects a realistic romance or social document. The main problem, I sus-pect, is the inevitable cultural loss that must occur when a work of art becomes distant in time and is by nature distant in culture. The major challenge for a comparativist is to understand the internalized assump-tions of one culture and articulate them in terms of another. Distance in time complicates the task. For Western readers of Chinese fiction, the unfamiliar mode of discourse is a further problem. The Western narra-tive tradition, deriving as it does from epic poetry, is plot-driven and tele-ological, whereas Chinese narrative proceeds by a succession of lyric tableaux. Each tableau functions primarily by persuading the reader to lay aside the sense of self and time and only secondarily by integrating this moment of experience into the larger temporal sequence of the narrative.[5] No one moment, or kind of experience, is intrinsically more significant than any other: All hold out equally the potential for literary and social insight and spiritual transcendence.

In this sense, the Chinese mode of narrative composition is ideally mated to the transcendental ideals of this novel. The experiences are equivalent. When we read *The Story of the Stone*, the vignettes in it that associate themselves in our minds, glinting in the vast landscape of the novel, are in principle co-spatial, co-thematic, and equipollent: equal in power and significance.[6]

This in itself can be a challenge to Western readers. The significance of events is not conveyed so much by their place in the narrative flow of the novel as associatively. An event that seems trivial in itself assumes the same value as obvious life events: a tile exchanged in a drinking game becomes a betrothal; an oaf's crude ditty is as weighty a guide to the vanity of existence as an immortal's long verse. This vignettism, by virtue of the potential equipollence of all events, is a paradigm not only for the kind of Buddhist enlightenment detailed in the novel but for the Chinese way of reading narrative as well.

No wonder a new reader may find *The Story of the Stone* hard to follow! And so rich is the text that, even after years of study and enjoyment, a reader will find it ever transforming. The world presented in it, once entered, is one to be experienced at will, in all its pleasure and heartache. It is also a world that, once entered, is almost impossible to leave.

Although this book is intended as an introduction for first-time readers of *The Story of the Stone*, the method of analysis detailed in the first chapter should suggest new ways for more advanced students and scholars to approach the text. There is only one way to embark on such an enterprise: with diffidence. *The Story of the Stone* is a recognized scholarly field (called *hongxue*, or *Dream of the Red Chamber* studies), with its own history and specialist journals, like Dante or Shakespeare studies in the West. The surge of interest in traditional Chinese fiction over the past few decades has made available to specialists many learned and fascinating studies. I hope to provide a bridge between the awakening of general interest and the more detailed study of particular aspects of Cao Xueqin's masterpiece.

The overriding, structuring image of the world in the novel is the garden, which becomes its center. The novel itself is like a garden, and a large one, since the reader may take first one path, then another, and always come upon something fresh with every change of season or direction. In this study I offer readers several walks in the garden, walks that I have taken but that are by no means the only ways to experience the text. Some landmarks that I have found essential in every promenade: the narrative frame of the Land of Illusion; Bao-yu's cardinal dream in chapter 5 (surely the greatest wet dream in world literature); the career of the Jias' mirror family, the Zhens of Nan-jing. These I discuss in chapter 1, but I refer to them in every chapter as they bind the narrative together.

My principle method of investigation is the same in all the following chapters: to select a theme or topos and follow it through the whole novel. The disciplinary focus of each chapter, however, is different. Chapter 2 investigates the inversion of ideal patterns of family conduct in the Jia household, its impact on the characters, and its significance as social criticism. Chapter 3 studies the role of medicine, especially the problem of retributory illness (*yuannie zhi zheng*)—illness with its etiology in a previous existence and so bearing upon a character's progress to spiritual emancipation in the present life. Chapter 4 treats poetry as an implement of social intercourse, especially among the inhabitants of the garden. Chapter 5 also investigates poetry, but as a direct vehicle of epiphany, a sudden guide to spiritual liberation.

In choosing these paths, I am all too aware of the paths not taken: the role of popular literature in the narrative; witchcraft and superstition; mysticism; the interweaving of Chinese and Manchu custom and belief; the life of the servants as shadows of the masters; foreign, especially European objects in use and imagination; food—there are always new prospects to be visited. My greatest hope is to encourage readers of *The Story of the Stone* to find their own way.

My overall method, the investigation of the relation of ideal and actual patterns, is based on a model from the social sciences but extends to every aspect of human experience, even transcendence of that experience. As a tool of literary analysis, it illuminates the irony essential to the novel as a genre.[7] It also illuminates the pathos and irony of human experience that is the ultimate subject, and object, of *The Story of the Stone*. The author reaches over time and culture to bring us into his world and gives us, through moments of insight into the experience of others, a sense of the possibility of transcendence, if not transcendence itself.

IDEAL AND ACTUAL, REAL AND NOT-REAL

We know rather little about Cao Xueqin's life. Various texts of the novel have the detailed and penetrating commentary of two critics who worked with the author through its long composition, and who were intimately associated with him from childhood. We are not sure of their relationship and know them only by their sobriquets "Red Inkstone" (*Zhiyan zhai*) and "Odd Tablet" (*Jihu sou*). Not only did they recognize Cao's world, its characters, and even its tiniest objects, but their advice and support were essential to him as he struggled to realize his artistic vision and purpose.[1]

Cao Xueqin appeared to have a complete draft several years before his death, but only the first eighty chapters are regarded as complete. The last forty, while following his intentions, were reconstructed from fragmentary texts by enthusiasts of a generation later, a writer of sample examination essays and poetry named Gao E (1740?–1815?) and an editor and bookseller named Cheng Wei-yuan (1747?–?). Critics passionately debate the authenticity of the last forty chapters. The question of how much extant text was in Gao E's hands, and how much he preserved or deformed, affects the interpretation of the novel as a whole. In this study *The Story of the Stone* is treated as a text of 120 chapters. The many textual difficulties of the last third of the novel create challenges for the reader, but they do not invalidate this part of the narrative.[2]

But *The Story of the Stone* is neither an autobiography nor just a social novel. The large narrative work as self-conscious cultural compendium is an ancient ideal in Chinese literature. Works of historiography, even before the *Records of the Historian* (Shi ji) of Sima Qian (144–90 B.C.), were compiled as representations of all notable deeds and events, doctrines, and ideals and thus were literary embodiments of the culture. Prose fiction derived much of its narrative technique from historiography and, in many instances, aspired to assume its scope as well.[3] The fact that this novel also embraces lyrical experience demonstrates the distinctive aesthetics governing the genre of prose fiction in the Chinese tradition.

Of all works of Chinese fiction, *The Story of the Stone* is the most comprehensive, and not just on the level of incidental detail. In the words of Andrew H. Plaks, "the work stands in its own cultural milieu . . . as an encyclopedic compendium of an entire tradition in a form that itself serves as a model against which to judge works of less imposing stature."[4] It is also an allegory of romantic love and spiritual transcendence and a complex exploration of the nature of existence and the function of art. The novel operates simultaneously in the empirical and cosmic realms of existence, and the metaphysical detail in it is as abundant as physical detail. Indeed, everything in the material world is material to the exegesis of the text. If a compendium implies the inclusion within small compass of a large subject or system, the larger subject of *The Story of the Stone* is life itself.

The novel focuses on the Jia family, originally from the city of Nanjing, which owes its status to the favor won by two glorious ancestors for outstanding service to their Manchu overlords. Although the temporal setting is not specified, it can be inferred from many details, including the structure of the imperial household, titles of princes and other officials, the geography of the capital city, and descriptions of the public aspect of social rituals.[5] During the Qing dynasty, members of the Chinese aristocracy could attain vast wealth and influence, yet they remained subject to the absolute authority of the ruling Manchus. The two Jia brothers received patents of nobility with the rank of duke (*gong*) and established their family compounds, the Ning-guo House of the older brother and the Rong-guo House of the younger brother, next door to each other in the vicinity of the imperial palace in Bei-jing.[6] Succeeding generations of Jia males are less successful, and the family fortunes both social and financial are definitely in decline. Tracing the Jias' collapse in the present generation, the novel sweeps from environments of unimaginable wealth, privilege, and refinement to the dregs and extremities of Chinese society.

The author's choice of a wealthy, extended family as the key structure of his narrative pays homage to the essential Confucian concept of the family as microcosm of the state. Confucian ideas of political structure depend on the family unit as its basis. According to Confucius, the ruler stands in relation to his subjects as a father to his children. If he acts in accordance with this ideal, his subjects will naturally respond with the passionate filial loyalty considered intrinsic to the human character, and all will be well in his domain. If problems arise, it is incumbent upon the ruler to rectify matters in the state as a father should in his own household, noble or humble. In the case of the Jia family, this model of filial relationship is complicated by the fact that the Jias themselves are Chinese bondservants to the Qing emperor, as was the author's own family. It is not that even the richest and most powerful Chinese nobles ever felt themselves to be near-equals of the emperor, but that under a native dynasty all the emperor's subjects were part of the same pyramid of power. Under the Manchus, there was a fundamental distinction, ruthlessly maintained, between the emperor and his trusted entourage, on the one hand, and the overwhelming majority of his subjects, on the other. When a son of the Jia household wears his hair elaborately braided into a queue (*bian*) fastened with half a dozen jeweled and gold clasps, the fact that he wears the queue in the first place is a sign of his subjugation to the Manchus.[7]

The fortunes of the Ning-guo and Rong-guo Houses reflect the precariousness of the existence of such Chinese families under a foreign dynasty and implicitly form a critique of that dynasty's rule. Although members of the Jia family extravagantly express their fealty to the emperor, their security is not guaranteed. Chinese in such positions of hereditary servitude enjoyed unusual privileges of access to and intimacy with the imperial household, but their existence could and often did change at the whim of their Manchu rulers. While the Jias' ultimate debacle is blamed on the failure of their elders to govern their own household well, the cataclysm that rips through the Ning-guo and Rong-guo Houses seems more like a natural disaster than the result of due process of law.[8]

To enter the world of the Jia family, the reader must step through a narrative frame set in a mystical realm called the Land of Illusion (*Taixu huanjing*). The Land of Illusion is a spiritual realm whose denizens have completely internalized the mystical doctrine of the unreality of worldly, particularly emotional, attachment (*qing*). *Qing* comprises and is generated by every stimulus that connects a person to the world and frustrates attempts to transcend it. Anthony C. Yu has translated *qing* as "desire," in a profound discussion detailing the cultural and spiritual manifestations of the term and linking this inclusive Chinese concept with a suggestive Western counterpart. His disquisition, however, is focused on *qing* as a concept and force in traditional Chinese culture, but without emphasis on the Buddhist implications that are so crucial to the narrative as a vehicle to enlightenment.[9] Because the narrative privileges Buddhist paths to liberation, at least for the protagonists, I prefer to translate *qing* as "attachment." "Desire," especially as used in comparative literary criticism, is appetitive, dynamic, and goal-oriented; whereas *qing*-as-attachment is more encompassing. Romantic and sexual desire are certainly important, even paramount, but they are not the only form of emotional connection implied.[10]

The object of *qing* is *se*, in some contexts rendered as "sex," but here the universe of material shape and form: the world our deluded senses perceive, giving rise to the impediments of attachment. This doctrine is essential both to Buddhism and Taoism as practiced in eighteenth-century China. The Taoist notion of the cyclical nature of existence and the insubstantiality of life was syncretized with Buddhist notions of transmigration and progress toward enlightenment, which meant liberation from *samsara,* or the cycle of rebirth and transcendence of material existence.[11]

In the Land of Illusion, under Greensickness Peak (*Qinggeng feng*), stands the Stone of the title (*SS* I.1.47). The name of the spot is literally "Green-ridge Peak," but here it has been translated by David Hawkes with reference to its near-homophonous pun, *qinggen*, "the root of [emotional] attachment." "Greensickness" is a disorder thought to be caused by lovesickness, the distraction of unfulfilled romantic longing and sexual desire.[12] That the Stone should have come to rest in this place signals that his career has been formed by entering into the illusion of romantic attachment; in other words, the physical inscription of the text on the Stone is the Stone's own account of his experience of *qing*/attachment. What the reader must realize is that attachment in *any* form is illusion and that liberation from attachment can come only through *dis*-illusion.

This Stone was originally made by the goddess Nü-wa during large-scale operations to repair a hole in the sky. For some reason he (the Stone is explicitly identified as male) was left over and discarded when the job was finished. As a magical object, the Stone had consciousness and therefore was full of restless disaffection, feeling his existence to be without purpose. He wandered about the Land of Illusion until he found the Crimson Pearl Flower (*Jiangzhu xiancao*). The Stone was so entranced by its beauty that he took to watering it daily with sweet dew (*ganlu*), which eventually transformed the Flower into a fairy girl. The sense of her obligation to the Stone weighed upon her mind, until finally she decided that the only way she could repay her benefactor would be to submit to a lifetime of suffering in the mortal world, where she could repay her debt, drop for drop, in tears.

The agents of the Stone's disillusionment and the Flower's payment of her debt of tears (*huanlei*) are the lame Taoist Mysterioso and the scabby-headed Buddhist monk Impervioso. When they meet the Stone, they agree to carve some mystical words on him and arrange for his incarnation as a human boy. The Stone needs to be liberated from two delusions that block his spiritual emancipation. The first is his feeling of rejection from Nü-wa's sky repairs because of some imagined defect. The second is his romantic attachment to the Crimson Pearl Flower. The purpose of sending him to experience the vicissitudes of a human life is to awaken him not only to the emptiness of the mundane world of emotional—especially romantic—attachment but also to the emptiness of longing itself.

When the story opens, the Stone under Greensickness Peak has in fact already completed his extension course in the "world of the red dust" (*hongchen shi*, i.e., the mundane world, especially the mortal realm of human affairs) and returned to his proper place in the universe. He has already lived a lifetime as the main character of *The Story of the Stone*, Jia Bao-yu, and achieved enlightenment by experiencing the passions of a mortal existence and awakening to their futility. Moreover, he has inscribed upon his own stone self a complete record of his experiences as a benighted mortal, to be read by anyone who would achieve enlightenment—in fact, the very text in the reader's own hands. Engaging in a philosophical and aesthetic argument with the Taoist adept Vanitas (*Kongkong daoren*), the Stone communicates the essential features of the experience leading to his enlightenment and invites him to read the inscription. Upon the first reading, Vanitas is unable to grasp its potential as a spiritual vehicle. The Stone admonishes him that his error is in reading his account as a book like other books and assuming the experience to be inauthentic because it is *vicarious*.[13] The Stone asserts that his story is unique because it is *authentic*: A reader who suspends disbelief will have exactly the same experience, but through reading rather than living the historical life. This is precisely what happens when Vanitas reads it through for the second time:

> As a consequence of all this, Vanitas, *starting off in the Void (which is Truth) came to the contemplation of Form (which is Illusion); and from Form engendered Passion; and by communicating Passion, entered again into Form; and from Form awoke to the Void (which is Truth).* He therefore changed his name from Vanitas to Brother Amor, or the Passionate Monk (because he had approached Truth by way of Passion).
>
> (*SS* I.1.51, *HLM* I.1.3, italics added)

In a mere sixteen characters (the parenthetical phrases were inserted by Hawkes), the author lays out the novel's emphasis on passion and experience as a vehicle for awakening to their vanity. It is a summary of the Buddhist process of enlightenment, which, according to the Stone, the reader can follow just by reading *The Story of the Stone*. The key terms—"void/truth" (*kong*), "form" (*se*), "passion" (or, as I have rendered it, "attachment," *qing*)—point to the nature of illusion itself. When the Taoist Vanitas changes his identity and faith by renaming himself Brother Amor (*Qing seng*, "the Passionate [Buddhist] Monk"), he acknowledges that the novel has proved an effective vehicle to enlightenment.[14] Its method? The text is so evocatively real that it provides objects of attachment to enlighten its readers as to the vanity of attachment and existence.[15] It is not a question of confusion on Vanitas's/Brother Amor's part or even a privileging of one vehicle to liberation over another. Distinctions between Taoist and Buddhist doctrines are neither substantively nor analytically important; in the realm of transcendence, these identities are as illusory as any other object of mind.

The process of enlightenment described by Brother Amor, namely reaching enlightenment through passion and experience, is the grand strategy of *The Story of the Stone*. When he first read the novel, Vanitas's delusion lay in his attachment to the characters and world of the Stone's experience. In Cao Xueqin's scheme of things, this is just as empty, just as illusory, as sexual desire, maternal love, or pity. By capturing not only the essence but the details of real life, it functions as a substitute for real life. And not just any life, but one in which the tides of desire and experience have been shown to lead to spiritual liberation. A second reading persuades Vanitas that he had actually fallen into the trap of attachment by reading the novel, until the narrative rescued him. His conversion to Buddhism is therefore a sign that he understands his previous "enlightenment" was illusory, as it was not grounded in experience of form and passion.

The Stone's incarnation as Jia Bao-yu, then, is not random. In order for him to fulfill his cosmic imperatives, the Stone needs an environment in which he can be exposed to the full range of emotional attachment and social aspiration. In fact, by virtue of his cosmic origin, the boy that the Stone becomes exists simultaneously on the mundane and transcendent planes—two different "worlds" within the unitary cosmos. Bao-yu is oblivious to this, but throughout the book the reader is reminded that, as the incarnation of the Stone, he has two full existences, until he achieves enlightenment and realizes that the two are one.

In this particular family, with all its privileges, pitfalls, and flaws, the boy Bao-yu will have his chance to fulfill the Stone's destiny. For readers plunging into this world, the process of attachment also begins—to the characters, to the plot, to the beauty and luxury of the place, to the nostalgia of time gone by. The sheer variety and magnificence of this environment are seduction enough to distract us from remembering its ultimate unreality.

Bao-yu is a boy born, it would seem, to resuscitate the family's former glory. He arrives in the world with a beautiful piece of jade (for which he is named—Bao-yu means "precious jade") in his mouth. The family takes this miracle as a sign that he is destined for great worldly success. In fact, it is a symbol of Bao-yu's origin as the Stone. In his human avatar no one, not even Bao-yu himself, can know what the jade *really* is. It is a tenet of Buddhist reincarnation that one can have no knowledge or memory of one's personal karma, the cumulative experience of previous lives that determines the rebirth and experience of the present life. Although Bao-yu's previous existence is the essence of his being, he has no access to it. Once in a while his "karmic amnesia" is jogged by a sense of déjà vu, but no illumination can come from that source.

As Bao-yu, the Stone has come "down" a step on the ladder of spiritual attainment. To become a human boy after being a magical stone in the realm of the immortals is definitely a demotion. As a human boy, the Stone will engage the illusion of his love for the Crimson Pearl Flower, incarnated in the Jia household as Bao-yu's incomparably beautiful, brilliant, and temperamental cousin, Lin Dai-yu. His love for her is reciprocated, but the course of true love does not run smooth. The Flower as Dai-yu cannot possibly fulfill her debt of tears if she finds fulfillment in love. How this drama plays out is the heart of the novel. The process of detachment at the heart of Buddhist enlightenment is a dynamic one, driven by emotion.[16] Unless the illusions that cloud human perception are powerfully challenged by adversity and loss, transcendence is blocked. It is only by experiencing the agony of attachment that one can realize its futility.

The mundane world of Bao-yu and Dai-yu continually evokes and intersects with the metaphysical world of the Stone and the Flower. Although an unenlightened being has, by definition, no conscious memory of a past life, the cousins do seem to "recognize" each other on their first meeting: Dai-yu finds Bao-yu "extraordinarily familiar," while Bao-yu asserts positively "I have seen this cousin before" (*SS* I.3.101, 103, *HLM*

I.3.29–30). Responding to this sense of affinity, Bao-yu asks Dai-yu if she has a jade to match his.[17] His jade has marked him from birth as different from other children, and he is frantically disappointed when she responds in the negative. But Bao-yu has asked Dai-yu the wrong question. They were the perfect match in the Court of Sunset Glow, the Stone and the Flower. The match for the earthly jade, however, is not jade (*yu*, the second character in both their names), but gold (*jin*), in the person of Bao-yu's and Dai-yu's cousin, Xue Bao-chai. From almost her first introduction, Bao-chai is Dai-yu's natural rival on every level: in beauty, in intellect, in family status. To Dai-yu's horror, she has a golden locket with an inscription that matches Bao-yu's jade perfectly. The imperatives of his present life will propel Bao-yu inexorably toward this match, the "affinity of gold and jade" (*jinyu yinyuan*).[18]

In a sense, the fates of all the characters in *The Story of the Stone* turn on the overpowering doctrine and metaphor of karma as a refuge from the ironies and frustrations of an individual's experience. Aspects of human existence that resist or even defy rational explanation are susceptible to explanation by causality and reincarnation. The Buddhist theory of karma, transmigration, and reincarnation is meant to encompass and rationalize the implications of causality. On the emotional level (and in the context of this narrative), it does not matter whether one is physically reincarnated, or not. It is the very notion of causality that is awesome. The understanding that the smallest, most thoughtless actions may have major consequences is a burden too great to bear. It seems unreasonable that the trivial actions of the present life might have such power, and produce such dire consequences, in the same lifetime. The cumulative force of many actions, over unknowable periods of time, makes more sense of momentous events. Because they have only one previous existence, Bao-yu and Dai-yu have entwined fates that are a simplified demonstration of the way karma plays out in everyday life, allowing us to understand how what seems an abstract force or principle actually shapes personalities, social interactions, and even physical attributes to fulfill their destinies.[19]

In chapter 1 of the novel, the narrator challenges the reader to appreciate the essential paradox of a *fictional* mundane world, which by definition cannot be "true" (*zhen*) or "false" (*jia*), "real" (*you*) or "not-real" (*wu*). Our guides to this world are two acquaintances, the unambitious scholar Zhen Shi-yin and his friend Jia Yu-cun, a young man determined to make a successful government career for himself. Zhen Shi-yin's name is a pun on the phrase "true matters concealed"; Jia Yu-cun's puns "false discourse." In a hazy dream, Zhen Shi-yin meets the Taoist and the Buddhist and gets a glimpse of the potential Bao-yu in the form of the jade with which the mortal boy will be born. The immortals leave Zhen Shi-yin suddenly under the gateway between the mundane world and the Land of Illusion, which is inscribed with this couplet:

> Truth becomes fiction when the fiction's true;
> Real becomes not-real where the unreal's real.
>
> (*SS* I.1.55, *HLM* I.1.5)

This is *the* signpost to transcendence and affects all levels of the book. The gateway presents the ultimate conundrum of the writing and experience of the novel. The paradox of the first line of the couplet pivots on the word for "time" (*shi*), the second on the word for "place" (*chu*). Truth and fiction interpenetrate in time, real and not-real in space. They appear together in a realm beyond either: "Truth becomes fiction *when* the fiction's true / Real becomes not-real *where* the unreal's real" (italics mine). There is every temptation to try to comprehend what this really means—to visualize, by mentally gazing at this inscription, the relation of truth and time, of reality and space, and the relation between these two relations. But the epiphany of the couplet is that the separation of these categories is illusory. Whatever the vehicle to enlightenment, when liberation is achieved the truth or fictionality, realness or not-realness of the vehicle—and the goal—evaporates.

The couplet therefore signifies not a hard and fast division between truth and falsity, reality and illusion, but the impossibility of making such distinctions in any world, fictional or "actual."[20] What is not quite clear from Zhen Shi-yin's dream is in which direction the sign is pointing—this way direct to the Land of Illusion? Or that way, through the mundane world? The gateway is like the paradoxical brain teaser where a card has inscribed on one side "The statement on the reverse of this card is true" and on the other side "The statement on the reverse of this card is false." If the "real" world is a wilderness of illusion, is the Land of Illusion a paradise of truth?

From the moment Zhen Shi-yin awakes, we are decisively in the mundane world. This world is meant to provide an accurate representation of quotidian existence, so rich in detail that, as the Stone / narrator warns, we fall into the same traps of attachment and delusion that he did and therefore, by reading the text, may have the same chances he did for transcendence through awakening to the vanity of attachment. Life in the world of the red dust contains within itself the very quality of unreality that, seen by the Stone's incarnation as one long series of losses and disillusionments, can produce the detachment necessary for transcendence.

Since the Stone's experience of the mundane world *is* his vehicle to enlightenment, the pairing of "real" and "not-real" must be translated to the lavishly detailed environment of the Jia household. In many studies of the novel, this translates into exhaustive, and exhausting, discussion of the biographical reality of details of the work of fiction—a manifestation of what Anthony C. Yu has called "the aesthetics of misplaced historicism."[21] Yü Ying-shih, in *"Honglou meng" de liangge shijie* (The Two Worlds of *The Dream of the Red Chamber*) jumped beyond biographical interpretations of *The Story of the Stone*, with their often over-ingenious attempts to locate biographically real persons, places, and events beneath the supposed camouflage of Cao Xueqin's writing.[22] His analysis draws the distinction between the two worlds of truth and fiction as they pertain to the characters, the reader, and the author. Yü's purpose was to restore invention both to the writer and to the text as a work of art, by associating "real" with "historically real" and "not-real" with "invented." He makes the crucial point that invention inevitably draws in some ways on a writer's awareness of reality, but is in no way limited by that reality. The author could freely imagine things and create persons and situations that completely transcend the limitations of his own biographical experience; moreover, he was not engaged in camouflaging real events for whatever reason. Yü is arguing for artistic freedom and a framework in which the themes of nostalgia and enlightenment support the novel as a work of art rather than just a puzzle obscurely keyed to his contemporary context.[23] His "two worlds" operate on two levels: On the artistic level there is a contrast between reality and imagination, while on the spiritual level the contrast is between "real" and "not-real." Both levels are essential to our appreciation of *The Story of the Stone*.

There is a further distinction to be made, however. Most characters in the novel itself do not see their daily lives as participating in the "real/not real" question. Their actions and responses relate to a more practical dichotomy, between *ideal* and *actual* patterns. This dichotomy is between two aspects of *reality*. By ideal patterns I mean social patterns that members of a society in general claim *should* obtain and even persuade themselves *do* obtain. Actual patterns are the ones that *do* obtain, and their significance lies in the extent to which they diverge from the ideal. Both the ideal and the actual affect the realities of a subject's life, with consequences that are entirely different from those in the "two worlds," the real and not-real, of *The Story of the Stone.*

The phrase "ideal and actual patterns" comes from a sociological model devised by Marion J. Levy Jr. for the analysis of family structure in general, and Chinese families in particular.[24] Levy's interest was in the scientific analysis of social patterns:

> This distinction [between ideal and actual patterns] is an ancient and an humble one, both in the general common sense of mankind and in the social sciences. It is so humble that we often tend to overlook the fact that some of our most general and useful theorems arise from applications of these concepts, e.g., 1) there are no people who do not distinguish between ideal and actual structures—regardless of their vocabularies; 2) in no society (or social system) do the ideal and actual structures coincide exactly; 3) some of the major sources of stress and strain characteristic of all societies (or social systems) inhere in the failure of the ideal and actual structures to coincide exactly; 4) some of the possibilities of integration and adjustment characteristic of these units inhere in the failure of the ideal and actual structures to coincide exactly (appearances to the contrary notwithstanding, this in not paradoxical when taken in connection with the preceding generalization); 5) the failure of the ideal and actual structures to coincide exactly for any society (or social system) as a whole is never explicable solely in terms of hypocrisy of the members of the system; and 6) exact coincidence of the two types of structures for any society (and probably for any social system as well) is forever out of the question for two reasons. The knowledge necessary would overload any probable cognitive mechanisms (in this case, those of human actors), and if there were not the cognitive problem stated, the perfect integration of systems of such coincidence would of necessity be highly brittle, leading to fracture of the general system by any change (including biological or geographical change) in the setting of the system concerned that had any implications whatever for actions in terms of the system.[25]

Levy goes on to explain that observations of social phenomena tend to be made in terms of ideal rather than actual patterns, and levels of social harmony are affected by how much coincidence individuals perceive between ideal and actual patterns. If ideals are seen as reasonable and perhaps attainable, there are high levels of social harmony.[26]

For our purposes, the great interest of the model is less in how a family like the Jias aspires to ideal patterns than in how far their family structure and organization falls short of the ideals to which it outwardly conforms. Sociologists tend to see ideal and actual patterns as existing on different planes, one abstract and one concrete. In *The Story of the Stone* they coexist, locked in a perpetual struggle that forms the underlying irony of the novel. Furthermore, this conflict is mapped out clearly and comprehensively on every level: personal, social, and spiritual. Subversion of authority is a fact of life in this world, yet the desire to adhere, or at least appear to adhere, to ideal patterns of conduct drives almost every character. These attempts are mocked as each actor finds that the task of living up to ideal patterns is a positive impediment to personal fulfillment. Depending on the individual's sensitivity, the gap between the patterns that should obtain and those that do obtain can be excruciating, even fatal.

Because of this conflict, "real" life contains a sense of its own unreality, which if one is so inclined can lead to *dis*-illusionment—literally, the shedding of illusions—and transcendence. This is the process followed by Vanitas as he translates himself into Brother Amor after reading the inscription for the second time. It is also the process followed by the novel's protagonist, Bao-yu. In an ideal Confucian world, social convention would not be a bar to personal fulfillment. Ideal patterns of conduct would be correct and beneficial by definition, promoting fulfillment through order, stability, and forbearance. This leaves no room for certain forms of individualistic behavior, notably romantic attachment, which lies outside the conventional mechanisms of betrothal and marriage.

In contrast, the author's notion of Buddhist transcendence favors romantic attachment as a source of conflict between the individual and society, and ultimately as a vehicle to enlightenment. This can almost be read as an enlargement of the old saying "fight poison with poison and fire with fire."[27] For a seeker of spiritual transcendence, disillusionment with the mundane imperatives of Confucian society provides a way to "fight the world with the world," and so achieve liberation. In the "actual" world of the novel, social convention and romantic fulfillment are perpetually at war, and their mutual hostility leaves plenty of room and opportunity for disillusionment, hence emancipation from the fetters of attachment that bind the individual to that world.

In Bao-yu's view, traditional Chinese social values are secondary to the elevation of sentiment and emotional attachment. Bao-yu's romanticism includes the idea that individualism and personal transcendence can be achieved only through opposition to social convention. What he does not understand is that his dissatisfaction with the patterns represented to him as ideal, and his struggle to transcend the actual patterns, will allow him to achieve enlightenment only when he becomes disillusioned with the idea of transcendence itself. In other words, when Bao-yu's romantic aspirations are systematically thwarted, rather than converting to ideals of social convention he chooses to disengage from society altogether.

In his prefatory remarks, Cao Xueqin explicitly states his wish to create a memorial *and* a vehicle for transcendence: "In this way the memorial to my beloved girls could at one and the same time serve as a source of harmless entertainment and as a warning to those who were in the same predicament as myself but who were still in need of awakening" (*SS* I.21, *HLM* I.1.1). When the "passionate monk" Brother Amor (as the Taoist Vanitas) first read the Stone's inscription, he deprecated its merits because it lacked an explicit dynastic setting and examples of moral grandeur. The Stone defended his work for its authenticity, its genuineness, its "real"-ness:

> "All that my story narrates, the meetings and partings, the joys and sorrows, the ups and downs of fortune, are recorded exactly as they happened. I have not dared to add the tiniest bit of touching-up, for fear of losing the true picture.
>
> "My only wish is that men in the world below may sometimes pick up this tale . . . and in doing so find not only mental refreshment but even perhaps, if they will heed its lesson and abandon their vain and frivolous pursuits, some small arrest in the deterioration of their vital forces."
>
> (*SS* I.1.50, *HLM* I.1.3)

In a novel that self-consciously proclaims that its fiction is no fiction, analysis of the gap between ideal and actual patterns, and the struggles of various actors to bring them into coincidence, mirrors the interpenetration and inseparability of real and not-real. Both author and narrator pledge themselves to the twin realms of the red dust and of transcendence. Indeed, as we know from Brother Amor's experience, attachment to form, which is illusion, is a means of awakening to the emptiness of all attachment. The model of ideal and actual patterns can apply not only to incidental detail but also to the transcendence that is the ultimate end of every sentient being. Not only can the inscription on the Stone awaken us to the illusory nature of existence in the novel, but it can lead us to understand that our own world is just as illusory as the fictional one.

Transcendence is presented as an ideal, and many of the characters achieve it, in one way or another. But the novel is not just a tract, a how-to-get-out-of-the-world handbook. The reader is irresistibly involved in the constant tension between ideal and actual in every sphere of the life of the Jias. The world outside the walls of the family compound assumes that they are fabulously wealthy—and so they have been, in part from grants and emoluments from the imperial treasury, in part from the large holdings in land granted them by the emperor and acquired by prudent ancestors. At this time, however, their expenditure so greatly exceeds their income that they are cruising toward bankruptcy. The intellectual and financial resources of the family should allow their sons to study and excel in the national examinations, so that they can serve their country and add further glory to their house. The actual situation is that it has been several generations since a Jia male passed the exams and received an official post on the basis of merit—all are getting by with inherited offices and purchased patents.

Into this family has come Bao-yu, born with a beautiful piece of jade (the symbol of his origin as the Stone, full of worldly longings) in his mouth. To be born with a jade in the mouth is a sign of superior spiritual awareness, but to the older generation spiritual awareness is not a desideratum. As the child grows and his eccentricities become more pronounced, he finds himself under ever-increasing pressure to conform to the gentry goals of completing his education, taking the imperial exams, and receiving a post by placing high in these glorious ranks. Bao-yu disdains such aspirations as the province of "career worms" (*lu-du*) and prefers to spend his time in the company of the many lovely girls of his own age—sisters, cousins, and maidservants—in whose behavior and minds he finds beauty, purity, and sensitivity to the impermanence of worldly things. This crucial aspect of his own personality, his aesthetic and spiritual sensitivity, is so alien to his society that even Bao-yu himself does not recognize its true nature.[28] Early on, the young Bao-yu attempts to assert his spiritual and emotional self by railing against his jade:

"None of the girls has got one," said Bao-yu, his face streaming with tears and sobbing hysterically. "Only I have got one. . . . And now this new cousin comes here who is as beautiful as an angel and she hasn't got one either, so I *know* it can't be any good."

(SS I.3.104, HLM I.3.31)

This passage has been interpreted as a sign of Bao-yu's obsession with his sexuality,[29] and this in turn has led to misunderstandings about the significance of chapter 5 ("Jia Bao- yu visits the Land of Illusion and the fairy Disenchantment performs the 'Dream of Golden Days' "). Although the novel's more popular title, *Honglou meng* (The Dream of the Red Chamber), is mentioned on the very first page of the first chapter, its significance crystallizes here in the song-cycle of that title, rendered by Hawkes as "A Dream of Golden Days." Chapter 5 is indeed important, but less as a turning point in Bao-yu's sexual awareness than for the foreshadowings of the fates of the girls in his life and the basis of Bao-yu's final liberation.

During a nap in the luxurious chamber of his niece, Qin Ke-qing, Bao-yu, aged maybe twelve, is given an opportunity to circumvent the tribulations of his mortal existence. The boy has a dream in which he visits the palace of the fairy Disenchantment (*Jinghuan xiangu*) in the Land of Illusion.[30] The dwellers in this land, it is important to remember, are not content to exist in blissful aloofness. Having completely assimilated the doctrine of emptiness, they exercise the overflowing compassion that attends this level of enlightenment to alleviate the suffering of unenlightened beings. As Bao-yu drifts into sleep, he follows a dream manifestation of his niece into the Land of Illusion. There he meets the fairy Disenchantment, who explains that she has agreed to plant in the boy the seeds of his awakening to the vanity of his existence at the urgent request of the spirits of his noble ancestors, who fear for the continued maintenance of their house. First and foremost, Bao-yu must be liberated from his attachment to the girls in his life, whose every action, feeling, and word engage his imagination and distract him from his duty to his ancestors.

During his tour, Disenchantment allows Bao-yu to read a set of poems in the Celestial Registers that reveal the girls' fates. The poems might as well be in Greek for all he can make of them, and so Disenchantment treats him to a pageant of poetry and music—"A Dream of Golden Days" (*honglou meng*)—which spells out the messages of the poems in the registers even more plainly.[31] With all his senses overstimulated, Bao-yu nods off. Since the boy will not absorb these poetic admonitions, he will be obliged to "awaken to the nature of emptiness by means of passion" (*yi se wukong*); in other words, he will have to endure the experiences detailed in the inscription on the Stone.[32] Exasperated by his obtuse innocence, Disenchantment startles the boy by confronting him with his true character: "The reason I like you so much is because you are full of lust. You are the most lustful person I have ever known in the whole world!" (*SS* I.5.145, *HLM* I.5.53). Bao-yu protests that he is not really "lustful" (*yiyin*), but here he makes precisely the mistake that Disenchantment warns against. She admonishes him:

> "In principle, of course, all lust is the same. . . . But your kind of lust is different. That blind, defenceless love with which nature has filled your being is what we call here 'lust of the mind.' . . . Because of this 'lust of the mind' women will find you a kind and understanding friend; but in the eyes of the world it is going to make you seem impractical and eccentric."
>
> (*SS* I.5.146, *HLM* I.5.53–54)

Bao-yu's problem is not sex per se but susceptibility to any kind of sympathy or emotional attachment. Disenchantment gives him a fairy bride, hoping that sexual initiation will "help you to grasp the fact that, since even in these immortal precincts love is an illusion, the love of your dust-stained, mortal world must be doubly an illusion" (*SS* I.5.146, *HLM* I.5.54).

The bride Disenchantment bestows on Bao-yu is her own younger sister, whose formal name, Jian-mei, means "Paired Beauties," rendered by Hawkes as "Two-in-one." This name prepares us to see what Bao-yu immediately sees: The girl combines attributes of the two heroines of the novel, Lin Dai-yu and Xue Bao-chai , in one perfect bride. That the dream bride combines attributes of both Dai-yu and Bao-chai shows that, on some level, Bao-yu is already aware of both girls' potential in his life and that he may already feel anxiety about the demands of social convention versus romantic attachment. The fairy bride's nickname, Ke-qing, happens to be the personal name of the niece, Qin Ke-qing, who has lent her gorgeous bridal bed for her uncle's nap. The pun on the name, *keqin*—"lovable, desirable"—suggests that both manifestations are embodiments of all that gives rise to passion.[33] In one brief dream, Bao-yu is wed to all the charms he might covet in the world, and when he wakes, teetering on the edge of the Ford of Error (*milu*), instead of realizing his narrow escape he plunges into a lifetime of romantic longing.[34] Like Zhen Shi-yin, he wakes up in the world of the novel; in Bao-yu's case, when he awakes from his nightmare of stumbling into the Ford of Error, he literally falls into it.

To provide a foil for Bao-yu's drive for individualism, and his family's aspirations for him, the author provides him with a double and his family with a mirror. These are the Zhens, another old family of Nan-jing. They are allied to the Jias on every level: in social rank and connection, in service to the empire, in symbolism. Their names are puns for the defining terms from the Land of Illusion: the surname Jia for "false," and Zhen for "true." While the Jias have removed to the capital, the Zhens remain in Nan-jing, but the families maintain contact and perform favors for each other. The most astonishing correspondence between the families is that the Zhens also have a son called Bao-yu, born a year after Jia Bao-yu.[35] The two boys not only share a name, but are very alike in appearance. Zhen Bao-yu even shares his double's sentimental tendencies, preferring the company of girls, despising boys as crude and impure, and mulishly resisting discipline or education. When Jia Bao-yu hears about his existence, he is both deeply shaken and hopeful—who can this unknown twin be? Is his existence a blow to Jia Bao-yu's sense of his own uniqueness, or is this a true friend, a soul-mate? The two Bao-yus first meet in a dream, each seeking the other, and when they are finally face to face seize each other's hands in delight:

> "So *you* are Bao-yu, and this isn't a dream after all?"
> "Of course it isn't a dream. . . . It couldn't be more real!"
>
> (*SS* III.56.86, *HLM* II.56.602)

Jia Bao-yu's remark "It couldn't be more real!" suggests a further pun: "The *Zhen* [Bao-yu] is the real one!" Jia Bao-yu awakes and finds himself face to face with his large bedroom mirror.[36] Why is he so sure that Zhen Bao-yu is the "real" one?

In terms of his own family's aspirations for him, Zhen Bao-yu becomes the ideal Bao-yu the Jias longed for. Jia Bao-yu, for a variety of reasons that are discussed particularly in the next two chapters, will not conform to gentry ideals of study and public service. At the end of the novel, after a serious illness and near-death experience, he sets his mind on quitting the world to become a Buddhist monk (chapter 116). After a similar illness, Zhen Bao-yu determines, just as decisively, to conform to society and seek his place there (chapter 93). When the "twins" finally meet in the flesh, their opposing aspirations are made plain. Jia Bao-yu is nauseated by what he regards as Zhen Bao-yu's complete capitulation to social convention. If this is "reality," he wants nothing to do with it.

But it is not just the two boys who mirror one another. The fortunes of the two families, even the careers of the heads of the households, form two identical waves in the same cycle, during a dynasty in which Chinese aristocrats faithfully served foreign rulers according to Confucian precepts, but in even more precarious circumstances than public servants of previous Chinese dynasties. Zhen Bao-yu's father, Zhen Ying-jia, is impeached and stripped of office and title, and his family fortune is confiscated. As the father struggles to redeem himself for the sake of his family, his traumatic experience may have influenced his son to turn to his family for support at last. Somewhat later, as if following in the Zhens' wake, the Jias face a similar round of impeachments and a confiscation. Jia Zheng's son sets his face in the opposite direction. Only one Bao-yu is the incarnation of the Stone. The Stone has his own cosmological imperatives, distinct from any illusory double. Jia Bao-yu does not leave his family desolate, but he only fulfills the bare essentials of his obligations. And while the text seems to approve his choice of leaving the mundane world to become a Buddhist monk, there are always doubts as to which Bao-yu is the "real" one, which aspiration is right, which human good is absolutely good. Jia Bao-yu, according to social convention and his family's hopes for him, may not be the boy he is supposed to be. As discussed in chapter 2, because of their deviations from their professed ideal patterns of conduct, the Jia family is not exactly the family it is supposed to be, either.

If ideal patterns could hold, there would be no reason to look beyond them for anything further. As soon as Jia Bao-yu sees through the illusion of his family's ideals, when he recognizes how wide is the gap between the ideals his father has tried to inculcate in him and his father's own inadequate fulfillment of them, he understands social convention as a force in and of itself, divorced from the ideal. For Jia Bao-yu social convention is irremediably a force opposed to self-fulfillment; for Zhen Bao-yu, it is a force that, properly maintained, can reestablish the ideal patterns and lead to self-fulfillment.

Without the spiritual superstructure of *The Story of the Stone*, we might think that, if only ideal social patterns held, there would be no need for liberation. Socially this might be correct, but, in spiritual terms, an ideal mundane world would still be a world of form and passion: illusion without substance. It is not just the negative experience of the world that must be transcended—it is all experience. Hate, greed, and despair are no more illusory than love, valor, and compassion. All participate in a karmic cycle that should ultimately free all beings from all attachments.

For Bao-yu, the division between his two existences—one as the Stone and one as the boy with the jade—and the necessity of both to his final emancipation is embodied in the two women, both his cousins, who become rivals for his affection. As mentioned above, the boy seems to have some subconscious awareness of their combined role. Underlying the two girls' distinct charms, style, aspirations, and intelligence is the symbolic fact that they are two complementary halves of a single ideal woman, who exists only in a dream.[37] As individuals, their differences are so compelling as to inspire passionate partisanship for one or the other. Critics wax choleric on the subject of Dai-yu's suffering or Bao-chai's venality, and students shout one another down on Dai-yu's self-centeredness and Bao-chai's martyrdom.[38] Within the story, their relationship is inevitably complex. On the one hand, they are both affected by the passions and jealousies that such natural rivals must inevitably feel. On the other hand, they are also natural allies, intimate members of the Jia family who never forget their ultimate status as "outsiders" and who therefore best understand the precarious nature of their intimacy. Neither one alone may be Bao-yu's ideal match, but they are certainly, for good and ill, perfectly matched to each other. We must keep in mind, however, it is not simply that one is "good" and the other "bad." As readers, depending on temperament and inclination, we may prefer one to the other, but sentimental preference is a sign of how deeply we are mired in the fictional world.

The two women embody different ideals: romance versus social convention, transcendence versus society, ethereal delicacy versus robust *belle tournure*. They also embody the conflict of ideal and actual. It is not that one of them stands for each side of the conflict. Rather, by their coexistence, and especially in their relation to Bao-yu, they ensure that the conflict remains at center stage at all times. Only one of them, Dai-yu, is the incarnation of an immortal. If her purpose is to achieve transcendence, she cannot do it through fulfilled love for Bao-yu, only through bitter suffering of blighted love. If Bao-chai's purpose is to restore the fortunes of her family and live as a paragon of social convention—well, fulfillment in love is not necessary for that, either. If Bao-yu must fulfill the Stone's purpose and liberate himself from the fetters of attachment, he nevertheless owes a debt of gratitude to those who make his disillusionment possible, and this entails fulfilling certain minimal obligations: providing his family with an heir, passing the national exams, reflecting credit on the family name. Both women are essential to his success, and each has some special quality to support it.

It is more fruitful to see their contrasts in terms of complementarity than opposition.[39] Dai-yu is not of this world; Bao-chai is. While, as a mortal boy, Bao-yu is oblivious to his place in the Land of Illusion until he is ready to leave the world, and his two full existences are separated most of the time, he still feels the pull of both, manifested in his physical attraction to Bao-chai in spite of his emotional commitment to Dai-yu. The ultimate split is not between Dai-yu and Bao-chai but between Bao-yu's two existences. The fairy Disenchantment intended Bao-yu's first "bride" to be the vehicle of his awakening, and so, ultimately, she is, but only through the duality of Dai-yu and Bao-chai. Bao-yu must endure nineteen years of existence as a human boy to recognize it.

2

"FAMILY TOGETHERNESS"

Patterns of Authority and the Subversion of Family Structure

According to Zhang Xinzhi (fl. 1828–1850), a nineteenth-century commentator on *The Story of the Stone*: "The entire text of the *Hung-lou meng* can be summed up in one phrase from the *Tso-chuan* [The Tso Commentary], 'condemnation for failure to instruct' [*shih-chiao*]."[1] In his reading, the Jia family's deviations from the principles of right conduct are the consequences of failing to inculcate the timeless values of the classics. Moreover, *shih-chiao* denotes progressively failing instruction; in other words, this is not a matter of a lesson missed but of consistently inadequate teaching and example over time.[2] This is indeed the progress of the Jias over the span of time detailed in the novel. Their decline begins with individual shortcomings and self-indulgences, which accumulate and accelerate until their downfall is not only inevitable but justified as the outcome of both individual retribution and social justice. Since, according to the ideal patterns of traditional Chinese education, individuals cannot deviate from right principles if they are correctly taught, wrong conduct is the result of poor instruction, which lays the blame at the feet of the oldest generation.

The twelfth song in the fairy Disenchantment's pageant, however, places this failure in a larger, cosmological context:

> The weakness in the line began with Jing;
> The blame for the decline lay first in Ning;
> But retribution all was of Love's fashioning.
>   (SS I.5.144, HLM I.5.53)[3]

While it is possible to read *The Story of the Stone* entirely as a social novel, doing so would disregard much of the book's moral and spiritual substance. It would also ignore the stated origin of the book, inscribed on the Stone under Greensickness Peak, whose name evokes the notion of attachment, or "love" (*qing*), here declared to be the vehicle of retribution. For characters and readers alike, emotional attachment—love, of course, but ultimately all kinds of attachment—is not just a facet of social life, it is a working-out of destiny. Although the immediate effect is likely to be destructive, ultimately it is a means to enlightenment. Any study of the Ning-guo and Rong-guo juggernauts, therefore, must consider both the temporal level of their deportment and the cosmic imperatives directing the conduct of individuals and the houses' decline.

Although romantic involvement and failure to instruct are the perceptible agents of the Jia family's downfall, on a more general level the story is bound up with the conflict between ideal and actual family patterns. In his account of a scant ten years in the life of a single (though much extended) family, Cao Xueqin shows how this conflict pervades every aspect of family life, and how it ultimately undermines both the outward structure of the family and the lives of its individual members.

The Story of the Stone as cultural compendium focuses on the Jia household as a microcosm of the empire. From at least the time of Confucius, the family has been not only the chief but the archetypal structural unit of Chinese society.[4] Primary loyalty in traditional Chinese society was to the family, outweighing all other social imperatives. Symbolically, the emperor was the country's "head of family" (*jiazhang*). Therefore the depiction of the fortunes of the Jias can be read not only as a gripping domestic drama, but also a literally ominous vision of the fortunes of China under Manchu rule in the eighteenth century.[5] As the narrative stands, no blame for the decline of the Jia family attaches to the imperial government—on the contrary, the emperor is cited again and again for his compassion and wisdom, and ultimately the Jias are spared total ruin by his mercy. But it is clear that their fortunes are precarious beyond their own failings, as they live in a state of constant uncertainty as to when, how, and why their loyalty and dedication may be tested.

The combined Jia households, the Ning-guo and Rong-guo establishments on Two Dukes Street, represent an "ideal" Chinese gentry family, in which all living generations dwell under one roof.[6] Three generations earlier, the brothers Jia Yan and Jia Yuan had won favor with the Manchu emperor and received high rank and honor, with appropriate emoluments. These patents are hereditary, but with each generation the rank is reduced, unless the service of a member of a new generation equals that of his ancestors. Each generation, therefore, becomes more and more urgently invested in public service and achievement, but the sons born into the two households seem less and less able or inclined to apply themselves to the task. Jia Yu-cun, himself a distant kinsman of the Rong-guo side, shows astonishment when his colleague Leng Zixing remarks:

"Nowadays both the Rong and Ning mansions are in a greatly reduced state compared with what they used to be . . . though outwardly they still manage to keep up appearances, inwardly they are beginning to feel the pinch. But that's a small matter. There's something much more seriously wrong with them than that. They are not able to turn out good sons, those stately houses, for all their pomp and show. The males in the family get more degenerate from one generation to the next."

(SS I.2.73–74, HLM I.2.15)

Leng Zi-xing happens to be married to the daughter of one of the Jia household retainers; even so, his disquisition on the goings-on in both the Ning-guo and Rong-guo Houses confirms the extraordinary level of outside scrutiny to which such affluent and successful families were subject. Yet, in such a large establishment, how strictly can order be maintained? Including family members, retainers, bondservants, and slaves, the inhabitants of the two compounds and their environs add up to some three hundred people—a sizable village comparable to the largest urban mansions in seventeenth- and eighteenth-century Paris or London.[7] Both households come in for criticism. The proper head of the Ning-guo House, Jia Jing, has given up his inheritance and moved to a Taoist temple of dubious reputation to concoct elixirs of immortality. Leng Zi-xing condemns Jia Jing's abdication of his responsibilities and blames his refusal to exercise any authority for the fact that his son, Jia Zhen, terrorizes his household and leads a life of unbridled self-indulgence. In the Rong-guo House, the elder son, Jia She, is the nominal head of household but, in fact, leaves all management duties to his younger brother, Jia Zheng. Jia Zheng, a stickler for convention, insists on deferring to his feckless brother in every detail, with the result that almost every aspect of the family management actually falls upon the women of the household. In matters of discipline of the extended clan, he even defers to his younger nephew, Zhen, who as head of the Ning-guo household is technically head of the senior branch of the family and therefore responsible for clan affairs.[8]

The older generation is caught in a cleft stick: On the one hand, they castigate their sons for failing to live up to their example; on the other hand, the failure of their sons is an indictment of their own ability to instruct them adequately. Further intimacy with the household reveals that the Jias consistently invert and subvert the ideal patterns of authority and the proper roles of family members according to generation, sex, birth order, and family status. In the eyes of the characters and the reader, these inversions are not necessarily negative; each one provides someone with a release from the pressures of daily life, even if the consequences may be destructive for the family as a whole. Sons avoid the authority of their fathers, daughters-in-law have control over the affairs of their mothers-in-law, wives defy their husbands, and maids manipulate their masters and mistresses. This is quite apart from instances of sexual misconduct. In a burlesque twist on the proper deportment of a faithful family retainer, Big Jiao, a venerable servant from the Ning-guo House, bawls for all to hear:

> "Who would have believed the Old Master could spawn this filthy lot of animals? . . . Up to their dirty little tricks every day. *I* know. Father-in-law pokes in the ashes. Auntie has it off with nevvy. Do you think I don't know what you're all up to? Oh, we 'hide our broken arm in our sleeve'; but you don't fool me."
>
> (*SS* I.7.183, *HLM* I.7.75)[9]

Big Jiao is the archetypal "faithful old retainer"—now eighty, he had saved his master's life in battle when both were young. This act of heroism and his advanced age give him a privileged place in the house, and he regards himself as an arbiter of family standards. The current generation sees him as an unruly old sot, who in his cups abuses all and sundry with impunity. In his own eyes, drink is a way to forget the humiliation of watching his master's children and grandchildren descend into iniquity; he speaks the truth about their conduct as a faithful retainer ought to do, and wails that he is going to the ancestral temple to weep before his master's tablet. Although his conduct is beyond the pale, Big Jiao embodies the paradox of the decline he laments: Jia family standards and authority since "the good old days" have slid to the point that, within earshot of his masters, a servant can shout his brains out about their filthy habits. Xi-feng, his older cousin, is livid when Bao-yu asks her to explain what Big Jiao's tirade means; however, Bao-yu's innocent questions are nothing compared to what awaits the Jias, when the misconduct of members of the Ning-guo and Rong-guo households spills decisively into the public arena.

One of the household's greatest deviations from ideal family patterns is the overwhelming power and authority of the matriarch, Grandmother Jia (*Jiamu*). This redoubtable lady embodies an essential contradiction of filial piety: On the one hand, younger family members are expected to respect and defer to their elders; on the other hand, once her husband has died, a mother is supposed to defer to the authority of the new head of household, her eldest son. As the only surviving member of her generation—who, moreover, remembers the glory days of their early ennoblement—Grandmother Jia commands deference from both the Ning-guo and Rong-guo sides. Her very age and robust health demand it: In China, longevity and good health are signs of moral superiority, which confers the favor of heaven. Because of her formidable personality, Grandmother Jia dominates both her sons absolutely. This ironic inversion of the mother/son authority pattern is by no means unusual; indeed, the irony is virtually built into the relationship by the time the mother has reached the *laonian* ("old age, elder") stage of life. Although the eldest son becomes head of the household after his father's death, he may be inhibited in exercising his authority over his mother because of the strict rules of respect due to *laonian* in general, and aged parents in particular.[10]

Jia Zheng is a straight arrow in matters of social convention and quite lacking in imagination. His deference to his mother is not just formulaic; he desperately seeks her approval. The fact that she prefers the lively company of her grandchildren, especially her adored grandson Bao-yu, is a source of resentment and tension. At a family party inhibited by his stiff presence, Jia Zheng protests when his mother suggests that he retire: "You have so much affection for your grandchildren, Mama. Can you not spare just a tiny bit for your son?" (*SS* I.22.447, *HLM* I.22.217). Even Jia She, in a rare appearance at a Mid-Autumn Festival, makes a tactless joke about the placement of an acupuncturist's needle, with the punch line "A mother's heart always inclines towards one side" (*SS* III.75.505, *HLM* II.75.831).

Grandmother Jia's preference for Bao-yu does not require his jade to explain. Jia She's son, Jia Lian, is capable enough in his way, but has long since failed to show any aptitude for the *cursus honorum*; instead he squanders his talent in shady financial deals that become more and more flagrant as the family's expenditure ever exceeds its income. Jia Zheng's promising older son, Jia Zhu, died, leaving a son of his own, Jia Lan, who is still an infant. Jia Zheng has another son by a concubine, Bao-yu's younger half-brother Jia Huan, but this boy shows aptitude for nothing but sneaking and sniveling. On the Ning-guo side, Jia Zhen keeps his son, Jia Rong, at his beck and call for the most menial tasks, and the youth is utterly cowed by his father's imperious and capricious demands.

For the Jia family, the jade's miraculous appearance has raised hopes that Bao-yu is destined to resuscitate the family's fortunes with a brilliant career in public service. This hope is doomed to disappointment, for the jade is a symbol of Bao-yu's origin under Greensickness Peak. The Stone must eventually resume its immortal shape after awakening to the vanity of earthly existence.

The child Bao-yu, however, knows nothing of his real purpose. His family sees him as charmed from birth, possessing physical beauty, extraordinary intellectual precocity in certain areas, and a natural, personal grace. Of course, his grandmother dotes on him! Her active interference in his upbringing all but exempts him from the ordinary pressures of study and filial obedience. Even so, as the child grows and his eccentricities become more pronounced, he finds himself under ever-increasing pressure to conform to the gentry goals of completing his education and placing high in the imperial exams.[11] Bao-yu has no interest in these aspirations. All he knows is that his preference for feminine company is paramount, and as a result he not only avoids masculine company whenever possible but positively despises any suggestion that his own maleness confers either privilege or obligation upon him:

> But there was another, zanier notion which contributed to this attitude. Let us try to explain it. Bao-yu had from early youth grown up among girls. . . . As a result of this upbringing, he had come to the conclusion that the pure essence of humanity was all concentrated in the female of the species and that males were its mere dregs and off-scourings. To him, therefore, all members of his own sex without distinction were brutes who might just as well not have existed. Only in the case of his father, uncles and brother, where rudeness and disobedience were expressly forbidden by the teachings of Confucius, did he make an exception—and even then the allowances he made in respect to the fraternal bond were extremely perfunctory. It certainly never occurred to him that his own maleness placed him under any obligation to set an example to the younger males in his clan.
>
> (SS I.20.407–408, HLM I.20.196)[12]

Grandmother Jia is not the only female to exert her authority on Bao-yu's behalf, over the norms of social convention and his father's wishes. The family receives an extraordinary honor when Jia Zheng's elder daughter, Yuan-chun, is selected as an imperial concubine. As a unique favor, Yuan-chun is allowed to make one visit to her home, for which occasion the Jias construct a garden paradise to receive her in proper style. Her exalted position as a member of the emperor's intimate entourage makes her a direct representative of imperial power, and her wishes are carried out with the dispatch one would expect in the case of imperial commands. During her visit, none of the Jia males, not even her father, is allowed to see her—she receives her own father's kowtow from behind a curtain. At the time, she weeps at this inversion of proper filial roles, but her position allows her, if the fancy takes her, to override her father's authority in the disposition of his household. Although Bao-yu is already fully adolescent, Yuan-chun, like all the other older women in the family, regards him still as a child, and he is the sole male admitted to her presence.

From the palace, Yuan-chun decrees that all her unmarried sisters and cousins be allowed to take up residence in the garden's various delightful buildings and pavilions. She also directs that Bao-yu should join them, even though Bao-yu is already long past the age at which customary rules of sexual segregation should be in force. Yuan-chun's directive enforces a systematic inversion of the ideal family patterns for the gentry. In traditional Chinese society, the sexes are supposed to be segregated after early childhood, the boys coming under their fathers' supervision, the girls remaining under their mothers.'[13] Obviously, Bao-yu has not been much subjected to his father's direct supervision. In the garden, he will be completely removed from male oversight. Bao-yu's presence in the garden is the motive force for most of the emotional and romantic dynamics of the novel. The fact that this subversion of ideal patterns of sexual segregation comes at the behest of one who derives her authority from her position as the emperor's concubine, and therefore functions as his direct representative, casts a shadow of doubt, or irony, on the vigilance of the ultimate head of household.

A child whose primary pursuit in life is sentimental attachment is not exactly what the family hopes for, although Bao-yu's position as the cherished favorite of the matriarch protects him from serious attempts to make him conform to discipline. Ideal patterns call for a son to respect and submit to his father's authority, which in turn nurtures the development of father-son solidarity and the proper conduits for the son's ultimate succession to his father's place in the family.[14] Grandmother Jia's protection of Bao-yu subverts this relationship, releasing the boy from the social conventions that oppress him. At the same time, however, Grandmother Jia's indulgence leads Bao-yu away from the path of filial piety because releasing him from his father's authority puts Bao-yu into direct conflict with him.

In part because of his thwarted authority and in part because of jealousy of his mother's favoritism, Jia Zheng's relationship with his son is fraught with mutual hostility and intolerance. Their fundamental misunderstanding began at Bao-yu's birth. Jia Zheng was the only family member who considered the jade an ill omen. At the celebration of Bao-yu's first birthday, when traditionally a child is shown an array of objects symbolizing possible career paths (books, musical instruments, tools, and so forth) and expected to chose his future career, the baby went straight for objects from a woman's boudoir—combs, bracelets, and cosmetics.[15] Jia Zheng automatically assumed that this pointed to a career as a libertine and grew chilly toward him. The gossiping Leng Zi-xing makes the same assumption, when he recounts Bao-yu's priceless remark: "Girls are made of water and boys are made of mud. When I am with girls I feel fresh and clean, but when I am with boys I feel stupid and nasty" (SS I.2.76, HLM I.2.16).

Jia Yu-cun sharply protests this inference. The fact that Bao-yu was born with a jade in his mouth shows that he is endowed with extraordinary spiritual awareness, and Jia Yu-cun pompously places him among other figures of unique talent at all levels of society throughout history:

> ". . . place them in the company of ten thousand others and you will find that they are superior to all the rest in sharpness and intelligence and inferior to all the rest in perversity, wrongheadedness and eccentricity. . . . Under no circumstances will you find them in servile or menial positions, content to be at the beck and call of mediocrities."
>
> (SS I.2.78–79, HLM I.2.17)

Jia Yu-cun's lecture provides a detailed cosmological explanation to set the stage for an epic father/son struggle. While Bao-yu is a young child, Jia Zheng looks sour over his lack of discipline, but dares not interfere with his own mother's authority. When Bao-yu's adolescence begins, he tries to take a stronger line, which Bao-yu resists with every fiber of his being. There is more here than adolescent rebellion following a spoiled childhood. There is dereliction on both sides. Bao-yu's resistance to the aspirations of his family and class reveals an equally severe set of failings in the person who is supposed to inculcate these values in him. Even with an indulgent grandmother, in an ideal household Bao-yu would respect Jia Zheng because his father by definition was worthy of respect. If it is indeed cosmically determined that a personality like Bao-yu's will reject domination by mediocrities, then his father is at a disadvantage from the start. While Jia Zheng cites chapter and verse about decorum, study, and ambition, he himself is a dismal failure in a public office granted to him by imperial fiat rather than earned by merit.

This does not prevent him from escalating pressure on Bao-yu to behave as an ideal son, even though from birth the boy has not conformed to these notions at all. Bao-yu lives in terror of his father's inquisitions, which are particularly dreaded because they are unpredictable—Jia Zheng calls his son in to recite lessons or compose poetry at a whim, not as a regular part of his course of study. Perhaps if his father consistently oversaw Bao-yu's studies, the boy would be better prepared and would have greater respect for Jia Zheng's drill. But these occasions, in Bao-yu's eyes, are like natural disasters, and the father's attitude is always contemptuous. The sessions are excruciating, not least because it is evident that Bao-yu is exceptionally bright. It is impossible for Jia Zheng to think anything but that his son is mulishly resisting his duty, and it is impossible for Bao-yu to think anything but that his father is tormenting him on purpose. When the call comes, Bao-yu always pleads for intercession from his grandmother or feigns illness—anything to avoid being called to his father's study.[16]

The occasions when Jia Zheng has such power over his son, then, are rare. Because of Jia Zheng's personal inadequacies and the overwhelming power of women in the family, he is usually thwarted in his sporadic attempts to discipline his son and oversee his development. As long as Bao-yu's defiances of propriety remain within the household, Jia Zheng tries to ignore them or at most remarks on them with sarcasm. When they threaten to expose the family to outside scrutiny, Jia Zheng's frustration, guilt, and jealousy explode in a burst of nearly fatal violence. The explosion and its aftermath reveal how completely the governance of the Jia household has departed from the ideal to which it outwardly conforms.

Jia Zheng's crucial confrontation with his son occurs in chapter 33. Bao-yu, preoccupied by the suicide of one of his mother's maids, Golden (Jin-chuan-erh, meaning "Gold Bracelet"), and feeling partly responsible because she had been peremptorily dismissed for flirting with him, is intercepted by Jia Zheng, who is disproportionately irritated by his unconscious sighs and general air of depression. The father is called away from his peroration by an emissary of the prince of Zhong-shun, who intimates that Bao-yu has seduced the prince's favorite actor away from his post at the palace, and requests that Jia Zheng use his authority to make his son divulge the actor's whereabouts. Jia Zheng is enraged by the implications of such an act of *lèse-majesté*, which is both an affront to the prince and a disgrace for himself as lacking in authority to prohibit such entanglements. Bao-yu is indeed a close friend of the actor, Jiang Yu-han (stage name Bijou, or *Qi-guan-er*), but disclaims any acquaintance with him.[17] The prince of Zhong-shun's chamberlain scoffs at Bao-yu's affected ignorance, pointing to Jiang's sash around Bao-yu's waist as proof of their intimacy. Thus cornered, Bao-yu changes his tune and suggests that Jiang can be found at his new house outside the city.

While Bao-yu's clumsy deception is typical of patterns of adolescent solidarity, his attempts to keep faith with his friend and conceal his whereabouts are totally inappropriate when faced with such a formidable representative of authority. As long as Bao-yu's intimacy with Jiang Yu-han did not interfere with the actor's service to the prince, boys could be boys. When the prince's chamberlain calls, however, maintaining personal loyalty to his friend positively threatens his own family's interests. Bao-yu's obtuseness is a sign of both his unusual reverence for sentimental attachment, and his extraordinary social immaturity. The chamberlain thanks father and son ironically and sweeps out to find the errant favorite.

Reeling from the mortification of this reprimand, Jia Zheng erupts in rage when Bao-yu's half-brother Jia Huan tells him of the maid's suicide and says that Bao-yu had attempted to rape her. This is sheer malice on Huan's part. Lady Wang, Bao-yu's mother, had overreacted to what she saw as Golden's potential to corrupt her "innocent" son; she slapped her and sent her packing, and then was filled with remorse when Golden threw herself into a well. But Huan, whose attitude toward his older brother mixes envy of Bao-yu's intelligence and beauty with contempt because Bao-yu refuses to assert his authority as elder brother, never misses an opportunity to cause trouble. Huan's obsessive jealousy shows another deviation from ideal patterns of family structure, which dictate that a concubine's children should take their position in family hierarchy strictly according to age precedent, not the relative status of the birth mother. All children were supposed to regard the primary wife as their mother and refer to their father's concubines as "aunt" (*yiniang*) regardless of their biological connection. Huan attributes his inferiority to the fact that he is a son of Jia Zheng's concubine, Aunt Zhao, but in ideal terms, that should make no difference. Huan's vicious fecklessness is partly a matter of his own temperament and partly due to his biological mother's nagging and meddling.[18] Beside himself with fury, Jia Zheng summons the unsuspecting (and, in this case, innocent) Bao-yu:

> Jia Zheng turned a pair of wild and bloodshot eyes on him as he entered. Forgetting the 'riotous and dissipated conduct abroad leading to the unseemly bestowal of impudicities on a theatrical performer' and the 'neglect of proper pursuits and studies at home culminating in the attempted violation of a parent's maidservant' and all the other high-sounding charges he had been preparing to hurl against him, he shouted two brief orders to the pages.
>
> "Gag his mouth. Beat him to death."
>
> (*SS* II.33.148, *HLM* I.33.332–333)

Unlike his brother Jia She, and his nephew Jia Zhen, Jia Zheng is not known for rages and beatings. Indeed, although there are references to previous spankings, this is the only explicit instance of such action by him in the novel. Jia Zheng is above all a man of words and principles: His words may be dry and his principles old-fashioned, but the nearest thing to this beating he has visited on Bao-yu has been the threat of a slapped face. His usual prolixities run through his mind as he confronts his son, but he is so utterly transported by rage that he falls headlong into disaster.

First, the savagery of the beating is extreme. Second, if he were actually to carry through with his resolve, he would commit the enormity of cutting off his family line. Bao-yu is the only surviving son of his principal wife, and it falls first on him to carry on the family name. To leave your house without posterity is the most unfilial act a man can commit.[19] To cut off the family line deliberately, and seek to justify it by indicting your son as a disobedient monster, is the direst self-indictment: Who is responsible for his upbringing and conduct? The fact that Jia Zheng has so far lost his self-control as to pass a death sentence in a blind rage, without considering the consequences for the family, shows that he has already abdicated his authority. Society accords him the right to punish his son, even to execute him if it seems justified, but not the right to murder him in an act of passion.[20]

Jia Zheng is challenged in the nick of time by his own wife, the ordinarily indolent and ineffectual Lady Wang. She argues that Jia Zheng's filial obligations to his own mother should deter him, but her husband's reasoning is just the opposite:

> "Don't try that sort of talk with me!"said Jia Zheng bitterly. "Merely by fathering a monster like this I have proved myself an unfilial son; yet whenever in the past I have tried to discipline him, the rest of you have all conspired against me to protect him.Now that I have the opportunity at last, I may as well finish off what I have begun and put him down, like the vermin he is, before he can do any more damage."
>
> (SS II.33.149, HLM I.33.333)

Affected by his wife's passionate grief, Jia Zheng suspends the beating and bursts into tears of frustration. Before he can recover the upper hand, Grandmother Jia arrives on the scene:

> "Kill me first! You may as well kill both of us while you are about it!"
>
> As much distressed by his mother's words as he was alarmed by her arrival, Jia Zheng hurried out to meet her. . . .
>
> "Surely, Mother, in such hot weather as this there is no need for you to come here? If you have any instructions, you should call for me and let *me* come to *you*." . . .
>
> "Oh! Are you speaking to *me*?—Yes, as a matter of fact I *have* got 'instructions,' as you put it; but as unfortunately I've never had a good son who cares for me, there's no one I can give them to."
>
> Wounded in his most sensitive spot, Jia Zheng fell on his knees before her. The voice in which he replied to her was broken with tears.
>
> "How can I bear it, Mother, if you speak to me like that? What I did to the boy I did for the honour of the family."
>
> (SS II.150–151, HLM I.33.334)

When Jia Zheng protests that what he did was "for the honour of the family," his womenfolk, over whom—as head of household—he is supposed to have complete authority, defy him by countering that *he* is failing in his filial duties himself, by threatening to cut off the family line and leave his mother without comfort and support in her old age, and no one to see to the ancestral rites after her death. And he is. The *jiazhang* is ultimately responsible for the conduct of the members of his household. A son will be a good son, *act* like a son, if his father *acts* like a father. If his son is disobedient and dissolute, that is the direct result of his own failure to discipline his son properly. If the women defy him and get away with it, he has no one to blame for their lack of respect but himself. It is not "fathering this monster" that is the fault; it is the lack of fathering that indicts Jia Zheng. His own mother throws this failure in his teeth, when she tearfully reproaches him, "And you say you have been punishing him for the honor of the family, but you just tell me this: did your own father ever punish *you* in such a way?—I think not" (*SS* II.33.151, *HLM* I.33.334).[21] Utterly crushed by his mother's speech, Jia Zheng realizes that the attempt to consolidate his power over his son has cost him what little power he had managed to retain.

After the beating, Jia Zheng's authority becomes even more remote. He sticks mainly to his desk at the office, while Bao-yu lives with his sisters and girl cousins in the garden. Grandmother Jia has won. Her authority and its reflected power in her epigones rule Bao-yu's adolescence. It would seem to be his ultimate release from duty, responsibility, and care, but this inversion of authority patterns does not pass without a full exploitation of its ironic implications, with tragic results for the entire family.

What Bao-yu cannot know is that the inversion of ideal patterns of authority that allows him to enter and remain in what he regards as the perfection of the world, the female domain, will ultimately result in almost universal ruin for the happiness and well-being of the girls whom he adores. Strictly speaking, Bao-yu's continued opportunity to associate freely with his sisters and female cousins, especially to be alone with them, is a violation of the incest taboo.[22] His presence in the garden is a constant reminder of the inversion of ideal authority patterns that blights the household around it and makes Bao-yu so eager to flee his father's realm.[23] While the children may feel free to create their own world, the adult world will reassert its authority as they become adults themselves and are forced to leave the garden. But even the garden is not immune to corruption, in spite of its guardians' protestations to the contrary. And as jealousy, covetousness, deviousness, and opportunism become rife among the garden's inhabitants, the very complacency of the family's authority figures will be their sharpest reproach.

In Bao-yu's mind, for the moment he can live unhindered in his single-minded pursuit of sentimental attachment. Designed as this environment seems to be for refined appreciation of the gentler emotions, passions run as deep in the garden as they do outside it. Here his "lust of the mind," as the fairy Disenchantment warned him, leads him ever farther from ideal patterns of filial aspiration, but ever nearer to disillusionment and detachment.

In the garden, Bao-yu's childish preference for his brilliant cousin Dai-yu develops into a romantic passion. Dai-yu reciprocates his love, but the attachment is doomed. We know from the first chapter of *The Story of the Stone* that Dai-yu is the incarnation of the Crimson Pearl Flower. She owes her sentient life to the nurturing attentions of the Stone (Bao-yu), who watered her with sweet dew in the Land of Illusion. In order to repay him, she has pledged him a lifetime of tears. This cosmic affinity is supported by their earthly affection, but in the garden the conflicts that will finally doom their romantic aspirations play themselves out.[24]

The greatest threat to their aspirations is Bao-chai. She is Dai-yu's equal in beauty and talent, and her superior in wealth. Worse still, her gold locket, the mate to Bao-yu's jade, implies a destiny against which Dai-yu feels powerless. In chapter 8, the two charms discover each other when Bao-chai asks to see the famous jade, and we read for the first time the mystical inscription promised the Stone in the Land of Illusion. The two poems are significant in inverse proportion to their aesthetic merit:

Magic Jade

Mislay me not, forget me not,
And hale old age shall be your lot.

(SS I.8.189, HLM I.8.80)

Bao-chai's attendants are astounded because their mistress owns a golden locket given to her by none other than the same scabby-headed monk who had engraved the jade! Interfering old busybody that he is, the couplets are a perfect match:

Ne'er leave me, ne'er abandon me:
And years of health shall be your fee.

(SS I.8.190, HLM I.8.80)

Here is the gold to enclose and enhance the jade, here is the woman who must be Bao-yu's perfect match. *In this existence.* The presence of the gold locket is a source of great embarrassment to Bao-chai, not just because of her sense of maidenly modesty, but because of the jealous obsession of Dai-yu.

Bao-chai seems aware of the implications of this correspondence, but Bao-yu is only briefly interested. On a subconscious level, the golden locket disturbs him, though. Some time later, Bao-chai is astounded to hear him cry out angrily in his sleep:

> "Why should I believe what those old monks and Taoists say? I don't believe in the marriage of gold and jade. I believe in the marriage of stone and flower."
>
> (SS II.36.203, HLM I.36.365)

The monk has placed the locket not so much to fulfill the destiny of gold and jade as to guarantee that the destiny of flower and stone will be fulfilled; or, rather, the destiny of gold and jade has been set to fulfill the destiny of flower and stone. In spite of the origin of these verses in the supramundane realm, they speak to distinctly mundane aspirations—health, long life, precisely the concerns of the family with all its practical mundane goals. But these are not the aspirations of the Crimson Pearl Flower and the Stone, nor are they the destinies of their present incarnations. The Flower's brooding on the locket will help her pay her debt of tears. The Stone's disregard of the locket will help him realize the necessary disillusionment with emotional fulfillment, the perceived lack of which (in his shame and disappointment at being left over from Nü-wa's celestial repairs) started him longing for worldly experience in the first place. The "affinity of jade and gold" (*jinyu yinyuan*) is the destiny of the present life; the "affinity of stone and flower" (*mushi yinyuan*) is the prior attachment. When Bao-yu soothes Dai-yu's spasms of jealousy by reminding her that *theirs* is the earlier affection and *theirs* is the stronger bond, he unknowingly has the force of karmic history on his side.

As suggested by his dream utterance, Bao-yu seems to have unconscious knowledge of the debt of tears. In chapter 36, Bao-yu deplores conventional notions of a glorious death and details *his* vision: to die surrounded by his beloved girls and have his body float away on a river of their tears. After witnessing a lovers' spat between one of his male cousins and an actress, however, he changes his tune:

> "What I told you the other night was wrong. . . . I'm not surprised that Father tells me I have 'a small capacity but a great self-con-

ceit.' I mean, that stuff about all of you making a river of tears for me when I die: I realize now that it's not possible. I realize now that we each have our own allotted share of tears and must be content with what we've got."

(SS II.36.210, HLM I.36.368)

Although the history of the love of the Stone and the Flower underscores the development of Bao-yu's love for Dai-yu, it is not necessary to explain their fates. These can be explained by the combination of indulgence and negligence among the guardians of the garden. While Grandmother Jia enjoys the beauty and retreat from care that the garden affords, she is resolutely oblivious to its evocation of the romance and escape found in her favorite theatrical entertainments—entertainments whose preference she shares with her impressionable grandchildren. In chapter 54, she delivers a swingeing condemnation of these dramas, explicitly exposing the gap between the ideals they claim to portray and their essential falsehood. In well-to-do households like the Jias', the kinds of ideal young men and women who lose their heads in romantic comedies would not do so in "real" life—they would be better protected against temptation by their solid upbringings and by the bevy of attendants who serve and protect them. Grandmother Jia snorts with contemptuous incredulity at suggestions that well-educated youths would toss aside their books for love or that well-conditioned maidens would toss aside their modesty and their duty to their parents for the first man who catches their eye. From her point of view, the authors' motivations are deeply suspect:

> "There's always a reason for it. . . . In some cases it's because the writer is envious of people so much better off than himself, or disappointed because he has tried to obtain their patronage and failed. . . . In other cases the writers have been corrupted by reading this sort of stuff before they begin to write any themselves, and, though totally ignorant of what life in educated, aristocratic families is really like, portray their heroines in this way simply because everyone else does so and they think it will please their readers. I ask you now, never mind *very* grand families like the ones they pretend to be writing about, even in average well-to-do families like ours when did you ever hear of such carryings-on?"

(SS III.54.31, HLM II.54.571)

Compare Grandmother Jia's protestations with the Stone's defense of his inscription to Vanitas in chapter 1. After his first reading, Vanitas pooh-poohs its merit—where are the exemplars of moral grandeur? The Stone protests that his is no formulaic historical novel or boudoir romance: "All that my story narrates, the meetings and partings, the joys and sorrows, the ups and downs of fortune, are recorded exactly as they happened" (*SS* I.1.50, *HLM* I.1.3). If there is any resemblance to the kind of fiction Grandmother Jia deplores, it is fortuitous—or is it? Vanitas gives the book a second chance: "He could see that its main theme was love; that it consisted quite simply of a true record of real events; and that it was entirely free of any tendency to deprave or corrupt" (*SS* I.1.51, *HLM* I.1.3). This emotionally and factually "authentic" narrative is the story in which Grandmother Jia finds herself, protesting that the shenanigans typical of novels cannot occur *here*. Strictly speaking, she is correct. No member of her family will defy his parents' wishes or elope or cause the kind of public scandal that is the lifeblood of romantic farces. This will not, however, prevent individual tragedy or public humiliation as the irregularities of her household are brought to light. Perhaps the inversions of ideal patterns resulting in actual disaster are what persuade Vanitas that this is a "true record" and absolve *The Story of the Stone* of the taint of corruption.

Grandmother Jia ignores the chief value of theatrical entertainments and fiction in her world, which is to provide, for a brief period, a romantic release from the pressures and obligations of social convention. These stories are a part of society's prescription for sublimating awareness of actual pressures. They function as palliatives to a world in which romantic love is not possible. For individuals like Grandmother Jia, who have internalized social convention and who recognize literary convention for what it is, these entertainments are harmless diversions from the actual world and the pressure to maintain the ideal patterns. She does not realize that her grandchildren and other denizens of the garden might believe that these works of fiction are *ideals*, and perhaps attainable ones.

Indeed, Bao-yu's first physical experience of passion is suffused with the memory and symbols of old tales as translated through the vicarious experience of fiction and theatrical entertainments. In chapter 5, the scene of his dream sexual initiation in his niece Qin Ke-qing's bedroom is as heavy with portents of disaster as with sensuality. The gorgeous bed hung with a canopy of pearls, the priceless paraphernalia of her vanity, even the sumptuous bedclothes are, in Bao-yu's mind at least, explicitly associated with fabulous beauties of history, legend, and fiction. Usually, the bedroom of a young wife in a gentry family would be decorated with items from her own home.[25] Qin Ke-qing is the adopted daughter of a poor scholar and certainly could not have brought such gifts to her husband's household. Nor are they likely to be Jia Rong's gifts to his bride; Rong is an only son, it is true, but his father keeps him on a tight rein and treats him with brutal contempt. He would be unlikely to have luxuries, even without their distinguished provenances. Where do these things come from?

It is possible that they come from Bao-yu's imagination. When he finds himself in the most intimate part of his niece's apartment, each object of her personal sanctum resonates for Bao-yu with old tales of great passion. For him, entering Qin Ke-qing's bedroom would be entering the heart of the world of female sexuality in all its opulence and mystery. Female accouterments come to life as objects of legend; he is touching them, imagining their use, vicariously drinking in every possible aspect of their existence. In this sense, Bao-yu himself may "create" these objects, with his niece unaware of the power her everyday cosmetics and furnishings could have for him.

On another level, just as significant and far more disturbing, the objects are quite real.[26] In the extant version of the novel, Qin Ke-qing dies of illness in chapter 13.[27] Bao-yu is deeply affected when he hears the news: He spits blood, an event read by his family as a sign that his distress has caused the blood in his heart to flood its banks. It is also a symbol of his deep attachment, if not precisely to Qin-shi herself, to the mystery of femininity she has represented for him. In Bao-yu's dream in chapter 5, however, a riddle in the Celestial Registers and a poem in the fairy Disenchantment's pageant show positively that Qin-shi is destined to hang herself when it is discovered she has been carrying on an affair with her father-in-law, Jia Zhen.[28] This puts the objects in her bedroom in a different light because almost every one, from the empress Wu Zi-tian's mirror to the quince that bruised the breast of the imperial consort Yang Gui-fei to the silk coverlet laundered by Xi Shi before she was promoted from laundress to favorite of the king of Wu, is associated with *femmes d'histoire*—"fatal beauties," women of destiny—who caused older men of great power to lose their heads and even their kingdoms.[29]

The furnishings of Qin Ke-qing's bedroom are symbolic of her transgression with her father-in-law. In an even larger sense, they are the objects of her *spiritual* dowry, and through the disaster of romantic attachment they all have the potential to enlighten lovesick individuals as to the vanity of passion. The spirit of Qin Ke-qing explains her heritage to Grandmother Jia's maid, Faithful (Yuan-yang), much later, after the dowager's death:

> "I once occupied the highest seat in Disenchantment's Tribunal of Love. My responsibility was the settlement of Debts of Passion. I went down into the human world, where naturally I was destined to become the world's foremost lover, my mission being to draw lovesick lads and lovelorn maidens with all speed back to the tribunal and the settlement of their debts. As part of this mission it was my Karma to hang myself. I have now seen through the illusion of mortal attachment, and have risen above the Sea of Passion to the Paradise of Love."
>
> (*SS* V.III.210, *HLM* III.III.1213)

Although critics have been bothered by the gap between Qin Ke-qing's fate as detailed in the poems from the Land of Illusion and her prosaic death by illness in the extant text, the nature of her transgression with Jia Zhen is not in doubt because of the myriad clues surrounding her life and death.[30] The affair is not explicitly narrated—no passionate trysts, no incriminating notes—yet Qin Ke-qing's incest with her father-in-law is systematically implicit. In addition to the portents of her bedroom, there are the poems in chapter 5, which not only describe a wanton nature but also state that she was driven by shame to hang herself when the affair was discovered. There are Big Jiao's tirades against the decline of his master's house. There are the bizarre splits in the responses, first to Qin Ke-qing's illness, then her death, in the extant version. In the first stages of her illness, everyone in the household, especially her mother-in-law, You-shi, is most solicitous. When Qin Ke-qing begin to decline, they are concerned not only for her but for the family line she must continue. But after her death in chapter 13, the conduct of her immediate family suggests something gone very wrong indeed: her husband Jia Rong's strange distance from all the arrangements, her mother-in-law's sudden incapacity and refusal to handle anything about the funeral, and, most tellingly, Jia Zhen's extravagant hysteria and grief. With his wife apparently disabled, Zhen pitifully supplicates Lady Wang to permit Wang Xi-feng to take over the funeral arrangements. When he approaches her for this favor, he is described as so debilitated that he must "support himself with a staff" (*zhu ge zhang*) (*SS* I.13.266–

267, *HLM* I.13.125). This is an allusion to the fact that he has lost the support of his wife (*zhang qi fu*), usually said of a man whose wife has died. In this case, You-shi is ill, but by no means in danger of dying. His cane symbolizes his unnatural dependence on his daughter-in-law, whom he mourns as his own wife.[31]

Even Qin Ke-qing's maids show their involvement: One kills herself and the other becomes Ke-qing's posthumous adopted daughter. Both actions are guarantees of silence. Although the suicide of one is ascribed to excess grief and the adoption of the other maid is regarded as a reward for her devotion to her mistress, terror of their employer Jia Zhen's wrath for their knowledge of his secret probably provoked these actions. The suicide will obviously be silent and, under the circumstances, would pass the required review of the case by the city tribunal. The adopted daughter would also remain silent, as a "child" would never, according to ideal patterns, reveal a "parent's" disgrace to the outside world. These symbolic children of Jia Zhen and Qin Ke-qing's union deflect the threat a biological child would have posed to the family's stability and honor. Jia Zhen insists on carrying out the funeral on a level of unprecedented extravagance—not even Grandmother Jia will go to her final rest with half the style or expense.

Textually speaking, Qin Ke-qing's death from an obscure illness is the ultimate cover-up for a transgression that violates natural and imperial law. Discovery of such a shame, whatever its outcome, would destroy both the family's internal harmony and public reputation. If Ke-qing had actually committed suicide, the situation would demand an external, official investigation that would disastrously expose the family to the outside world. Suicide was considered a legitimate, though drastic, form of protest against the household system of authority. Suicides were therefore considered in the category of "wrongful death," presumed to be motivated by unendurable cruelty and injustice and required investigation by the city tribunal. Furthermore, during the Qing dynasty the results of suicide inquiries were reported directly to the emperor.[32] On the level of the prose narrative, the illness conveniently blocks this and hushes up the true cause of death. For Jia Rong's wife to die without issue is a blow to the family. But one has only to look at Jia Zhen's behavior to gain an idea of what her death really meant to him.

These events, occurring before the garden is even built, are an example of the deviation from ideal patterns in the Jia household. The minor inversions of family patterns that assert themselves on a quotidian basis are ultimately just as harmful. The insidious erosion of the garden as sanctuary is due largely to the kind of mismanagement that results when authority is either in incompetent hands or in the wrong hands. Wang Xi-feng, the wife of Jia She's son Jia Lian, has charge of household management, not only of the Rong-guo side but also, when You-shi is incapacitated after Qin-shi's death, temporarily of the Ning-guo side as well. She is widely recognized as an extremely capable woman, who declines to hide her light under a bushel. Because of her ready wit and forceful personality, she is Grandmother Jia's favorite. When she is put in charge of the household, she technically has authority over her own mother-in-law, Lady Xing, and her own aunt, Jia Zheng's consort Lady Wang. According to ideal patterns, Lady Xing should have charge of the household management; if her husband has abdicated his responsibilities in favor of his younger brother, then Lady Wang should be in charge.[33] In the Rong-guo House, Lady Xing actually has her hands full trying to keep a lid on Jia She's extravagances and tempers, while Lady Wang only rouses herself to action with the greatest difficulty, as when Bao-yu's life is in danger in chapter 33. Both ladies are just as happy for Xi-feng to have the burden of their proper responsibilities, although the praise and favor she receives for her efforts is also a source of jealousy.[34]

When Xi-feng is disabled by a miscarriage (chapter 54), Lady Wang has as much as she can handle managing Grandmother Jia. Running the garden is beyond her, and so she appoints three deputies, denizens of the garden, to manage affairs there. The first is Li Wan, the widow of her son Jia Zhu. The second is Tan-chun, Jia Zheng's daughter by his concubine, Aunt Zhao, and sister of Jia Huan. The third is Bao-chai, who is her sister's daughter. Although they are all able young women, particularly Tan-chun and Bao-chai, none are ideally suited to manage the garden. Li Wan is a self-effacing young widow, whose lack of a living husband deprives her of his authority. Tan-chun is the unmarried daughter of a concubine. Her youth and innocence would diminish her authority, to say nothing of disqualifying her from overseeing matters having to do with married members of the family or staff.[35] Bao-chai is an unmarried cousin of a different surname, technically an outsider, whose participation in Jia household affairs would be regarded outside the family as a grave irregularity. In short, none of these internal governors of the garden is actually suited to the task of household governance, even if they are not positively disqualified. In household management, only married women are supposed to have the necessary authority to oversee all domestic matters. While Xi-feng is an honorary member of the garden's society, her status as a married woman disqualifies her from residence—the "children" in the garden are supposed to be innocent. This interlude underscores the inversion of ideal patterns represented by the garden's society, as its own members are by definition disqualified as governors, while its proper governors are a priori a contaminating influence.

Li Wan regards her own participation in the household administration as strictly temporary and does not undertake any independent judgment or action. In spite of being unmarried, Tan-chun is able to assume her proper status because of her intelligence and well-developed sense of self-respect. Bao-chai herself is mortified when her aunt asks her to conduct disciplinary surveillance in the garden and, as soon as possible after this, arranges to move back in with her mother, out of the garden entirely. Bao-chai is in her own way as punctilious as her Uncle Zheng and infinitely more aware of the implications of what is going on around her. Her removal from the garden allows her to dissociate herself from the destruction that she rightly assumes will result from such irregular patterns of authority.[36] Tan-chun must remain, and her frustration is palpable.

Bao-chai and Tan-chun see perfectly clearly that inversion of proper structures of authority means *no* authority; at least, no authority recognized or condoned by the ideal patterns to which the family aspires. The elders of the household assume that, since the children are doubly sequestered—in the garden and within the family compound—they are somehow timelessly held in childhood and innocence. The children themselves are far more aware than any of their elders that childhood is ending. And although the adults may be oblivious to what is happening in the garden, many of the young people see all too clearly what is going on in the adult world from which they are presumably sheltered. When there are so many servants and such bustling activity, not all members of the household can be incorruptible. Furthermore, so many members of the elder generation are known not for their attention to business and their strong management but, rather, for negligence and avoidance of responsibility. Li Wan turns a blind eye and minds her own affairs, but Tan-chun and Bao-chai are aware that the family is vulnerable. Both try their best to preserve the family from taint of corruption, but there is not much these two young girls can do.

It is from Tan-chun that we hear the first news of the debacle of the Jias' mirror-twin family, the Zhens. Shocked when a serving-girl discovers a purse decorated with erotic figures in the garden, Lady Xing and

Lady Wang unleash a vice squad of toadying servants on all the garden's inhabitants to weed out elements of sexual corruption. As seen in her abrupt dismissal of her own maid, Golden, for flirting, Lady Wang abhors the appearance of licentiousness, and she uses this opportunity to purge the garden of any maids who might conceivably use their sexual attractions to gain favor with Bao-yu. Tan-chun knows that before the Zhens were visited with an imperial confiscation, they carried out a similar investigation of their own servants. Such drastic measures mean that the family has no basis of solidarity on which to operate, no reliable internal trust or loyalty to support them when attacked from the outside. Tan-chun shows her solidarity with her personal staff by denying the inquisition access to their effects, insisting that she be searched first. As the inquisitors reluctantly comply, Tan-chun bitterly warns Xi-feng, Lady Wang's unwilling lieutenant, of the implications:

> "I must say, I cannot understand this eagerness to meet trouble half-way. The searching will begin soon enough in this household when the day of the confiscation arrives. . . . No doubt our time too is coming, slowly but surely. A great household like ours is not destroyed in a day. 'The beast with a thousand legs is a long time dying.' In order for the destruction to be complete, it has to begin from within."
>
> (*SS* III.74.471, *HLM* II.74.813)[37]

Lady Xing and Lady Wang's raid on the garden is conducted for the express purpose of keeping the young people who live there innocent. The result is a fiasco. Whatever the state of innocence of the garden's inhabitants, such an investigation cannot help but shake the foundations of that innocence. This event, more than any other, shocks them into awareness of the force of time.[38] Although Bao-yu's cousin Ying-chun is the first to go, almost all the girls are of marriageable age and soon will face the exigencies of their society's demands on their sex. Several of the garden's inhabitants are already well aware of their danger and are none to eager to make the transition from childhood to marriage.[39]

Most appalled at the prospect, on the girls' behalf, is Bao-yu. From his own observations, there is little potential for female fulfillment in marriage; indeed, what he sees of marriage makes it a fate to be dreaded for girls. According to him, "A girl before she marries is like a priceless pearl, but once she marries the pearl loses its lustre and develops all sorts of disagreeable flaws, and by the time she is an old woman, she's no longer like a pearl at all, more like a boiled fish's eye" (*SS* III.59.138–139, *HLM* II.59.632). His observation proves true, with a couple of notable exceptions. He even has some insight into what causes this deterioration. Thrust aside by the grim female retainers assigned to remove the maid uncovered as the owner of the licentious purse during the raid, he exclaims: "Strange, the way they get like this when they marry! It must be something in the male that infects them. If anything they end up even worse than the men!" (*SS* III.77.534, *HLM* II.77.849).

While the serving women laugh at his assertion that "all girls must be good and all women must be bad" (ibid.), Bao-yu has hit on the etiology of this seemingly universal erosion of the female spirit. He is not speaking merely of exterior beauty but internal contentment. Distraught over his cousin Ying-chun's wretched fate in marriage to a battering libertine, Bao-yu laments to Dai-yu: "Why is it that the minute they're grown up, girls are married off and have to suffer so?" (*SS* IV.81.33, *HLM* III.81.894). What he does not understand is that he himself is deeply implicated. Bao-yu will inflict upon his own wife—Bao-chai—precisely the kind of injury that causes the deterioration he has observed. Marriage marks the beginning of this destruction, except in those rare cases of happy marriages. And since romantic inclination is not a factor in selecting a marriage partner, those who are romantically inclined are almost certain to be disillusioned.

This is essential in the destinies of the Stone and the Flower. In the garden the children were left to their own devices, which in Bao-yu's and Dai-yu's case means carrying out the imperatives of their previous existence in the Court of Sunset Glow with no inhibition or interference from any outside authority. Seldom does their relationship progress harmoniously—quite the contrary. The two lovers never seem to reach an understanding (except in their dreams), and their constant bickering and mutual wounding ensures that Dai-yu's tears will flow to repay her debt. When Bao-yu flatly declares to her, "If you died, I should become a monk" (*SS* II.30.95, *HLM* I.30.301), Dai-yu upbraids him for such an extravagant and inappropriate resolve. But he speaks simple truth; he will indeed make good this vow when he comes to accept her death. At this point, however, the prospect seems like fantasy, in view of the encumbrances on both Bao-yu and Dai-yu.

Even their plainest declarations either go unspoken or unheard—by the right person. In chapter 32 Dai-yu overhears Bao-yu rhapsodizing on her superiority to all others, and her emotions run through the catalogue of love. But when Bao-yu runs after her to make his declaration in person, she declines to hear, slips away, and leaves Bao-yu to make a passionate pledge to his maid Aroma (Xi-ren) by mistake. This slip not only deprives Dai-yu of emotional gratification but will bring about the lovers' romantic ruin. Aroma is alarmed by her master's words, which she understands were meant for Dai-yu, and concerned that a scandal will occur. When she learns of his parents' plan to betroth him to Bao-chai, she is the one to carry the tale of Bao-yu's true love to Lady Wang, which will set in motion the plot to trick Bao-yu into the marriage.

The cousins' preference for each other is recognized by everyone around them, and despite all their quarreling and misunderstanding they take their special relationship for granted. But it cannot set a social pattern. Ideally, marriage is a matter of family politics and economics.[40] As a choice for Bao-yu in betrothal and marriage, Dai-yu is disqualified because she is an orphan without fortune, unable to bring in the sumptuous dowry desperately needed by the debt-ridden Jias. Furthermore, her sickly constitution makes her unlikely to survive to produce an heir.[41] As a patrilineal first cousin, she is regarded as slightly "closer" kin than a matrilineal cousin, and although she still bears a different surname from Bao-yu, the "more distant" relation of a matrilineal cousin would be regarded as an advantage.[42] Bao-yu's cousin Bao-chai is the family's choice, because of her family's wealth and because her robust health and equable temperament make her more likely to withstand the pressures of the Jia household and produce an heir. Besides, Bao-chai possesses the golden locket, which was given to her by Bao-yu's own abiding guardian monk, with the injunction that she should marry someone with a jade to match. When the senior ladies begin to discuss Bao-yu's betrothal, this is taken as a sure sign of a "predestined affinity" (*tianpei de yinyuan*)—which it is, but not quite in the way they think. Although these considerations would indeed be vital to the family when selecting a bride, when Grandmother Jia seems surprised to hear of Bao-yu's preference for Dai-yu, the reader is incredulous. What makes matters far worse, however, is the elaborate deception concocted by the women to bring about Bao-yu's marriage to Bao-chai.

Dai-yu has always feared that her hopes for marriage with Bao-yu would be ignored. She looks everywhere for omens, good and bad. An old woman bringing a present of lychees from Bao-chai sings out: "No wonder our Madam says that Miss Lin and your Master Bao were made for one another! She really does look just like a fairy!" (*SS* IV.82.61, *HLM* III.82.908). Preparing for bed, Dai-yu broods: "I know Bao-yu loves me more than anyone else. But Grannie and Aunt Wang still haven't mentioned it! If only my parents had settled it for us while they were still alive . . ." (61–62, 909). She then slips into a nightmare in which she imagines all the hopeful possibilities lost, and the true detachment of her Jia kin is seen in the harshest, but ultimately truest light. She dreams that her father is alive and has arranged a betrothal for her. Her nightmare grandmother coldly explains "It's no use. . . . All girls marry and leave home. You're a child and don't understand these things" (63, 910). Even the dream Bao-yu seems prepared to give her up if she wants to leave. When she cries that she cannot bear to be separated from him, he reminds her of the universal expectation her residence with the Jias created:

> "If you don't want to go, then stay here. . . . You were originally engaged to me. That's why you came to live here. Has it never occurred to you how specially I've always treated you? Haven't you noticed?"
>
> Suddenly it all seemed clear. She really was engaged to Bao-yu after all! Of course she was!
>
> (65, 911)

The nightmare ends as Bao-yu insists on showing her how true he is. He cuts open his chest to show her his heart, finds it is no longer there, and falls to the ground. Dai-yu wakes in a cold sweat, and remembers: "Mother and father died long ago. Bao-yu and I have never been engaged. . . . What ever could have made me have such a dream?" (66, 911).

One does not have to delve too deeply to find the emotional source of the dream, but it has a powerful social logic as well. The fact that the Jias took Dai-yu in after her mother died, but while her father was still living and able to provide for her materially if not emotionally, would have been enough to suggest to the outside world that she was Bao-yu's intended bride. Their further intimacy through childhood and residence in the garden made it look that much more certain. Although it would be inappropriate for a son to express a marriage preference, it would never have occurred to Bao-yu that he needed to express it at all—he regards the match he desires as a fait accompli. In chapter 28, Bao-yu catches a glimpse of Bao-chai's plump and pretty arm and muses, "If that arm were growing on Cousin Lin's body . . . I might hope one day to touch it. What a pity it's hers! Now I shall never have that good fortune" (SS II.28.66, HLM I.28.285). When Dai-yu's maid,

Nightingale, probes his intentions, he states flatly, "Let me try to put it for you in a nutshell. In life we shall live together; in death we shall mingle our dust. Will that do?" (*SS* III.57.101, *HLM* II.57.611). Even if his parents had other ideas, Bao-yu would have expected his grandmother's subversion of his parents' authority to assure that his wish would be granted. Grandmother Jia might well have capitulated to Bao-yu's wishes if he had thought to speak plainly to her of his preference—did she not herself suggest that they were fated to be wed when she remarked:

> "It must be my punishment for something I did wrong in a past
> life to have to live with a pair of such obstinate, addle-pated lit-
> tle geese! . . . It must be fate. That's what it says in the proverb,
> after all:
> 'Tis Fate brings foes and lo'es tegither."
> (*SS* II.29.91, *HLM* I.29.298)[43]

Xi-feng's frequent teasing of the two also seems to take their union for granted, even after the family has begun to discuss its plans for Bao-yu's betrothal in secret. The members of the household who should look to the proprieties strangely ignore these appearances, but to the outside world the only possible way to break this implicit betrothal would be with Dai-yu's death. As it happens, Dai-yu spits blood upon waking from her nightmare, and this marks the beginning of her final decline.

The first mention of Bao-yu's betrothal, in chapter 84, focuses on the "predestined affinity" of Bao-yu's jade and Bao-chai's gold locket. Jia Zheng is reluctant to make concrete plans for Bao-yu until he shows some signs of settling down to a serious course of study and understanding his responsibilities in life. Surprisingly, his main concern seems to be for the happiness of the bride: "Without a marked improvement on his part, any alliance we might hope to arrange would be doomed, and would certainly be a regrettable error for the young lady concerned" (*SS* IV.84.96, *HLM* III.84.929). His mother bristles at his implied criticism of her role in rearing Bao-yu:

> "I know that it's your decision! . . . and that I'm an interfering old
> busybody! But let me say just this: even if I *did* rather spoil him
> when he was little, and even if he isn't quite as grown-up and re-
> sponsible as you think he ought to be, I still think he has always
> been a nice, well-mannered, honest boy. I think you're quite

wrong to treat him as a ne'er-do-well, or as some sort of threat to a young girl's happiness."

(ibid.)

It is wonderfully ironic that Jia Zheng seems to have so much more insight into what makes a good match than his mother does. One could hardly accuse him of sentimentality, yet again and again, his intuition for the happiness of the girls is far truer than that of the most experienced woman. It was Jia Zheng who foresaw Ying-chun's disaster and tried to remonstrate with his elder brother. When he arranges a match for Tan-chun, he chooses well—hers is one of the few happy marriages in the entire novel.

Although Jia Zheng was reluctant to betroth Bao-yu to Bao-chai in the first place, it was out of consideration for Bao-chai, not because he feared Dai-yu would die of a broken heart. The deception that results in this unhappy marriage is only possible because in chapter 94, when a group of spring-flowering crabapples ominously bursts into bloom in the autumn, Bao-yu loses his jade. The household responds to this crisis with predictable hysteria, and Bao-yu rapidly descends into idiocy. Hoping to bring him around, over his father's express objections Grandmother Jia decides to marry him to Bao-chai as soon as possible. Aroma warns Bao-yu's mother of his passion for Dai-yu, and the senior ladies conspire to trick Bao-yu into marriage by telling him that Dai-yu will be his bride. Dai-yu, finally confirming her worst fears, vomits blood and prepares for death. Although it is Grandmother Jia's neglect and inadvertent connivance that brought matters to such a pass, when confronted with Dai-yu's final decline, the old lady speaks most harshly to this point:

> "I simply cannot understand it. Ours is a decent family. We do not tolerate unseemly goings-on. And that applies to foolish romantic attachments. If her illness is of a respectable nature, I do not mind how much we have to spend to get her better. But if she is suffering from some form of lovesickness, no amount of medicine can cure it and she can expect no further sympathy from me either."
>
> (*SS* IV.97.342–343, *HLM* III.97.1066)

Of course, it is precisely the family's passive collusion in these "unseemly goings-on" that has aggravated the problem, at least on the mundane level. Because of the cosmic foreshadowing, we have known from the beginning that this can be the only outcome. But the earthly tragedy is compounded. Whatever Bao-chai's feelings for Bao-yu may have been, there is plenty of evidence that she does not relish the match, in part because of violations of the proper marriage rituals the Jias force upon her to hasten it, in part because the bridegroom is seriously ill and thus unequipped to gratify her emotionally or sexually. And no one knows better than she where Bao-yu's real preference lies. In this sense, Bao-chai becomes a sacrifice, for the sake of both the Jias' family stability and continuance and Bao-yu's and Dai-yu's liberation from the red dust. When Bao-yu lifts his bride's veil and sees the wrong woman, he collapses. At that very moment, Dai-yu dies in agony, convinced that her love has abandoned her.

Bao-yu's bride, however, must struggle to bring about harmony and fulfillment in the family realm, mocked by the knowledge that her husband preferred another and would have refused her if he had been in his right mind. In practical terms, Bao-chai is the ideal bride for the Jia *family*. She is just not the ideal bride for Bao-yu, and therefore the process of deterioration noted by him in his discourse on the stages of womanhood—the progress from pearl to fish's eye—must begin. When Bao-yu sees his lively cousin Shi Xiang-yun a few weeks after her marriage, he is astonished to observe that she looks radiant, even prettier than she did before she was married, and he wonders: "I always imagined that Xiang-yun would change once she was married. . . . But to hear her talk now, she seems quite the same as ever. Why has marriage made *my* wife more modest and bashful than before, more tongue-tied than ever?" (*SS* V.108.161, *HLM* III.108.1179).

The answer is that Xiang-yun is happy; Bao-chai is not. Again and again, marriages are observed to stifle and beat down, even physically batter women, until whatever spirit they have dissipates in frustration and despair. The young Xi-feng, passionately attached to Jia Lian, deteriorates exponentially as his compulsive infidelities insult and degrade her, until her entire being is consumed by sexual jealousy and her only outlet is the relentless pursuit of money. Ying-chun is done to death outright by a vicious batterer, but others die more slowly. Dai-yu, denied the man she loves, at least goes to her grave a priceless pearl.

Bao-chai attempts to confront her own suffering, from both bereavement for her friend Dai-yu and her husband's rejection, by confronting Bao-yu with the fact of Dai-yu's death. In this she actually defies her new in-laws to snap him out of his protracted fit. Bao-yu is wild with grief, but his mind is cleared of the fog that descended upon him with the loss of his jade. Unfortunately for Bao-chai, facing up to Dai-yu's death points Bao-yu to his ultimate liberation. After all, the Stone and the Crimson Pearl Flower were incarnated as human beings not to fulfill their love but to transcend the illusion of love. None of Bao-chai's well-reasoned persuasions or attempts to win her husband to her notions of social duty or marital commitment can change that. Much earlier, after Bao-yu had been so badly beaten by his father, Bao-chai remonstrated with him that the episode should allow him to make a new beginning and willingly follow Jia Zheng's authority and intentions. Bao-yu reacted with scorn—why should girls worry about such nonsense? Much of the strength of his affinity with Dai-yu came from the fact that she agreed with him that striving for fame and career were a waste of time. The underpinning of this affinity is their preexisting attachment and their present destiny. Bao-yu and Dai-yu are both beings to whom it matters nothing whether they get on in the world because neither is destined to be integrated into that world.

Although the history of the Stone and the Flower prefigures the development of their love, it is not necessary to explain the events in the narrative in human terms. Observing Bao-yu's misery, Dai-yu's maid Nightingale muses:

> "What a dreadful pity it is that our Miss Lin never had the fortune to be his bride! Such unions are clearly determined by fate. Until fate reveals itself, men continue to indulge in blind passion and fond imaginings; then, when the die is cast and the truth is known, the fools may remain impervious, but the ones who care deeply, the men of true sentiment, can only weep bitterly at the futility of their romantic attachments, at the tragedy of their earthly plight. *She* is dead and knows nothing; but *he* still lives, and there is no end to his suffering and torment. Better by far the destiny of plant or stone, bereft of knowledge and consciousness, but blessed at least with purity and peace of mind!"
>
> (*SS* V.113.255, *HLM* III.113.1243)

But this *is* the destiny of plant ("Flower," *caomu*) and stone ("Stone," *shitou*). Although this is quite unknown to Nightingale, on further consideration the bitter irony of her words gives way to understanding of their truth. Unconscious as she is of her mistress's original nature, Nightingale has seen through the illusion of romantic attachment more clearly than any other member of Bao-yu's household, including his own wife, with the possible exception of his cousin Xi-chun. This contrary younger sister of Jia Zhen is terrified of what she sees of sex and marriage around her and wishes to escape to the cloister. Even the ignorant little novices from the Convent of the Savior King, when they come to visit her, seem to understand these apprehensions:

> "A nun leads a hard life, it's true, harder than a young lady in a rich family. But we're *saved*! Even if we can't hope to become Buddhas or Saints, at least by keeping up our devotions we may someday be reborn as men. And that would be sufficient reward in itself. At least then we would escape the endless trials and tribulations of womankind. You are still too young to understand, miss; but let me tell you, when once a young lady leaves home and marries, it is all over with her. She must spend the rest of her life a slave to her husband's will."
>
> (*SS* V.115.270, *HLM* III.115.1253)

This is something that Xi-chun understands all too well. As Jia Zhen's sister, is her puritanical reaction to the conduct of the Ning-guo House really so surprising? That she should seek refuge in the cloister, to the point of attempting suicide when the family denies permission, is a sign of how truly desperate matters are. In this light, her verse in the Celestial Registers, "Alas, that daughter of so great a house / by Buddha's altar lamp should sleep alone!" (*SS* I.5.135, *HLM* I.5.48), is not a condemnation of life in a nunnery but, rather, an indictment of a household that seems to hold out no prospect of a decent life for its female members. Better to opt out of society altogether than to be overwhelmed by the injustice of the world against women.[44]

When the senior women of the household finally yield and allow Xi-chun to become a nun, Bao-yu not only supports her but urges his mother to allow Nightingale to have her wish to serve Xi-chun in her hermitage. The Stone and the Flower voluntarily submitted to the tribulations of a mortal existence in order to awaken to the bliss of their proper nature, "without knowledge or feeling" (*wuzhi wujue*). Nightingale does not yet realize that this is a state of transcendence, rather than unconsciousness. In other words, ignorance is bliss, but only if you come to choose ignorance after acquiring experience and knowledge. Nightingale believes that complete lack of consciousness would be a happier state, considering the prospects for happiness around her, than the miseries of sentient life. She does not connect unconsciousness with enlightenment, but for her the process of detachment has begun. For the moment, detachment from the mundane world may comfort her as she prepares for a better existence beyond this unhappy one.

The tragedy of Bao-yu and Dai-yu is only one, albeit a most heartwrenching one, of the consequences of internal mismanagement and negligence that determine the larger family debacle. The Jia household's internal disarray and deviation from ideal patterns of conduct mirror external acts of mismanagement, negligence, and even crime that do not go unnoticed and unpunished. After Jia Zheng returns from an assignment at a distant post, where he has been impeached for allowing his servants to accept bribes and practice extortion, the family reception to welcome him home is rudely interrupted. A detachment of the imperial secret police, known as the Embroidered Jackets, swarms through both the Ning-guo and Rong-guo Houses to conduct an official confiscation. A confiscation is a raid directed at a citizen who is perceived to be defying and even undermining imperial authority with illegal activities, and its purpose is to dispossess him utterly of both the fruits of his crimes and the wherewithal to continue them. The official charges, however, seem more directed at personal moral conduct than genuine threats to imperial authority.[45]

Although the entire family is in danger of losing everything, only one member of each household is actually indicted. Charges are read against Jia She for conspiring to ruin a man whose collection of antique fans he coveted, which led to the man's suicide. Jia Zhen is indicted for corrupting the sons of noble families by encouraging gambling and debauchery and for intimidating a man into giving up his promised bride, You-shi's stepsister Er-jie, so that she could marry Jia Lian illegally, during a period of national mourning. In the course of the raid, Jia Lian's apartment yields Xi-feng's records of all the loans she had extended at illegal rates of interest to feather her own nest and to meet the family's expenditures. The apartments of Jia She and Jia Lian are stripped of almost all their material possessions.

The looting would certainly have spread to the other apartments had it not been for the intercession of the prince of Bei-jing. This prince has taken an interest in Bao-yu ever since meeting him in Qin-shi's funeral procession, and his solicitude forces the fanatical commander of the Embroidered Jackets to call off his minions before they can empty the Rong-guo mansion entirely. Even so, the losses to Jia Zheng are considerable, and the only member of the family whose possessions are untouched is Grandmother Jia. On the Ning-guo side, no such intervention is made, and all that cannot be carried off is smashed to pieces.[46]

What is most striking, as the Jias attempt to recover from this disaster, is the emphasis on the shame brought upon the family by the failure of their domestic structure. Following ideal patterns, families should be able to manage six generations under one roof or continue for nine generations without a division of property.[47] Here Jia Zheng's and his mother's shortcomings converge to produce disaster, and both in their own way take the blame. Whatever the blow to their material well-being, it is the blow to their family integrity and prestige that could be mortal, and both mother and son struggle valiantly to soften the blow.

Even though he is neither charged with a crime nor implicated in one, Jia Zheng sustains the public face of the blame. When questioned by the presiding prince over the promissory notes at illegal interest rates in Jia Lian's apartment (which are not even his nephew's, but Xi-feng's), he immediately offers, "I have, alas, been insufficiently diligent in supervising my household. I was completely unaware of these activities" (SS V.105.121, HLM III.105.1152). Alone with his thoughts, he castigates himself that he is responsible for the disaster because of his failure to inculcate proper standards in the younger generation (shi wo bu neng guanjiao zizhi) (SS V.106.129, HLM III.106.1159). Grandmother Jia sounds the same theme as she prays to Buddha for the family's deliverance:

> "The blame for all of these misfortunes must rest on my shoulders, for having failed to teach the younger generation the true principles of conduct.... Have pity on me, Almighty Heaven, and heed my devout supplication; send me an early death that I may atone for the sins of my children and grandchildren!"
>
> (SS V.106.134, HLM III.106.1162)

The old lady's entreaty is dramatic, but when Xi-feng reproaches herself for her role in the family's ruin, Grandmother Jia consoles her, "This whole nonsense was started by the men.... It was nothing to do with you" (SS V.107.150, HLM III.107.1172).[48] Yes and no. If Xi-feng's usury and extortion were the product of her own initiative, the fact that she could carry out such audacious plans shows either that she was insufficiently mindful of her husband's authority or that he was negligent in asserting his authority and supervising his wife's activities. This is the true nature of the inversion of ideal patterns of authority in the Jia household: The women are intelligent and act independently, the men are either too distracted or too dissipated to oversee their activities. Both come to grief, and the men, ostensibly the guardians of the ideal patterns, must shoulder the public shame.

Jia Zheng's greatest humiliation is actually at the moment he is officially acquitted of any wrongdoing. He is summoned before the Privy Council, the emperor's own judicial court, for questioning. When asked about the activities of his elder brother and nephew, he admits:

> "I have truly endeavoured to be diligent in the performance of all [my] official duties, but I fear I have completely neglected to keep my own household in order. For this inexcusable shortcoming on my part, for my abject failure to instruct my sons and nephews in the true principles of conduct, for my base ingratitude to the throne, I can only beg that His Majesty will punish me with fitting severity."
>
> (SS V.107.140, HLM III.107.1166)

The emperor then pronounces sentence. Thoughts of the Jias' loyal and distinguished ancestors keep him from imposing the heaviest penalties allowed by the law. Jia She's and Jia Zhen's titles and official positions are forfeit, their estates are confiscated, and the family name disgraced. The two men are sentenced to military service at the far reaches of the empire. Severe as these disgraces are, the worst blow is for the member of the family who feels the stigma most deeply: "Jia Zheng has for many years held provincial posts in which he has served conscientiously and prudently, and he is absolved from the consequences of his failure to govern his household correctly" (142, 1167). The emperor declines Jia Zheng's offer to show his repentance by donating all his hereditary emoluments and accumulated property. Jia Zheng has been obliged, by his own sense of personal integrity, to take responsibility for his negligence in the domestic sphere, which he regards as the ultimate cause of all the misconduct of every member of the extended household. The throne agrees with him, but "absolves" him. What greater confirmation of his mediocrity and inadequacy could he face?

Jia Zheng's appearance before the throne, taking his lumps for his family's deviations from ideal patterns of conduct, alludes ironically to the presentation of one Zhang Gongyi during the reign of the emperor Gaozu (r. 618–627) of the Tang dynasty. Zhang was renowned for the extent and peace of his household, which contained many branches and generations and remained intact through nine generations. The emperor summoned him for the express purpose of honoring him for this accomplishment. When asked how he managed to do it, Zhang took up a brush and wrote the character *ren* (forbearance) one hundred times.[49] Zhang Gongyi's honor and Jia Zheng's disgrace are a striking illustration of the contrast between ideal and actual patterns that would certainly not have been lost on Bao-yu's wretched father.

Jia Zheng invoked his duties at the office to excuse his inattention to household matters, fondly relying on his nephew to oversee domestic affairs. Jia Lian, however, cannot be the *jiazhang*—who must be a member of the older generation. Jia She may eschew his responsibilities, but Zheng cannot. In all fairness, he is by temperament not one to avoid his duty, especially when the family is in the public eye. Intellectually he understands the obligations of his position, and according to ideal patterns this should be enough. But as the example of Zhang Gongyi illustrates, understanding of the rules must be tempered by insight and compassion to maintain harmony. It is precisely in the intuitive, human realm that Jia Zheng loses his way, and he therefore has little understanding of how the principles to which he so assiduously adheres translate into day-to-day life. Certain matters—the household deficit, insubordination among the servants, sexual misconduct—he cannot face and so avoids confronting them as long as they stay within certain bounds. This is not forbearance; this is negligence. Negligence is easy to commit, but forbearance is hard. Unfortunately, when the buck stops, Jia Zheng cannot claim that—whatever the ideal patterns may be—according to actual patterns his household is typical, even doing rather well in the circumstances. Neither public scrutiny nor his own sense of personal integrity can exonerate him. The imperial grace he receives is grace indeed.

After the family's fortunes reach this nadir, Bao-yu's jade is returned to him by the monk who has been his ever-vigilant guide (chapter 115). Bao-yu swoons, and the monk leads him back to the Land of Illusion, where he has a second chance to read the Celestial Registers to learn the fates of the women in his life. This time, when he awakens he remembers every detail. He knows the futures of those whose lives concern him, all beyond his power to interfere. Moreover, he understands his true nature and recognizes his jade for what it is: not a life-preserving talisman or a signifier of worldly success, but merely a metaphor for his origin, the spiritual form to which he will inevitably return.

Although the family again hopes that the jade will restore its fortunes, the reappearance of the jade prefigures a most unexpected kind of change. Bao-yu's second reading of the Celestial Registers has settled his doubts and fears about his beloved girls, and he sets himself upon the path to personal liberation. His constant arguments with Bao-chai about the different kinds of spiritual life are now resolved in his own mind, but she is puzzled when he seems to cede to her remonstrations about duty and commitment: "Doing well in the examination is not that difficult. And what you said about *never achieving anything else* and making *some return for heaven's favor and our ancestors' virtue* is very much to the point . . ." (*SS* V.118.330, *HLM* III.118.1294). Although Bao-chai's sympathies are all with the ideal patterns of Confucian society, she understands the pull of the mystical side of consciousness and human striving on her husband, and his words fill her with foreboding.

In order to discharge his mundane obligations, he must father an heir to carry on the family line and tend to the ancestral sacrifices; fulfill his grandmother's dying wish that he bring glory to the family by passing the national examinations; and show his respect for his own parents. In apparently their only act of sexual intercourse, Bao-chai has become pregnant with a son. In the short time left before the exams are held, Bao-yu puts aside all but the required books and focuses on them perfectly, ignoring all other tasks. On the great day, when Bao-yu is about to leave home to sit for the metropolitan examinations, Bao-chai has a premonition that she will never see her husband again:

> Bao-chai had already perceived the strangeness of the conversation. . . . Not daring to express this presentiment of hers openly, Bao-chai held back her tears and remained silent. Bao-yu came up to her and made her a deep bow. It seemed to them all such an eccentric way to behave, and no one could imagine what it was supposed to mean; nor did anyone dare to laugh. The general amazement increased when Bao-chai burst into floods of tears, and Bao-yu bade her farewell:
>
> "Coz! I'm going now. Stay here with Mother and wait for the good news!"
>
> "It's time for you to go," replied Bao-chai. "There is no need to embark on another of your long speeches."
>
> "Strange that you should be urging me on my way," said Bao-yu. "I know it is time to go." . . .
>
> "Off I go! Enough of this foolery! It's over!" . . .

Only Lady Wang and Bao-chai were sobbing inconsolably, as if they were parting from him for ever.

(SS V.119.337–338, HLM III.119.1300)

After finishing his exams (in which he places a glorious seventh), Bao-yu again links up with the monk who encouraged his incarnation as the Stone in the first place and vanishes. Having begotten an heir and placed high in the national exams, Bao-yu has in fact discharged almost all his obligations according to the ideal family patterns. As a final gesture of his understanding of his family obligations, he appears before his father, who is on his way home to Bei-jing from burying Grandmother Jia in Nan-jing, and bows before him. He could not leave the world without showing his respect for his father. With this evidence of Bao-yu's irrevocable departure from the mundane world, Jia Zheng assumes that his son has reached illumination and, in so doing, shows some genuine illumination himself:

> "You do not understand," he said with a sigh. "This was indeed no supernatural apparition; I saw these men [Bao-yu, Impervioso, and Mysterioso] with my own eyes. I heard them singing, and the words of their song held a most profound and mysterious meaning. Bao-yu came into the world with his jade, and there was always something strange about it. I knew it for an ill omen. But because his grandmother doted on him so, we nurtured him and brought him up until now. . . . But the truth of the matter must be that he himself is a being from a higher realm who has descended into this world to experience the trials of this human life. For these past nineteen years he has been doted on in vain by his poor grandmother! Now at last I understand!"

(SS V.120.360–361, HLM III.120.1315)

Jia Zheng here underlines the difficulty of reading omens and comments on the paradox of understanding them only after the fact. Throughout The Story of the Stone, there is a pattern of omens taken as good, as pointing toward success according to the ideal patterns of social aspiration, which do not turn out as expected. Jia Zheng's first daughter is born on the supposedly lucky first day of spring (from which she gets her name, Yuan-chun), but is separated from her family forever by her promotion to the imperial bedchamber and dies young after a lonely and empty life in the palace. Some crabapple trees in

Prospect Garden, thought to be dead, burst into flower out of season in the inauspicious autumn. Grandmother Jia reads this as signaling good fortune for the marriage of Bao-yu and Bao-chai, but in fact it presages the loss of Bao-yu's jade, the death of the imperial concubine, and the death of Dai-yu. The jade itself, thought to mark Bao-yu for worldly success, is in fact a symbol of his otherworldly origin and his inevitable return to the spiritual realm.

Although spiritual transcendence might seem incompatible with social convention or emotional attachment, in *The Story of the Stone* both are necessary companions on the path to enlightenment. It is only when emotional attachment and romantic longing are systematically thwarted by the imperatives of social convention that spiritual aspirations become a conscious alternative. This is true for Bao-yu as the incarnation of the Stone and ultimately for the reader as well. Although Buddhist detachment and transcendence are defined in opposition to the worldly, Bao-yu's worldly attachments *are* his expedients to enlightenment. It was for this experience that the Stone was incarnated in the first place: Without having experienced emotional *attachment*, he could not achieve *detachment*. Because the Stone recorded his experiences exactly as they occurred, without any embellishment, the monk Vanitas was able to reproduce this process merely by reading *The Story of the Stone*. We know that it was the author's intention to help those of us "who are still in need of awakening." The promise of the inscription is that even people who lack Bao-yu's karmic heritage of needs and propensities can reach enlightenment through reading his story, as Vanitas did. Although the experience is *vicarious*, the Stone suggests that, by sticking absolutely to the "facts," narrating events exactly as they occurred, he allows the reader to experience his existence fully and reproduce his results. The author plays on the interpenetration of lyrical and narrative experience in his work: By following the vicarious experience of the narrative, one can achieve integration with that experience and reach a lyrical epiphany.[50]

Strange as it may seem, the purpose of the Stone seems to have been understood implicitly by at least two characters within the narrative. The first is Jia Zheng, who despite his apparent lack of imagination finally understands his son's true nature and is able to let him go. The second is Bao-chai.

It is not that the affinity of jade and gold has "triumphed" over the affinity of flower and stone. The strength of the Stone's prior attachment to the Crimson Pearl Flower has indeed carried him through the delusions of the world of his incarnation. Bao-yu's existence focuses on two personal crises: the romantic climax, when Bao-yu is tricked into marrying Bao-chai at the very moment of Dai-yu's death, and the spiritual climax, when Bao-yu quits the world so that the Stone can return to the Land of Illusion. These events are momentous not just to him but his entire family by virtue of the vital interdependence of the social, emotional, and spiritual levels. The marriage of jade and gold will bear fruit: Bao-chai will bear the son to carry on the family line and possibly reverse the decline in the Jia fortunes. But there is a further question—how does all this fulfill Bao-chai? This is a question left unanswered. Although Bao-yu chooses to leave the world rather than engage it, his arguments with his wife do not favor his side. Bao-chai's remonstrations with Bao-yu and others throughout *The Story of the Stone* are conservative, often to the point of priggishness.[51] Nevertheless, she gives voice to the aspirations of loyal subjects based on traditional ideal patterns, and even her husband cannot answer her. Indeed, he admits the justice of her admonitions and fulfills the letter, if not the spirit, of his mundane obligations. One could argue that the national sensation caused by Bao-yu's disappearance in chapter 119 accrues more benefit to his family than any mundane career could have done. Because Bao-yu places seventh on the national lists, he is summoned to an audience at the imperial palace. His nephew Jia Lan goes to represent the family, and he explains the family relation to the Jia imperial concubine and that his uncle has disappeared to become a Buddhist immortal. When the emperor reads Bao-yu's examination paper, he marvels at its brilliance. As a sign of respect for Bao-yu's genius, and out of tenderness for Yuan-chun's memory, the emperor pardons Jia She and Jia Zhen, and ultimately pronounces a general amnesty throughout the empire. By entering the gate of Buddhism, Bao-yu causes the emperor's mercy to extend to the farthest reaches of the land.[52]

This passage, starting from the inquiry about Bao-yu's identity and culminating in the declaration of the amnesty, has the high bathos of a Gilbert-and-Sullivan denouement, except that the hero does not reappear to live happily ever after. Within the frame of the novel, albeit in far more verbose terms, it echoes Vanitas's original reading of *The Story of the Stone* and offers a secular counterpart. Quite a testimony to the power of literature!

It is left to Bao-chai to carry out the imperatives of Confucian society and attempt to adhere to ideal patterns in rearing her son. She has opted for the world of duty and convention and must find her justification there. In this, Bao-chai is a more accomplished double of her sister-in-law, Li Wan. Li Wan was reared in a wealthy household, but limited to a minimal level of education as a matter of principle, so that she would not have exaggerated expectations for her life as a wife and mother. Bao-chai is profoundly learned in medicine and the arts, yet in her remonstrations with her cousins Shi Xiang-yun and Lin Dai-yu she advocated ignorance as better for women, as their horizons of expectation would be low after marriage, even in a wealthy household. Her meticulous preparation for becoming a wife serves her well in her premature "widowhood." Like Li Wan, she will care scrupulously for her only son and support her mother-in-law in the household management. Recreation is strictly circumscribed, escape limited to the vicarious experience of plays and fiction—except in extreme cases like her husband's, by leaving the world to become a monk, or like her friend Dai-yu's, through death.

Bao-chai is like her own locket: splendid, precious, but mostly hidden under a sober exterior. It adds an extra pathos to her earnest words—with all she has to offer, very little of it will give her happiness. But that is not the point, at least not on the cosmic level. Nevertheless, the author's voice resounds throughout the tale with nostalgia and regret. It is one of the essential paradoxes of existence as defined by *The Story of the Stone*.

3

PREEXISTING CONDITIONS

Retributory Illness and the Limits of Medicine

If fondness for the representation of *materia medica* is any indication, readers of *The Story of the Stone* might well think that Cao Xueqin missed his calling in life. The pageant of doctors, patients, folk remedies, and pharmaceuticals in *The Story of the Stone* shows a profound concern with illness in all its aspects—its physical and emotional effects, its paraphernalia, and its social and spiritual significance. The frequency and variety of illness in the novel is another facet of the novel as cultural compendium. Cao's descriptions of illness and medical practice are by no means incidental or generic. Each disorder is matched to its sufferer on his or her deepest organic and spiritual levels, which means that Cao's astonishingly detailed and accurate clinical profiles mesh perfectly with the allegorical imperatives of the individual characters.

This is especially significant when we consider the allegorical frame of the novel. We first meet the Stone-who-will-be-Bao-yu at the base of Green-ridge/Greensickness Peak in the Land of Illusion. The Chinese pun on this place name makes this crucial allegorical signpost almost a throwaway phrase,[1] but it points to a disorder that affects the lives of many of the important characters in *The Story of the Stone*. In its most dire form, it is hopeless and even fatal. When Grandmother Jia speaks of "lovesickness" (*xinbing*) as plaguing the adolescent members of her household, she is referring to a series of symptoms that were recognized by doctors in both East and West in premodern times, but have never fully coalesced into an organic illness. "Greensickness," as it is called in the West, is also known as the "disease of virgins," and since the seventeenth century has rejoiced in the clinical name "chlorosis."[2] It is regarded as a disease of unmarried females, though it is by no means unknown among unmarried males. Greensickness in both sexes is thought to be caused by frustration of sexual desire and unfulfilled romantic longing. Symptoms include unhealthy pallor, heart palpitations and shortness of breath, headaches, intermittent fevers, and a general feeling of lassitude. In females it is often accompanied by amenorrhea. Although the symptoms can be treated, the universal cure is marriage.[3]

The older ladies of the Jia family regard this disorder as almost an inevitable part of adolescence and therefore may be blind to the presence of more serious illnesses, with tragic results. The notion of *qinggen*, however, goes far beyond lovesickness. By using this pun as the point of origin for the Stone, the author sets the stage not only for a tale of romantic longing and desire but for a more complex intertwining of medical and spiritual viewpoints, fusing details of the mundane world with the potential for transcendence of that world. The ultimate purpose of the inhabitants of the Ning-guo and Rong-guo Houses is to awaken to the vanity of worldly existence and return to the realm of emptiness. According to the experience of Brother Amor, this is achieved by entering into the realm of form and experiencing the illusion of attachment, then realizing the true liberation of emptiness through disillusionment with the possibilities of attachment. At the base of Greensickness Peak, Cao Xueqin plants a sign: *Here is where attachment begins*.

Cao's vision of traditional Chinese medicine does not depend on religious dogma. Medicine as a discipline in China was, and remains, a humane system in a humanistic discipline, in which illness is regarded not as a sequence of biochemical events but, rather, as disruptions of patterns of human behavior that should be in accord with prevailing external and environmental conditions.[4] The purpose of Chinese medicine is to maintain for each person a constant level of "optimal functional effectiveness."[5] Each individual has his or her unique set point for this equilibrium; hence the Chinese emphasis on the patient in the context of his or her physical and emotional environment. When a person falls ill, the doctor's goal is to restore the patient's organic equilibrium. This may be achieved either by environmental changes or by the use of drugs—China's premodern pharmacopoeia is the most extensive in the world, and Cao Xueqin's knowledge of its intricacies is exhaustive.

If the patient's dysfunction has persisted for long enough to do permanent physical damage, it will be impossible to restore the original equilibrium. Even in such cases—Qin Ke-qing and Dai-yu, for example—it is essential to determine the origin of the dysfunction with the greatest possible accuracy, not in pursuit of a complete cure and restoration of function, but in the hope of stabilizing the patient's condition (to prevent further deterioration) and ameliorating the patient's discomfort. The doctor's visit should establish the proper level of the patient's vital functions, then analyze whatever functional disturbances may be responsible for the disruption of equilibrium. The purpose of Chinese diagnostic medicine is to identify a patient's departure from optimal function in a rigorous and verifiable manner, to determine the direction of the deviation, and if possible identify the agent or pathogen responsible for the disruption.[6]

This method is traditionally not very effective against infectious diseases; however, it is extremely effective against functional disorders (organ dysfunction or even failure) and chronic illnesses. This is the most common sort of disease described in *The Story of the Stone*. Slight indispositions, such as chills, colds, or stomach upset, tend to be treated without fanfare—a dispersant for a cold, fasting for a jumpy stomach. Sometimes the shrewd application of folk wisdom is also efficacious, as with Grannie Liu's cure of Xi-feng's daughter, Qiao-jie, in chapter 42. Although Grannie Liu's connection to the Jia family is distant and tenuous, when she visits her superaffluent relations, they all respect her judgment in matters of health. She pulls no punches when consulted:

> "Children of well-to-do folks are brought up so delicate, their bodies can't stand any hardship. And for another thing, when young folks are cherished too much, it overloads their luck. It might be better for her if in the future you tried not to make quite so much of her."
>
> (*SS* II.42.325, *HLM* II.42.430)

Grannie Liu's remarks have weight not just because of her age and experience but because she is a shrewd observer of human nature, combining well-seasoned common sense with a fund of insights drawn from popular superstition. Her diagnosis of Qiao-jie's indisposition illustrates the author's awareness of the interdependence of physical and psychological factors in the etiology of illness. The little girl may have caught a cold; more likely she may simply be out of sorts from the previous day's excitement—too many sweets, too little rest, too much stimulation. Grannie Liu consults a popular almanac, *The Jade Casket* (*Yuxia ji*)[7] and attributes the cause to the child's encounter with a "flower spirit" (*huashen*), but this is a metaphor for a common problem among toddlers. The girl might indeed be sickly, but, with all the attention focused on her, what can a child do but make a scene?

Although Chinese diagnostic medicine excels in the discernment of obscure etiologies, the allegorical frame of *The Story of the Stone* adds a spiritual dimension to illness and suggests the possibility of complicating factors that are by definition unfathomable; namely, *retributory* factors. A "retributory illness" (*yuannie zhi zheng*) is caused by an individual's karma; that is, the cumulative moral state of all actions of all previous lives. As there can be no knowledge of the acts of a previous existence, it is impossible to discover the true etiology of such afflictions. Medical practitioners are understandably reluctant to assign symptoms to retributory causes; how can a doctor get a complete medical history if he requires information from a previous existence for a diagnosis?

In *The Story of the Stone*, the metaphorical implications of any illness virtually overwhelm the organic ones. Yet what the complication of karmic factors really illuminates is the need to consider a human being, or, in this case, a character in a work of fiction, as a whole. Once the dimension of retributory factors is admitted, any illness can indeed be a metaphor, but the doctors do not forget that it is still illness and that the patient suffers.[8] Although the complications of retributory factors may sometimes make a cure impossible, in *The Story of the Stone* more often than not the doctors practice good medicine and arrive at the correct diagnosis. It is not their fault if, because of psychological or retributory factors, their medicine does not work. This is still sometimes the case with medicine even in the late twentieth century; the diagnosis may be correct, but the patient dies.

Retributory illness is more than just making "the punishment fit the crime."[9] In cases of such illness in *The Story of the Stone*, Cao Xueqin creates clinical profiles that suit their allegorical imperatives down to the last clinical detail. Each case is unique, as if the person and the disease were meant for each other. In serious cases, life-threatening or life-defining, we might say from the clinical point of view that the disease defines the individual.[10] From the perspective of a society that has embraced the doctrine of reincarnation, it is the individual's karma that determines the disease. The necessary retribution for the unknown actions of previous lives might become manifest as a genetic or congenital syndrome or cause a character to contract some dire illness as punishment for the misdeeds of a previous existence. In either case, the reader constantly moves between the narrative necessity of a character's condition as it relates to the cosmic structure of the novel and deep pity for suffering in the present moment, uncomforted by any notion of rightful indemnity or allegorical transcendence.

Much of traditional Chinese medicine, like Hippocratic or Galenic medicine in the West, is efficacious metaphorically or analogically rather than physiologically. This orientation lends itself to allegorical interpretations of illness. Take as an example the case of Jia Rong's wife, Qin Ke-qing. Her case is vexed from the start because we know from the

Celestial Registers and from the fairy Disenchantment's pageant in chapter 5 of the novel that the author's original plan was that she should hang herself in a garden pavilion, when her adultery with her father-in-law, Jia Zhen, was discovered by her maids.[11] In the poems, she still hangs; but, on the level of the prose narrative, Qin Ke-qing's death comes from a slow, wasting illness, the main symptom of which is amenorrhea. In its first stages, everyone in the household is concerned not only for her but for the family line she must continue.

After a series of doctors have failed to alleviate her symptoms, a distinguished scholar by the name of Zhang You-shi is called in. He declines to hear the medical history before he has felt the patient's pulses. Reading the pulse (*maili*) was the primary mode of diagnosis in the treatment of gentry women, except in exceptional circumstances. The sight of a woman's face was regarded as dangerously distracting; indeed, when a doctor strange to the Jia household is called in to examine Jia Lian's secondary wife, You Er-jie, the sight of her lovely face so rattles him that he makes a decisively wrong diagnosis. Doctors trained themselves to perceive far more from the pulse than is recognized in Western medicine. Examination of the several pulses in the two arms, arterial and venous, permitted insight into the workings of the internal organs and detailed description of disrupted body harmonies.[12] Qin Ke-qing, her face and body screened by curtains from the doctor's sight, places her arms on a large armrest and exposes both arms to the wrist. The doctor regulates his breathing so as to be able to count the rate, then feels each pulse for several minutes. He then withdraws with Jia Rong to the outer room and describes the nature of the pulses, with a detailed account of their implications for her current symptoms:

> "If the heart is generating fire, the symptoms should be irregularity of the menses and insomnia. A deficiency of blood and blockage of humor in the liver would result in pain and congestion under the ribs, delay of the menses beyond their term, and burning sensations in the heart. A deficiency of humour in the lungs would give rise to sudden attacks of giddiness, sweating at five or six in the morning, and a sinking feeling rather like the feeling you get in a pitching boat. And if the earth of the spleen is being subdued by the wood of the liver, she would undoubtedly experience loss of appetite, lassitude, and general enfeeblement of the whole body. If my reading of the lady's pulse is correct, she ought to be showing all these symptoms. Some people

would tell you that they indicated a pregnancy, but I am afraid I should have to disagree."

(SS I.10.226, HLM I.10.101)

The doctor's deduction of his patient's symptoms is complete and correct. The complementarity of *yin* and *yang* has been disrupted, and as a result several zones of bodily functions, associated with various of the five elements, are going haywire. Furthermore, the doctor infers from the pulses that the patient is high-strung and emotionally sensitive. The fact that a tendency to late menstrual periods has gone untreated provokes grave concern:

> "There is the cause of the trouble. If she could have been treated in time with something to fortify the heart and stabilize the humours, she would never have got into this present state. What we have now, I am afraid, is an advanced case of dehydration. Well, we shall have to see what my medicine can do for her."

(SS I.10.227, HLM I.10.102)

Dr. Zhang then writes out a learned prescription for "a decoction to increase the breath, nourish the heart, fortify the spleen and calm the liver" (227, 102). His prescription also, incidentally, includes many substances considered effective in treating menstrual irregularity and in tranquilizing the mind. Ginseng is regarded almost as a panacea for restoring physical vitality. In Qin Ke-qing's case, the fact that she has ceased to menstruate makes the doctor suspect a little too much sexual vitality. The liver is the organ thought to store blood; it therefore regulates blood volume according to physical activity and, in women, regulates menstruation. Deficiency of blood and blockage of the liver thus could result in amenorrhea, but such symptoms would suggest sexual overexertion to be the cause.[13] The ginseng is therefore combined with white peony root (*paeonia lactiflora*) and licorice root (*glycyrrhiza*) to moderate its action in sexual vitality and instead fortify the spleen and lungs, replenish her breath (*qi*), and calm her mind. Lotus seeds (*nelumbo nucifera*) and jujubes (*ziziphus jujuba*) also nourish the blood and have a tranquilizing effect; in combination they are good for palpitations.[14] Note that the prescription is balanced between physical and emotional symptoms, all of which have been discerned through the reading of the pulse.

When Jia Rong asks whether his wife's life is in danger, the doctor warns him that such an illness, untreated in its early stages, is not easy to shake off and leaves the young man no doubt that the prognosis, while not hopeless, is poor. Whether the doctor may have a further intuition of the complicating factors in Qin-shi's case is not explicit. The prescription's emphasis on calming the blood and tranquilizing the mind suggests that he suspects emotional complications beyond his power to interfere. The secret cause of Qin Ke-qing's illness, her incest with her father-in-law, is the source of the underlying distress that the doctor could literally feel in her pulse and that he warns Jia Rong will defeat even a correct diagnosis and treatment.

The substitution of a gynecological disorder for hanging points metaphorically both to a retributory cause from sexual excess and to the family "disorder" incest brings. As the primary wife of the only son of the Ning-guo House, Qin Ke-qing would seem to have as her main function to provide the house with a male heir. Incest with her father-in-law cannot be allowed to bear fruit. A son born of such a liaison would create dire tensions in every facet of the family's existence. It could destroy her marriage and her father-in-law's, disrupt the succession of the Ning-guo House, anger the spirits of the ancestors, and, if the facts became known to the outside world, bring down imperial wrath on the entire family. Qin Ke-qing's illness explains why she was unable to conceive not only on the practical level but on the symbolic level as well.

Although the incest may be the present cause of her indisposition, her karmic drive to commit incest was determined in a previous existence, when she was chief arbiter on the fairy Disenchantment's Tribunal of Love, with special responsibility for debts of passion (fengqing yuezhai). When Qin Ke-qing's spirit reveals her true nature to Faithful in chapter 111, she not only enlightens the maid as to her own capacity for pure love but leads her to liberation by showing her how to free herself from her earthly woes. The phantom loops a sash over a beam, reminding Faithful that the original Qin Ke-qing hanged herself and inspiring her to follow the same path. We can therefore read back to her "illness" to understand that it is only the actual death in chapter 13 that is *not* hanging.

The essence of a retributory illness is that the suffering incurred is *necessary*, not just as punishment for unknowable misdeeds of past lives but as a vital expedient to salvation in the present one. The suffering is real; for those with fatal illnesses, physiology overwhelms even allegory. In a work of fiction, characterizations demand just the right illness for each one afflicted: symbolically, spiritually, and clinically. It is a measure of the realistic detail of the novel that so many of the illnesses with which the various members of the Jia family are afflicted are described in sufficient detail to permit a fairly confident guess at a diagnosis. A major caveat is in order, however. If a character suffers from a disease we can identify with some confidence, and we analyze this diagnosis metaphorically in order to understand the character's role in the allegory, this by no means "explains" the character or his/her significance. It is merely a facet of a text whose realistic detail is so compelling that the reader easily forgets the allegorical frame and the Stone himself. To explain all the significance of a compelling existence on the basis of one insight, however brilliant, would be unworthy of the complexity of the author and his creation.

In *The Story of the Stone*, the destiny imposed on a character suffering from a retributory illness by unknowable karma seems the only possible destiny of the current life. In the case of Jia Rui, a member of one of the lesser branches of the far-flung Jia clan, his death could be ascribed to influenza complicated by secondary infections (perhaps bacterial pneumonia and kidney failure). But why this self-loathing closet homosexual should have developed his fatal attraction to Wang Xi-feng cannot be explained by her "masculine" style of attractiveness alone.[15] A string of psychoanalytical possibilities—the logic of fixing on an unattainable object ("the toad on the ground wanting to eat the goose in the sky" [*laihama xiang chi tian'e rou*]) (SS I.11.242, HLM I.11.111)[16] to justify his lack of normal sexual relations, the frustrations of his stifling existence under his grandfather's thumb, the rage of his class inferiority to his (by Chinese standards) near relations, the maddening tedium of instructing boys who defy his authority year in and year out—still do not prepare the reader for the horror of his death.

Jia Rui is the grandson of Jia Dai-ru, the punctilious master of the Jias' clan school. This institution was established by the Ning-guo and Rong-guo Houses to educate their own boys and as a charity so that the less-affluent members of the clan might also be educated. Jia Rui functions as his grandfather's factotum, and the boys are united in despising him for his inadequacies. Terrorized by his grandfather and fawning on any boys who can afford to treat him, he is useless in the classroom for teaching or discipline. Physically unattractive, he sublimates his sexual longings by aiding and abetting the older boys in a ring of homosexual activities that amount to countenanced prostitution.

Jia Rui's decline is precipitated by a fateful meeting with Xi-feng. He becomes completely infatuated with her, waylaying her in a "chance" encounter in the Ning-guo gardens, calling on her in her private apartments, and generally making a nuisance of himself. It is totally inappropriate for a man not of her own blood kin to pursue such contact with her, and Xi-feng immediately catches his drift. Instead of telling him off, however, Xi-feng decides to egg him on to teach him a lesson. She arranges an assignation with him and locks him in a freezing courtyard for a night. Jia Rui is so absorbed in his seduction that it never occurs to him that Xi-feng has tricked him, and when she sees that he is a glutton for punishment she arranges yet another meeting. This time Jia Rui is caught, literally with his pants down, by his cousins Jia Rong and Jia Qiang (foster-brother to Xi-feng's husband, Jia Lian). They extort hush money from him, empty a chamber pot onto his head as he waits for them to unlock the gate, and then let him go. Raging with humiliation, he still cannot give up his fantasy:

> Rushing into his own room he stripped off his clothes and washed, his mind running all the time on how Xi-feng had tricked him. The thought of her trickery provoked a surge of hatred in his soul; yet even as he hated her, he longed to clasp her to his breast. . . . From that time on . . . he longed for Xi-feng with unabated passion.
>
> (SS I.12.249, HLM I.12.116)

Not surprisingly, Jia Rui spins into a physical decline:

> Unable, even now, to overcome his longing for Xi-feng, saddled with a heavy burden of debt, harassed during the daytime by the schoolwork set him by his exacting grandfather, worn-out during the nights by the excessive hand-pumping inevitable in an unmarried man of twenty whose mistress was both unattainable and constantly in his thoughts, twice frozen, tormented and forced to flee—what constitution could withstand so many shocks and strains without succumbing in the end to illness? The symptoms of Jia Rui's illness—a palpitation in the heart, a loss of taste in the mouth, a weakness in the hams, a smarting in the eyes, feverishness by night and lassitude by day, albumen in the urine and blood-flecks in the phlegm—had all manifested themselves within less than a year. By that time they had produced a complete breakdown and driven him to his bed, where he lay, with eyes tight shut, babbling deliriously and inspiring terror in all who saw him. Physicians were called in to treat him and some bushels of cinnamon bark, autumn root, turtle-shell, black leek and Solomon's

seal must at one time or another have been infused and taken without the least observable effect.

(SS I.12.250, HLM I.12.116–117)

Why do none of these remedies work? From this list of pharmaceuticals, the doctors clearly have some notion of the real root of Jia Rui's problem. They perceive dehydration due in part to fever, in part to masturbation. Because of this excessive *yang* Jia Rui's kidneys are in danger of permanent damage. As in the West, the kidneys are related symbolically and diagnostically to the testicles in Chinese premodern medicine. Cinnamon bark (*cinnamonum cassia*) in combination with a preparation of freshwater turtle-shell nourishes *yin* and subdues *yang*, to counter dehydration due to long-term night fevers. Cinnamon also bonds with "autumn root" (*aconitum carmichaeli*) to treat kidney deficiencies manifested as chills, cold limbs, and soreness and weakness in the lumbar region. "Black leek" (*allium tuberosum*) fortifies the liver and kidneys, while "Solomon's seal" (*polygonatum oderatum*) nourishes *yin* to promote production of body fluids and strengthen the stomach.[17]

These medicines are appropriate for treating the patient's symptoms, but they cannot touch the cause of the illness. All of Jia Rui's senses are blasted by his passion. The pharmaceuticals cannot have any effect because the influenza, pneumonia, and kidney failure are in fact secondary complications. The primary diagnosis is unrequited sexual passion, and there are only two cures for that: to have his love requited, or to awaken to the vanity of love. Since the object of Jia Rui's passion is hopelessly out of reach, reciprocity in love is out of the question. Jia Rui is literally being consumed by his own *yang* energy, which might be brought into check by the doctors' prescriptions if the patient were not fanning the flames with anger and longing. When everything else has been tried, a savior appears:

> One day a lame Taoist appeared at the door asking for alms and claiming to be able to cure retributory illnesses. Jia Rui, who chanced to overhear him, called out from his bed. . . .
>
> "Holy one, save me!" he cried out again and again.
>
> The Taoist sighed.
>
> "No medicine will cure your sickness. However, I have a precious thing here which I can lend you which, if you look at it every day, can be guaranteed to save your life."
>
> <div align="right">(<i>SS</i> I.12.251, <i>HLM</i> I.12.117)</div>

With this, the Taoist produces the "Mirror for the Romantic" (*fengyue baojian*) and offers it to Jia Rui.[18] He explains that the mirror comes from the Land of Illusion, and "was fashioned . . . as an antidote to the ill effects of impure mental activity" (251, 117). Although both sides of the mirror are highly polished, the Taoist admonishes his patient that *he must look only into the back*. If he obeys, he will be cured in three days. When Jia Rui follows his instructions, he is scared silly by the grinning skull that appears, holographically as it were, in the shining surface. Rejecting this stern memento mori, he looks into the forbidden front, where his fate awaits him:

> There inside was Xi-feng beckoning to him to enter, and his ravished soul floated into the mirror after her. There they performed the act of love together, after which she saw him out again. But when he found himself once more back in his bed he stared and cried out in horror: for the mirror, of its own accord, had turned itself round in his hand and the same grinning skull faced him that he had seen before. He could feel the sweat trickling all over his body and lower down in the bed a little pool of semen that he had just ejaculated.
>
> Yet he was still not satisfied, and turned the face of the mirror once more towards him. Xi-feng was there beckoning to him again and calling, and again he went in after her. He did this three or four times. But the last time, just as he was going to return from the mirror, two figures approached him wearing iron chains which they fastened round him and by which they proceeded to drag him away. He cried out as they dragged him:
>
> "Wait! Let me take the mirror with me . . . !"
>
> (*SS* I.12.252, *HLM* I.12.118)

No doctor would have been able to help Jia Rui. In the present life, he has too many reasons to conceal the root of his problem: fear of his puritanical grandfather, terror at the enormity of his intended transgression with Xi-feng, rage and humiliation at the treatment he received from her. If his problem is karmic, and his destiny destruction by passion, it is so deeply buried that only an epiphany can liberate him. If it is his karma that has driven him, apparently against his nature, to be attracted to Xi-feng and thus to his own destruction, it is also his karma that drives him to reject his cure and salvation.

The mirror the Taoist offers is a symbol of his unenlightened mind.[19]

If he fails to understand the symbol, then the image in the back of the mirror is a further explanation of the vanity of his passion. The skull is not only his own fate but the fate of the object of his lust, who so enticingly appears on the "front" to destroy him. There is no ontological distinction between the amorous Xi-feng in the front and the hideous skull on the back. Therefore the mirror contains both his temptations and the means to transcend them. Unfortunately, Jia Rui embraces his delusion so completely that, when the messengers of death come for him, he begs to take the mirror with him! Can he still be unaware that he has already got it with him? Although Xi-feng may be the embodiment of his delusions, the mirror gives him a chance to awake to the emptiness of the "real," but in spite of all his suffering he resists to the end.

This is as low as you can go in spiritual terms. Jia Rui is literally a "jerk": Shown the explicit means to salvation, he overlays it with his delusion and dies, his stiffening body mired in an icy patch of semen. When the distraught Jia Dai-ru and his wife try to burn the mirror, the Taoist snatches it away and scolds them: "Who told him to look in the front! It is you who are to blame, for confusing the unreal with the real!" (253, 118). Certainly Jia Rui's woes seem to be largely self-inflicted. But in spite of the depth of his degradation, the reader feels only pity and horror. Physically and morally unattractive as Jia Rui may be, what the reader confronts is his pitiful humanity, a specter almost too painful to endure.

The severity of Xi-feng's treatment of Jia Rui on the mundane level demonstrates her ruthlessness and lack of compassion. On the cosmic level, it suggests the possibility that the luckless man might owe Xi-feng a karmic debt for unknowable damage in a past life. An incident in chapter 4 illustrates this belief. In his first magistracy, Jia Yu-cun confronts a case of manslaughter, which because of social factors is impossible to prosecute as the law demands. The guilty party is none other than Bao-chai's brother, Xue Pan, whose vast wealth and position as purveyor to the imperial household make him a scofflaw. A court usher offers his master a way out by suggesting that the crime was based on a karmic problem not a temporal one. He urges his master to declare that "the dead man, Feng Yuan, owed a debt of *karma* to Xue Pan from a former life and 'meeting his enemy in a narrow way,' paid for it with his life" (*SS* I.4.116, *HLM* I.4.37). Jia Yu-cun nervously dismisses this course as "too risky," but the fact that such a specious strategy for the administration of justice can even be mentioned in a court of law indicates the general acceptance of karmic factors in bizarre twists of fate. The sad case of Feng Yuan turns on *his* sudden conversion from confirmed homosexuality when he falls in love with a woman also coveted by Xue Pan. His death at the hands of Xue Pan's bullies foreshadows Jia Rui's death by more devious but ultimately just as violent means.

The two characters explicitly linked in sickness and in health are the protagonist, Jia Bao-yu, and the love of his life, Lin Dai-yu. They have the most complete and organic characterizations in the novel, including the attachment of their previous lives, which has linked them in a fatal bond in the present one. For Dai-yu, love for Bao-yu is the death of her. Not only her pathologies but Bao-yu's as well are essential to the fulfillment of her destiny. Dai-yu's respiratory afflictions and Bao-yu's neurological disorder mesh to ensure that the two will be perpetually off balance, and tears will flow from joy, fear, frustration, misunderstanding, and hopeless longing.

Dai-yu suffers from tuberculosis, a disease that in China, as in the West, is associated with romantic agony.[20] She recounts to her grandmother how a monk (Impervioso himself, of course) warned her parents of her doom:

"I have always been like this. . . . I have been taking medicine ever since I could eat and have been looked at by ever so many well-known doctors, but it has never done me any good. Once, when I was only three, I can remember a scabby-headed old monk came and said he wanted to take me away and have me brought up as a nun; but of course, Mother and Father wouldn't hear of it. So he said, 'Since you are not prepared to give her up, I am afraid her illness will never get better as long as she lives. The only way it might get better would be if she were never to hear the sound of weeping from this day onwards, and never to see any relations other than her own mother and father. Only in those conditions could she get through her life without trouble.' Of course, he was quite crazy, and no one took any notice of the things he said."

(SS I.3.90, HLM I.3.24)

For something no one paid any attention to, the monk's words — as recited by Dai-yu — were evidently an important part of the Lin family mythology. The monk's prescription was perfectly correct if the purpose of the child's existence was to be happy and healthy in this lifetime, an outcome her family passionately desires. Their very love for their only child, however, causes them to choose the course that will bring disaster in this lifetime. Dai-yu speaks these words to the very marriage kin (*qin*) who will love, cherish, and drive her to her death. But from the narrative frame of chapter 1, we know that this destiny is to be her greater fulfillment, for the Crimson Pearl Flower cannot return to the Void until she has fulfilled her debt of tears. Dai-yu's parents, mired in the delusion of their attachment, consign her, on the one hand, to a life-time of misery, but, on the other hand, to the path to salvation.

Dai-yu's sickly constitution is essential to her uniquely ethereal beauty, and part of the delusion of Bao-yu's attachment to her is his refusal to realize that the beauty he so cherishes proclaims his love's mortality.[21] In spite of the whole family's vast solicitude for Dai-yu's illness, this willful oblivion contributes materially to the fulfillment of the debt of tears.

Tuberculosis (*mycobacterium tuberculosis*), romantically termed "consumption" (*laozheng* or *laoqie zhi zheng*) because of its wasting effect upon the body, was endemic to China in the eighteenth century, as indeed it was to all of the old world. In Europe the majority of the population was exposed, especially in urban areas. The bacillus could infect the body at any time, although it would not necessarily progress into the active form of the disease. It is airborne and spreads rapidly in areas of dense population.[22] In a household like that of the Jia family, exposure, though not necessarily infection, would be virtually universal. Many of the Rong-guo staff are described as suffering from consumption. One of Bao-yu's principal body servants, Skybright (Qing-wen), is rapidly carried off by the disease after her brutal dismissal from the household at the hands of Lady Wang (chapter 77), and her later replacement, Fivey (Wu-er), also suffers spells of active infection from the disease before she enters service in Bao-yu's apartments.

Tuberculosis was naturally more likely to become malignant in a delicate organism, and, from her first appearance, Dai-yu is the ideal candidate. The family notices "the frail body which seemed scarcely strong enough to bear the weight of its clothes, but which had an inexpressible grace about it" (*SS* I.3.90, *HLM* I.3.24). She has suffered from illness since infancy, and her abstemious eating habits have left her in a state of chronic malnutrition, with very low resistance to any kind of infection.[23] If we recall her origin in the Land of Illusion, the match is even more complete. Dai-yu's delicate charm evokes both her illness and her identity as the Crimson Pearl Flower. When Bao-yu first sees his cousin, his impression conjures up both her present and her past identities:

> Habit had given a melancholy cast to her tender
> face;

Nature had bestowed a sickly constitution on her
    delicate frame.
Often the eyes swam with glistening tears;
Often the breath came in gentle gasps.
In stillness she made one think of a graceful
    flower reflected in the water;
In motion she called to mind tender willow shoots
    caressed by the wind.

                              (SS I.3.102–103, HLM I.3.30)

The sickly body is the necessary manifestation in the present life of the Crimson Pearl Flower, whose grace and beauty are evoked by the images of a flower reflected in the water and the wind-stirred willow shoots. As Dai-yu herself confirms, she has always been ill, although the precise nature of her illness has not been understood (except by Impervioso). Because she is not robust and has a poor appetite ("Eating perhaps no more than five meals in every ten" [SS II.35.183, HLM I.35.353]), it is assumed that her system requires stimulation, and therefore she is treated with such nostrums as "Ginseng Tonic Pills" (renshen yangrong wan) or "Deva-King Cardiac Elixer Pills" (tianwang buxin dan).[24] These remedies do nothing to improve her constitution, and she is well aware of her vulnerability. Like many sufferers from chronic, debilitating illness, Dai-yu tends to appear self-absorbed because of her preoccupation with her physical limitations. Realizing that this is a disadvantage, she tends to be touchy and unpredictably abrasive. The result is that even Dai-yu herself assumes that her almost paranoid quickness to take offense is a trait of her character, rather than the cumulative effect on the psyche of growing up with a chronic, incurable disease. Even events that should bring her joy tend to return her mind to her deteriorating condition. Overhearing Bao-yu proclaiming his preference for her to Xiang-yun and Aroma, she is both thrilled to have her hopes of his devotion confirmed and full of foreboding for the future:

"I feel so muzzy lately and I know my illness is gradually gaining a hold on me. (The doctors say that the weakness and anaemia I suffer from may be the beginnings of a consumption.) So even if I *am* your true-love, I fear I may not be able to wait for you. And even though you are mine, you can do nothing to alter my fate."

                              (SS II.32.132, HLM I.32.323)

After his terrible beating at the hands of his father in chapter 33, Bao-yu sends Dai-yu a token of his complete confidence in their intimacy: a pair of plain, everyday handkerchiefs, carried to her by a baffled maid simply to reassure her that he is thinking as much of her as of himself. Not only does this evoke the tradition of lovers exchanging small personal objects, especially personally used ones, as signs of affection; the choice of handkerchiefs, which presumably he has used for his own tears, is a gesture of love and understanding of her grief. In a flash she understands the significance of this strange gift:

> "I feel so happy . . . that in the midst of his own affliction he has been able to grasp the cause of all *my* trouble.
>
> "And yet at the same time I am sad . . . because how do I know that my trouble will end in the way I want it to?
>
> "Actually, I feel rather amused. . . . Fancy his sending a pair of old handkerchiefs like that! Suppose I hadn't understood what he was getting at? . . .
>
> (*SS* II.34.167–168, *HLM* I.34.344)

Dai-yu is so moved by this eccentric but perfect communion that she gets out of bed, calls for ink, and composes three poems on the spot, writing them on the plain handkerchiefs themselves. But the enhanced level of emotional fulfillment provokes her disease to a new level, as well:

> She . . . was preparing to write another quatrain, when she became aware that her whole body was burning hot all over and her cheeks were afire. Going over to the dressing-table, she removed the brocade cover from the mirror and peered into it.
>
> "Hmn! 'Brighter than the peach-flower's hue,' " she murmured complacently to the flushed face that stared out at her from the glass, and, little imagining that what she had been witnessing was the first symptom of a serious illness, went back to bed, her mind full of handkerchiefs.
>
> (*SS* II.34.168, *HLM* I.34.345)

Like Jia Rui, Dai-yu receives from her mirror only the message she wishes and ignores the truth it holds.

While Dai-yu's health always worsens under emotional stress, her illness tends to flare up at regular seasonal intervals, for example, after the equinoxes (*SS* II.45.395, *HLM* II.45.466).[25] In chapter 45, Bao-chai suggests that the doctors' prescriptions may treat her symptoms, but not their cause, and the result is that Dai-yu's vitality is ever more drained. Bao-chai protests that she should have been expected to improve in adolescence, but Dai-yu is fatalistic about it:

> "Every year all through spring and summer you have this trouble; yet you're not an old lady, and you're not a little girl any longer. You can't go on in this way indefinitely."
>
> "It's no good," said Dai-yu. "This illness will never go away completely. Look what I'm like ordinarily, even when I'm not ill."
>
> Bao-chai nodded.
>
> "Exactly! You know the old saying: 'He that eats shall live'? What you ordinarily eat, when you're not ill, doesn't seem to nourish you or build up your resistance. That's one of your troubles."
>
> Dai-yu sighed.
>
> > "'Life and death are as Heaven decrees; and rank and riches are as Heaven bestows them.'
>
> These things are not in human power to command."
>
> (*SS* II.45.396, *HLM* II.45.466–467)

Bao-chai, who has observed Dai-yu more carefully than have the doctors, insists that their medications are overheating her depleted system and preventing her from taking any nourishment from her food. She prescribes a syrup made from bird's nest, for its high protein content, and sugar, for energy, and generously offers to provide the necessary ingredients herself. This moment of genuine sympathy between the two rivals for Bao-yu's affection is part of a sustained rapport. On the mundane level, the syrup, and the sympathy, do some good. On the cosmic level, Dai-yu's own observation is correct—the illness will never improve. Bao-chai's insight is limited to her cousin's physical organism; she cannot conceive of the preexisting conditions that will render all ministrations futile.

One obstacle to Dai-yu's treatment is the assumption, shared by the elder members of the family, that her emotional sensitivity and paranoia are matters of her peculiar temperament, rather than symptoms of the profundity of her illness. After Dai-yu's dreadful nightmare in chapter 82, her maids and cousins panic when she coughs up "a thick wriggling strand of dark red blood" (*SS* IV.82.68, *HLM* II.82.913). Grandmother Jia is rather peeved when she hears that Dai-yu is ill again and gives the order for the doctors attending Bao-yu (who is ill from suffering a version of the same nightmare, at exactly the time Dai-yu had hers) to look in on her:

> "Dear oh dear! How illness and misfortune seem to pick on those two! Ever since Dai-yu was a little girl, it's been one thing after another. Now that she's grown up, it is time she learned to take better care of her health. She's too highly strung, that's her trouble."
>
> (SS IV.83.77, HLM III.83.919)

But the attending physician, Doctor Wang, finally understands the organic nature of her problem—in this lifetime:

> "This condition should manifest itself in the following ways: dizzy spells, loss of appetite, frequent dreams, and fitful sleeping in the early hours; during the daytime a tendency to take offence for no reason and a generally apprehensive attitude towards other people. Some might attribute all these to a peculiarity of temperament, but they would be mistaken. They are organically related to a deficiency of Yin in the liver, with a concomitant diminution of cardiac vitality."
>
> (SS IV.83.78–79, HLM III.83.920)

Doctor Wang attributes her lung damage to this deficiency of the liver: "The hepatic humour, unable to disperse naturally, has encroached upon the spleen (*Earth*), with consequent loss of appetite. The extreme distemper has also caused a reversal of the elemental sequence, and the lungs (*Metal*) have certainly been damaged" (79, 920). In other words, the kind of attenuated physique and morbid sensitivity associated with tuberculosis is thought to have its cause in a malfunction of the liver, which effect cascades into the other internal organs and manifests itself as this disease. The fact that Dai-yu lives in aggravating emotional circumstances makes it impossible to disentangle the strands and root out the illness. Ungenerous as Grandmother Jia's uninformed observation is, she is correct, deep down—her diagnosis of "lovesickness" (chapter 97) reflects the preexisting condition, the debt of tears, which Dai-yu inexorably pays off.

It is indeed tragic that the character traits that make Dai-yu so difficult are something she cannot help—they have organic causes and arise from her illness. When someone suffers from a chronic illness, it can be impossible to separate the personality from the disease, in part because long-term accommodation to disease becomes an integral part of the social persona. But although the effects of long-term illness might excuse aspects of Dai-yu's behavior, this does not mean that her temperament is not genuinely hers. Dai-yu's character traits have their roots in her previous existence as the Crimson Pearl Flower, and therefore the ultimate etiology of Dai-yu's illness is also in the Land of Illusion. The fairy whose mind was tormented by her sense of obligation to the Stone who tended her has inevitably passed this angst on to her human avatar. Dai-yu's character is more hers than anyone, even she herself, can know.

The fortunes of Dai-yu's health follow her hopes and fears for romantic fulfillment. She nearly succeeds in starving herself to death when she overhears a mistaken rumor that Bao-yu has been betrothed (chapter 89), then recovers almost immediately when the rumor is contradicted and she can hope once more. Yet they repeatedly misread each other's cues and fail to take the steps that would change their karmic destinies. Even at the last possible moment:

> Although there were a million things she wanted to tell him, her consciousness that they were no longer children inhibited her from showing her affection by teasing him in the old way, and rendered her powerless to express what was preying on her mind. Bao-yu for his part would have liked to talk with her sincerely and offer her some genuine comfort; but he was afraid of aggravating her illness by offending her in some way. . . . Theirs was a true case of estrangement in the very extremity of love.
>
> (SS IV.89.210, HLM III.89.992)

When Dai-yu finally confirms that Bao-yu has indeed been betrothed to Bao-chai, she allows her illness to have its way at last. She vomits blood. Medication "to check the Yin and to halt the flow of blood" (SS IV.97.342, HLM III.97.) has no effect. She dies in bitterness, the last gasp of her debt of tears, unaware that Bao-yu is true to her.

Doctor Wang verified that the touchiness that made Dai-yu so difficult to approach was not a matter of temperament, but the result of her illness. From her origin in the Land of Illusion, we know that her illness depends on her destined love for Bao-yu. Is Bao-yu, for his part, merely clueless? Or is he, like Dai-yu, also afflicted in some organic way?

In the introduction to volume I of his translation of *The Story of the Stone*, David Hawkes notes: "Bao-yu is an almost clinical picture of the kind of child whom old ladies refer to in lowered voices as 'a very strange little boy.' "[26] The clinical picture can now be recognized as that of attention deficit disorder (or A.D.D.). The novel's copious and precise detail of Bao-yu's life from approximately age nine to nineteen makes it possible to diagnose him according to many different standards and systems. Although "diagnosis" of a fictional character will always have the quality of a jeu d'esprit, the correspondence between what we know of Bao-yu and the characteristics of people diagnosed with A.D.D. is compelling because it makes sense of so many otherwise baffling aspects of his character. Bao-yu is universally recognized as a very odd little boy who grows into a highly eccentric young adult. With an understanding of the characteristics of A.D.D., *The Story of the Stone* becomes a history of a classic case.[27]

It is not my intention to reduce Bao-yu to a clinical curiosity. If Bao-yu "has" A.D.D., it does not explain everything in the book, nor does it detract from the vast sea of social, historical, psychological, and religious interpretations of the novel. The possibility of this common neurological disorder is only a facet of Bao-yu's character, albeit a very significant one. What it may do is give us a better sense of Bao-yu, and just possibly his creator, as they relate to their shared fictional universe. It certainly sheds light on the novel as roman à clef.[28] The beauty of the diagnosis is that it makes Bao-yu's character, and his characterization, consistent rather than capricious.

Attention deficit disorder was first described by George F. Still in 1902, but only within the past two decades has it come to the attention of the general public. Still was the first to describe the disorder as having a physiological, rather than moral or psychological, basis. A.D.D. is a physiological impairment of the faculties of self-control, especially in the areas of sustained attention, organizational ability, and temper.[29] A.D.D. tends to run in families. While girls may be afflicted, the disorder is far more likely to appear in boys, especially if there is a family history of it.[30]

One of the disorder's significant symptoms, hyperactivity, is well recognized, to the point of being overtreated. Although hyperactivity is indeed often present, the specter of the "motor-driven kid" is only one manifestation of the disorder. For children and adults, the core of the A.D.D. affliction is that it causes them to act unthinkingly on any and every external stimulus, indiscriminately, instead of sustaining their selected focus through ordinary distractions.[31] People whose A.D.D. goes undiagnosed often make heroic attempts to compensate for their disability, frequently by means of self-imposed programs of discipline that allow them, at least in full adulthood, to integrate successfully into society.

What is not so widely known is the prevalence of less overt symptoms of the disorder. Hyperactivity has a mental counterpart, namely, extreme distractibility, which can include obsessive fascination with particular activities, often to the detriment of everyday affairs. One result of this distractibility is debilitating procrastination. Typical of people with A.D.D. is a "faulty" perception of the nature of linear time, with consequent lack of awareness of the passage of time and inability to think and plan ahead. They are also unusually impulsive, and their impulsiveness can manifest itself in acting inappropriately on a momentary whim, wild mood swings, and irrational, sudden, and violent losses of temper. All these problems contribute to the sense of dissociation from their social context and a difficulty in basic social relations.

A.D.D. is widely known and studied in China, where it is called "hyperactivity syndrome" (*duodong zonghe zheng*).[32] Studies recognize the genetic nature of the disorder and its prevalence among men and boys.[33] Although *The Story of the Stone* has never been mined for information about this topic, the novel testifies to the relentless heredity of violent temper and other extreme behaviors that are symptomatic of A.D.D. Jia Zhen, head of the Ning-guo branch of the Jia household, is known for murderous rages resulting in savage beatings for the servants and especially his own son for apparently trivial offenses. The nominal head of the Rong-guo branch is Bao-yu's uncle, Jia She. He not only has these rages but is criticized for other kinds of erratic behavior, particularly obsession with objects beyond his reach, a symptom of A.D.D. identified as "insatiability."[34] Jia She's pursuit of his obsessions makes him oblivious to his duties as head of the Rong-guo House, but his irresponsibilities, while indulged, do not pass unnoticed. Whether it be his mother's favorite maidservant or a set of splendid antique fans, Jia She pursues them implacably, and woe to those nearby when he is thwarted. Again, the father is particularly liable to take it out on his own son, in one case gashing Jia Lian's face with a handy, heavy inkstone. As noted in chapter 2, in traditional Chinese society a father is certainly within his rights to beat his son, but when the punishment goes beyond discipline into grave physical harm, the father runs the risk of offending the ancestor spirits by threatening to cut off the family line. For both Jia Zhen and Jia She, there is a pattern of these assaults, and the terrifying thing is that no one can either anticipate or deflect them. One of the Jia family's faithful retainers, Old Mrs. Lai, comments sharply on the short-comings of the males of both households. Jia She and Jia Zhen are both criticized for their violent fits of rage, which because of their inconsistency make the servants despise them.[35]

But the main character of *The Story of the Stone* is Bao-yu, and he is our most complete case. A brilliant and beautiful boy, surrounded by wealth and luxury, marvelously exempted from the ordinary pressures of study and filial obedience by the all-powerful protection of a doting matriarch—Bao-yu could easily be seen as a boy whose moods and whims are the result of being just plain spoiled. But Bao-yu is in fact extraordinarily sensitive to the feelings of others, especially the young girls, his sisters, cousins, and even maidservants, with whom he is surrounded and whose company he prefers to anyone else's. That an essentially sensitive and diffident boy should frequently become an utterly self-centered and violent monster is hard to explain, until we consider the possibility of A.D.D.

We first encounter Bao-yu when he is about ten years old and comes to his grandmother's apartments to be presented to Dai-yu. Their attraction is instant and mutual. The cousins even seem "familiar" to each other, and Bao-yu, seeking confirmation of their kindred spirit, asks her:

> "Have you got a jade?"
>
> The rest of the company were puzzled, but Dai-yu at once divined that he was asking her if she too had a jade like the one he was born with.
>
> "No," said Dai-yu. "That jade of yours is a very rare object. You can't expect everybody to have one."
>
> This sent Bao-yu off instantly into one of his mad fits. Snatching the jade from his neck he hurled it violently to the floor as if to smash it and began abusing it passionately.
>
> "Rare object! Rare object! What's so lucky about a stone that can't even tell which people are better than others? Beastly thing! I don't want it!"
>
> The maids all seemed terrified and rushed forward to pick it up, while Grandmother Jia clung to Bao-yu in alarm.
>
> "Naughty, naughty boy! Shout at someone or strike them if you like when you are in a nasty temper, but why go smashing that precious thing that your very life depends on?"

"None of the girls has got one," said Bao-yu, his face streaming with tears and sobbing hysterically. "Only I have got one. It always upsets me. And now this new cousin comes here who is as
beautiful as an angel and she hasn't got one either, so I *know* it
can't be any good."

(*SS* I.3.104, *HLM* I.3.31)

In spite of having been warned about Bao-yu's unmanageable temper by his own mother, Dai-yu is mortified to have been the provocation
for what seems to her a shocking scene, and has to be comforted by Bao-
yu's chief maid, Aroma: "You mustn't take on so, Miss. . . . You'll see
him do much stranger things than that before he's finished. If you allow
yourself to feel hurt every time he carries on like that, he will always be
hurting you" (*SS* I.3.106, *HLM* I.3.32). In Dai-yu's case, the misery caused
by Bao-yu's eruptions will abet the debt of tears. As for the rest of the
household, clearly Bao-yu's scenes are well known, and, to the best of
their ability, his relatives and servants accommodate him, giving him
relatively little incentive to learn to self-regulate. Bao-yu is actually
rather less subject to the rages typical of the males in his family than to
the impulsiveness, obsessive fascination, and the loss of concentration
typical of people with A.D.D.

Bao-yu's dream in chapter 5 had a dual purpose: to warn him of the
inevitable fates of the girls to whom he is so attached and to initiate him
sexually so as to demystify the illusion of love for him. His guide in the
Land of Illusion, the fairy Disenchantment, admonished him by pointing out his great weakness: "obsessive longing" (*chiqing*) and "lust of the
mind" (*yiyin*). Although these terms are usually taken to refer to Bao-
yu's preoccupation with emotional, particularly romantic, attachment,
they also describe the "fits" that Bao-yu experiences when overwhelmed
by emotion.[36]

Bao-yu's impulsiveness is also suggested by a pattern of alternating
activity and quiescence—*dongzhongjing, jingzhongdong*. Andrew H.
Plaks analyzes this aspect of Bao-yu's character as a manifestation of
the structural principle he calls "complementary bipolarity," in which
apparently opposing principles are in fact mutually implicating and de-
pendent.[37] It is also suggestive as a description of the ways in which the
idiosyncrasies of Bao-yu's character drive the plot and thus affect the
structure of the narrative. His cousins call him "Busybody" (*wushi
mang*—literally, "busy to no purpose") (*SS* II.42.339, *HLM* II.42.437).

Bao-yu's A.D.D. usually manifests itself in situations requiring self-motivation and creates problems by annoying or simply confounding his attendants or his relatives. For example, Bao-yu decides to do some calligraphy, makes a great to-do about setting up his desk and implements, and then whips off three characters, throws down his brush, and rushes off, leaving his maids in the debris, not knowing whether to clear up or wait until their master should deign to return to his desk (SS I.8.196–197, HLM I.8.84–85). Another time, he conceives a desire to conduct a memorial service for Golden, the maid who drowned herself in shame when she was dismissed for flirting with him. Without any hint of his intentions, he gallops out at daybreak with his most trusted page, reins in his horse at a deserted area beyond the city, and demands an incense burner, fire, and three kinds of precious incense for his ceremony—and is quite put out when the bewildered Tealeaf explains that these items are not readily available. Bao-yu's insistence that their breakneck speed precluded bringing these supplies with them is an ex post facto excuse; he was focused only on his need to commune with Golden's spirit far from his domestic enclosure and never gave a thought to the accouterments. Back at the mansion, the household is in an uproar because he is missing an important birthday party. Grandmother Jia herself is so worried that she wants to have all his pages whipped because of her grandson's thoughtless disappearance, and only strenuous intercession prevents this punishment for Bao-yu's impulsiveness from being carried out (SS II.43.353–363; HLM II.43.445–449).

Perhaps the most striking instances of the effects of this typical impulsiveness are when Bao-yu attempts two perfectly ordinary, age-appropriate activities: kite-flying and fishing. The desire to participate fully in these essentially social activities with his sisters and female cousins puts him in a desperate situation. When he tries to fly a kite, his frustration with the simple but necessary sequence of fine-motor tasks throws him into a passion, which he struggles to control for fear of alienating the girls (SS III.70.390, HLM II.70.768–769). Here, at least, Dai-yu has the sensitivity to deflect a major scene, but Bao-yu's later fishing expedition is excruciating. Distressed by his cousin Ying-chun's tales of her brutal husband, he is unable to fix his mind on anything until he overhears his sister, Tan-chun, and three of his female cousins enjoying fishing in the artificial lake in the garden. Bao-yu proposes a game in which if a player catches a fish, it means a year of good luck, but, for those who catch nothing, it means a year of bad luck. Politely declining until each of the girls has taken her turn, and each one has caught a fish, Bao-yu winds himself up into action:

Walking solemnly down the jetty, he sat at the water's edge in the pose of the Fisherman Sage. Unfortunately, at the approach of this human shadow, the fish took refuge in the far end of the pond, and for all his exertions in the higher art of angling, a long time seemed to pass without the slightest sign of a bite. When once a fish did venture near and deigned to blow a few bubbles near the bank, he jerked the rod and scared it away.

"Oh dear!" he sighed. "It's no good. The trouble is that I'm so confoundedly impatient, and the fish are so slow on the uptake. We must be incompatible. I shall never catch anything at this rate. Come on now, help me! *Feel* yourself being drawn, there's my brave little fish!"

There was a peal of laughter from the girls. Then before anyone could say a word, the line seemed to move a fraction. A bite at last! The sage yanked in for all he was worth. The rod crashed into a protruding rock and broke clean in two. The line snapped, and the hook (with whatever it may or may not have secured) sank without a trace. This final stroke of virtuosity had his audience in stitches. Tan-chun called out:

"I've never seen such a clumsy fool!"

(*SS* IV.81.38, *HLM* III.81.897)

Fortunately for Bao-yu, he is called away from the scene of this fiasco by an urgent summons from Grandmother Jia. The portent of a year of bad luck is carried out in the text, as he loses his magic jade, falls temporarily into imbecility, and is married by means of a cruel deception to his cousin Bao-chai instead of to Dai-yu.

While Bao-yu's fits of temper and his impulsiveness are suggestive, it is their combination with his extreme distractability and inability to concentrate that are conclusive for a profile of A.D.D. These symptoms manifest themselves in drifting off into daydreams and losing awareness of where he is, even if he is gawping inappropriately at one of his female relatives. His distractability lets him in for much embarrassment. He has already given his heart to Dai-yu, yet he is often found staring abstractedly at Bao-chai, whose beauty and intelligence are equal to, though very different from, Dai-yu's. Although Bao-yu can lapse into a trance and stare at anyone, Bao-chai is particularly sensitive because of the suggested affinity of her gold locket with Bao-yu's jade. She and Dai-yu are both very familiar with Bao-yu's "trances," but neither of them is able to laugh them off.

Dai-yu seizes every opportunity to tease him about Bao-chai and the locket, in order to probe Bao-yu's feelings for her. Occasionally, she goes too far and pushes Bao-yu into scenes that are both frightening for her and very possibly compromising to their reputations. An episode in chapter 32 demonstrates how Dai-yu's and Bao-yu's ailments mesh and feed each other. Dai-yu overhears Bao-yu praising her to Aroma and Xiang-yun as the paragon among the girls of his acquaintance, and she is both overjoyed and alarmed: overjoyed that she is not mistaken in her sense of Bao-yu's attachment; alarmed that if he praises her in front of others, their secret love will be discovered. Weeping, she retreats, but Bao-yu follows her and impulsively tries to wipe away her tears. She rebuffs him fiercely and adds fuel to the fire by upbraiding him for attentions to Xiang-yun. Bao-yu flies into a rage, and the terrified Dai-yu tries to soothe him. When he reveals that he understands very well the nature of her teasing, and the reason for it, she is overwhelmed with emotion and leaves. Bao-yu, focusing all his efforts on his emotional crisis, is oblivious to everything external, including the person to whom he struggles to declare himself. At this moment, Aroma comes up to him to give him a fan that he had left behind. Bao-yu, still literally stupefied, does not perceive that he is speaking to the wrong girl and delivers a passionate avowal of love to his maid. Knowing full well that she is not the intended object, Aroma is horrified and shakes her master out of his trance (SS II.32.133–135, HLM I.32.325).

Hilariously and tragically, this scene alludes to a scene from the several versions of Romance of the Western Chamber (Xixiang ji), in which the lovesick Zhang Jun-rui mistakes the maid Hong-niang for her mistress, Ying-ying, in the dark, and passionately declares his love to her.[38] Here the mistake occurs in broad daylight—not remotely believable without Bao-yu's extreme distraction. The fact that Western Chamber is the favorite romance of both Bao-yu and Dai-yu and the source of much of their self-definition as lovers adds to this irony. At the time this is a source of acute embarrassment to all concerned, and it later provides the motive for the family's elaborate deception of Bao-yu in the choice of his wife.

Bao-yu's inability to concentrate and his extreme distractability tend to be passed over as personal eccentricities in the intimate circle of female domestics and relatives with whom he prefers to spend his time. The family, however, does not expect him to remain in the Garden of Total Vision forever. As he approaches marriageable age, Bao-yu comes under more and more direct pressure from his father to give up his childish ways and apply himself to the arduous preparation necessary to pass the national examinations. As the only Jia male of his generation with any hope of passing, Bao-yu cannot ignore the exhortations of his stiff-necked father, although the thought of the conformity of the civil service appalls him.

A scapegrace only son is a common enough figure, and Jia Zheng attributes his son's unwillingness to study to willful perversity, especially since he well knows that there are times when Bao-yu seems to work with almost unnatural concentration. Given sufficient pressure and motivation, Bao-yu often exhibits what is referred to as "hyperfocus," a characteristic of people with A.D.D. that allows them in some circumstances to execute projects with astonishing efficiency and brilliance.[39] Until the very end of the novel, Bao-yu shows this only in his attention to his relationships with various women in his life and occasionally in his poetry composition, appreciation of novels and plays, and enjoyment of music. Although the traditional course of study for the national examinations is distinctly uncongenial to Bao-yu, this is not just a matter of temperament. Bao-yu is truly unable to carry out the assignments he has been set. His native endowment of intelligence is evident in his articulate speech and his poetic talent, but it does not carry him through the slogging necessary to survive one of Jia Zheng's inquisitions. The prospect of being examined by his father brings out every aspect of Bao-yu's A.D.D., especially his inability to concentrate and plan ahead.[40]

Typically, Bao-yu neglects his studies completely while his father is away on government assignments and then frantically tries to catch up when Jia Zheng's return looms. His mother recognizes his symptoms well and remarks during one of his spurts of application: "It's too late to begin sharpening your weapons on the field of battle" (SS III.70.383, HLM II.70.765). Even Bao-yu has to admit the justice of her words, as he ruefully contemplates the task before him.

> "I ought to have had more sense," he told himself. "One really ought to do a little bit every day, to keep in practice."
> (SS III.73.436, HLM II.73.794)

Of course, left to their own devices, that is precisely what people with A.D.D. cannot do. Although Bao-yu is brilliant enough on those texts that have caught his fancy, the systematic study of the traditional corpus is simply beyond him. When his father finally forces him to attend school every day, his homework still poses an agonizing problem.

Bao-yu bolted his supper, had his reading-lamp lit and sat down straight away to revise his basic texts, the Four Books of Confucian Scripture. One glance at the first page, however, with its columns of heavily annotated text, and he began to experience a familiar sinking feeling. He tried flicking through one volume, and the general drift seemed clear enough; but the moment he went into it in any detail, it seemed to slip from his grasp. He turned for help to the marginal commentaries, he read the expository essays, keeping up the struggle till late in the evening.

"Poems are easy," he thought to himself. "But I can't make head or tail of this stuff."

He sat back, gazed at the ceiling and was soon lost in a daydream.

(*SS* IV.82.53–54, *HLM* III.82.905)

This passage describes a typical attempt by a boy afflicted with A.D.D. to apply himself to a large and admittedly tedious task, with only a promise of intangible results in an indefinite future. Without an explicit and attractive structure for his studies, there is no way he can manage them.[41] In order for Bao-yu to find a way to fulfill his family's expectations, he must find a way of purging his life of the distractions that relentlessly thwart his every attempt to concentrate.

Miraculously and tragically, Bao-yu finds a solution. The inevitable cosmological resolution to the story of the Stone meshes with the social and emotional imperatives that so oppress the Stone's human avatar. These combine to provide a brilliant literary denouement and a plausible resolution for Bao-yu's disorder. They also suggest that, whether Bao-yu's disorder is considered as an illness or a character trait, it has an explicit karmic purpose. In the absence of appropriate drug therapy,[42] the only way for Bao-yu to be able to concentrate is to find a way to structure his life and resist the distractions that plague him. Moral fortitude is unavailing; the distractions themselves must be eradicated or drastically reduced. Here fate and a newly awakened sense of self-preservation come to Bao-yu's aid.

By the time Bao-yu is about eighteen years old, he seems to show some signs of adjusting to his disorder, at least as it relates to those to whom he is closest. After years of mutual misunderstanding and hurt, Bao-yu and Dai-yu seem to have reached a new level of intimacy, which Bao-yu attributes to their new maturity: "When I was younger . . . and Dai-yu was rather more childish in her ways, somehow I always managed to upset her by saying the wrong thing. Nowadays I think more about what I say, and she takes offence less easily" (*SS* IV.92.243–244, *HLM* III.92.1011). Just as Bao-yu seems to have gained in his ability to communicate with Dai-yu, however, he is faced with a new calamity. The celestial scheme for the lovers is that they must lose each other. The Stone and the Crimson Pearl Flower can appreciate the emptiness of romantic attachment only after they have actually experienced its futility and awakened to love's folly.

On the mundane level, this is easily accomplished when the time comes to select a bride for Bao-yu, and his family betrothes him to Bao-chai instead of Dai-yu. The deception that results in his unhappy marriage is possible only because, at the time when family pressures on him to conform to social norms begin to overwhelm him, Bao-yu loses his jade. With all his history of distraction and carelessness, this is the one thing he has never mislaid, and it is not his fault now. As if in sympathy with his emotional predicament, the jade simply vanishes from its accustomed place on the bedside table. The household responds to this crisis with predictable hysteria, and Bao-yu suffers a complete mental and emotional breakdown. The family desperately hopes to turn him around, and so in spite of his debilitated state they decide to proceed with his marriage to Bao-chai, decoying Bao-yu with the promise that he will marry Dai-yu. At the very moment his bride is revealed to be Bao-chai, Bao-yu collapses, and Dai-yu dies, convinced that her love has abandoned her (chapters 97–98). When Bao-chai confronts Bao-yu with the fact of Dai-yu's death, he refuses to believe it. He faints and, while unconscious, receives instruction from a stranger that fulfillment of his desire cannot be sought in the realm of death because "Dai-yu has already returned to the Land of Illusion and if you really want to find her you must cultivate your mind and strengthen your spiritual nature" (*SS* IV.98.372, *HLM* III.98.1082). When he awakes, Bao-yu accepts the death of his beloved with profound sorrow, but otherwise seems resigned to his fate.

Unfortunately for Bao-chai, Bao-yu's resignation is hardly what it seems. His revelation ultimately points him to the way of overcoming all his mundane woes—and, incidentally, of bringing his A.D.D. under control. Bao-yu realizes that, in order to meet Dai-yu again, he must follow her not to the realm of death but to the spiritual realm—the Land of Illusion. After his errant jade has been returned by a mysterious monk—the same monk known to the Stone in its previous existence at the base of Greensickness Peak—Bao-yu follows that monk in a dream to the Land of Illusion and has a second chance to read the Celestial Registers to learn the fates of the women in his life. This time, when he awakens he remembers every detail. He knows the futures of those whose lives concern him, all beyond his power to interfere. Moreover, he understands his own true nature and recognizes his jade for what it is: no life-preserving talisman, no signifier of worldly success, but merely a metaphor for his origin, the spiritual form to which he will inevitably return.

None of his household understand, of course:

> He lay pondering one by one the experiences of his wandering soul, and as he did so a glazed look came over his eyes. To his great delight, he found that he could remember every detail of his dream, and he chuckled aloud with satisfaction:
> "So! So!" . . .
> When the family saw him behaving in this strange fashion, laughing one minute and crying the next, *they could only think of it as a symptom of his old fit.*
> (SS V.116.294, 296, *HLM* III.116.1269–1270, italics added)

What the women cannot know is that Bao-yu's revelation has given his life an overriding focus: to discharge his essential duties to his family and then fulfill his duty to himself by quitting the mundane world altogether as a wandering Buddhist monk.

Bao-yu has three earthly obligations: to provide his family with a male heir, to pass the national examinations and so carry out his grandmother's wish for him to bring glory to the family name, and finally, more intimately, to show his respect for the father to whom he could never draw close. In consummating his marriage to Bao-chai, Bao-yu in fact fathers a male heir. Awakened to the vanity of all human endeavor, Bao-yu utilizes the short time before the examinations to greatest advantage in his preparations. Taking a final leave of his wife and family, Bao-yu giggles to himself as he leaves his old life behind. He passes the exams, capturing seventh place, and disappears forever.

For Bao-yu, perfect knowledge of the ends of all the uncertainties of his life has freed him from distraction for the first time. His spiritual liberation is also liberation from the shackles of his disorder, and he begins an entirely new existence. It only remains for him to show his respect for his father, and on a snowy evening, Jia Zheng is astounded to see before him the apparition of his son in the guise of a mendicant Buddhist monk.

Bao-yu bows three times, with an expression between joy and sadness, and then is gone. Jia Zheng is left to explain the meaning of this encounter and shows some genuine insight into his son's nature:

> "When did you ever see Bao-yu willingly work at his books? And yet if once he applied himself, nothing was beyond his reach. His temperament was certainly unique."
>
> (SS V.120.361, *HLM* III.120.1317)

The jade, however, is *still* only a metaphor. Bao-yu did not need to be born with a jade in his mouth to be marked as special from birth. His beauty, intelligence, poetic gifts, and personal charm promised great things. But the strategies necessary to fulfill these hopes were precisely what would be impossible for a Bao-yu with A.D.D. to implement, as indeed it had been impossible for so many of his close male relatives. The fact that so many Jias before him had failed to distinguish themselves raised the pressure to unbearable levels, giving the young man ample reason to seek release. Bao-yu's enlightenment after his second visit to the Land of Illusion gives him an alternative, one that suggests a flash of genuine *self*-knowledge. The life of a mendicant Buddhist monk is far simpler, more "monochromatic" than his life in the Garden of Total Vision—and much more manageable for someone with A.D.D. The Stone's inexorable destiny, therefore, parallels Bao-yu's drive to achieve genuine, personal liberation. The choice to "leave the world" to become a monk may be a manifestion of Bao-yu's awakening to the vanity of human endeavor, but it is also an effective act of self-preservation.

This, more than anything else, distinguishes Jia Bao-yu from his doppelgänger, Zhen Bao-yu. Until only a year or two before both boys were to take the national examinations, reports of Zhen Bao-yu's preferences and behavior were so similar that Jia Bao-yu expected to find in Zhen Bao-yu a true double and the ideal friend for whom he had always longed. They had even shared a physical and spiritual crisis, in dreams that marked the turning points of dangerous illnesses. In these dreams both were illuminated as to the futility of their attachments to the females in their lives, but upon awakening they are set on divergent courses. Jia Bao-yu becomes a monk, while Zhen Bao-yu becomes what his double calls a "career worm." The blatant approval for Zhen Bao-yu's reform shown by the elders of his family and Bao-chai disgusts Jia Bao-yu, who sees his double as having "sold out" to the pressures of the mundane world to conform to his class expectations and aspirations.

But, because of his A.D.D., Jia Bao-yu does not have Zhen Bao-yu's option of a complete reform at the eleventh hour. The mirror images *are* different. Zhen Bao-yu's change of course and heart is possible because his shortcomings really were a matter of overindulgence and eccentricity. Although these are aggravating factors in Jia Bao-yu's case, they are not the whole story. Zhen Bao-yu is Jia Bao-yu's double, without the jade *and* without the A.D.D. He represents the possibility of "if only . . ." and incidentally reveals that if only Jia Bao-yu had not been encumbered by his jade, or if he had not had his fundamental disability, he might not have been so interesting and sympathetic a character. Moreover, if his future had really been under his control, the pressures of his life would certainly have kept him from reaching enlightenment and blocked the reader also. When Jia Bao-yu makes a supreme effort, marshalls all his brilliance and focus and places seventh in the exams, we cannot suppress a thrill at his triumph. It is not just that he has so decisively outmatched his priggish double. In so doing he has found the way to a genuinely higher understanding, which we too are free to emulate: if not to enlightenment in the spiritual sense, then to a new perspective on the seemingly inextricably tangled human destinies of the novel.

From the viewpoint of mainstream Chinese society, especially as represented by Bao-yu's wife, leaving the world to become a monk means abandoning one's entire social identity. A mendicant monk simulates reincarnation, at least on the emotional and spiritual levels; he affects being without existence previous to his conversion and creates a new identity for himself. An example of this insistence on a new identity involves Bao-yu's distant relative, Jia Yu-cun. Jia Yu-cun was able to take the national examinations because of the financial support of his patron Zhen Shi-yin, who subsequently met with a series of personal disasters and became a wandering Taoist adept. When Jia Yu-cun meets his former patron years later, he is almost unrecognizable. This is not only because Jia Yu-cun is confused by his changed appearance but also because the old man deliberately appears to know nothing, *nothing* of any existence they may have shared. For those still enmeshed in the world of illusion, those who "leave the family" (*chujia*) bail *out*; but those who choose this option call it "entering the gate" (*jinmen* or *rumen*). The flicker of recognition on Bao-yu's face when he takes his leave of Jia Zheng must be his last worldly acknowledgment.

Although the last third of the novel—forty chapters—has been much edited by a hand other than the author's, there is no question that Bao-yu followed his creator's original intentions. In literary terms, the emotional and cosmological imperatives merge to make Bao-yu's choice consistent with the novel's sense of closure. It is also consistent with Bao-yu's sense of both family duty and self-preservation. But what of his relation to his creator? Some of Cao Xueqin's own prefatory remarks to *The Story of the Stone* are compelling:

> Having made an utter failure of my life, I found myself one day, in the midst of my poverty and wretchedness, thinking about the female companions of my youth. As I went over them one by one, examining and comparing them in my mind's eye, it suddenly came over me that those slips of girls—which is all they were then—were in every way, both morally and intellectually, superior to the "grave and mustachioed signior" I am now supposed to have become. The realization brought with it an overpowering sense of shame and remorse, and for a while I was plunged in the deepest despair. There and then I resolved to make a record of all the recollections of those days I could muster—those golden days when I dressed in silk and ate delicately, when we still nestled in the protecting shadow of the ancestors and Heaven still smiled on us. I resolved to tell the world how, in defiance of all my family's attempts to bring me up properly and all the warnings and advice of my friends, I had brought myself to this present wretched state, in which, having frittered away half a lifetime, I find myself without a single skill with which I could earn a decent living.

(*SS* I, Introduction, 20, *HLM* I.i.i)

In spite of this direct statement by the author, our knowledge of Cao Xueqin's life is limited, especially the early years that *The Story of the Stone* is supposed to document. From the remarks of his two commentators, Red Inkstone and Odd Tablet, we know that they struggled with the author in what seemed the hopeless task of bringing the novel to completion.[43] In their remarks on the history of the composition of *The Story of the Stone*, we have a very suggestive portrait of a man who shared not only his past and his sensibility with his fictional hero but possibly his A.D.D. affliction as well.

The commentators' remarks on the evolution of Cao Xueqin's manuscript suggest that, beyond the usual struggles of a literary genius to bring his artistic vision to fruition, the author's inspiration was constantly blocked and frustrated. While eking out some sort of living as a painter, and perhaps as a tutor, Cao Xueqin worked on his manuscript for at least twenty years, until he died. Even the chapters he finished are full of contradictions and inconsistencies, signs of a work under revision. As Red Inkstone and Odd Tablet describe the process in bits and pieces throughout their commentaries, Cao Xueqin would write, then divide his book into chapters, then redivide it a different way. Given a revision to do, he would procrastinate, work on another part, change a previous section to accommodate his original text, go on a drinking binge, lend out or lose a chunk of the manuscript, forget the names of his characters, insert some entirely new material, drop the whole project, and freeze up. It took the combined efforts of his devoted editors to keep him going, and when Xueqin died in 1763, Red Inkstone mourns that he still left the book unfinished.[44]

This is more than an untrammelled artist possessed by the overmastering demands of creation. Red Inkstone and Odd Tablet speak of his frustration (and theirs) with his inability to set down all the material he could so well articulate, his impulsive treatment of the manuscript, and, above all, his constant distraction from his great task. It was not that Xueqin was crushed by working to support his family, for, while he may indeed have been living in poverty in his later years, there is no indication that he was ever overburdened with the responsibilities of "making a decent living." As cited above, he admits to "having frittered away half a lifetime." In his own preface, and through his novel's hero, he describes with heart-rending accuracy a deficient sense of time, a frantic awareness that time is slipping away, and an inability to seize his opportunities and bring his project to fruition.

Without wishing to indulge in a biographical fallacy—that only someone with A.D.D. could have written such a convincing case study—the parallels between Xueqin's personality and Bao-yu's lead irresistably to the idea that the author may well have suffered from the disorder he so unflinchingly and accurately describes in his hero. If this is so, the novel's spiritual climax demonstrates Xueqin's ability to envision a cosmological and emotional resolution that was beyond his own grasp. Bao-yu's decision to sever his earthly ties, especially his family ties, to become a wandering Buddhist mendicant is significant not because he converts to Buddhism per se but because this conversion provides him with a means to opt out of society altogether.

Here the artistic imperatives of the novel and the personal aspirations of the author diverge. Devotees of *The Story of the Stone* have argued endlessly over Bao-yu's solution: Is it a heroic act of self-liberation or a callous escape? Whatever answer the reader chooses, Cao Xueqin has constructed a narrative that makes this end both psychologically and allegorically inevitable. But what of the author's solution? If his hero can opt out of society altogether, why couldn't *he*?

By all reports, Buddhist transcendence was simply not an option for Cao Xueqin. Some sense of personal obligation weighed heavily on him, and he could not renounce it. The original obligations may well have resembled those faced by Bao-yu: to produce an heir, to pass the national examinations, to restore the family name to its past glory. But Cao Xueqin's son died, and several attempts to pass the exams ended in failure. The last obligation, however, he fulfilled. Through most of his adult life he labored to "create a memorial" of the people and the way of life he had known, which were so quickly passing beyond anyone's knowledge. Vexed and contradictory as the text of the novel may be, it has immortalized the author and his world beyond his wildest imagining.

4

A WORLD APART

Poetry and Society in the Garden of Total Vision

Poetry is everywhere in Bao-yu's world. Couplets are inscribed on doorways, on paintings, even on rocks in the Garden of Total Vision. The dramatic entertainments that are part of every family occasion, from public holidays to birthday parties, are largely in verse. Poetry composition is an essential social skill for men and women, although women's poetry seldom reaches an audience outside their intimate realm, and women may be deeply conflicted about the role of poetry in their lives. Because *The Story of the Stone* is a microcosm of society, it shows not just poetry but the social practice of poetry, both as private expression and public display. The main characters to whom we become so attached have internalized poetry and a poetic view of life and continually relate their literary knowledge both to their sentimental inner life and to their understanding of the world around them.

Poetry in the day-to-day world of *The Story of the Stone* includes poetry composed by the characters as a tool of social intercourse and poetry as an ornament of everyday life. In the textual history of *The Story of the Stone*, poetry composed by the characters has another dimension: It often preserves the tracks of earlier plots, characters, and devices, which were later, intentionally or unintentionally, edited out of the prose narrative. The inconsistencies of the poetic and prose levels of the novel, which have been well studied by experts in the novel's textual history, illuminate the gap between the author's original intentions for his story and characters and the final, though unfinished version. It appears that, as revisions were required, either by Cao Xueqin himself or by his editors, the last things to be changed were the poems.[1]

But even without these tantalizing inconsistencies, we would have an extraordinarily rich range of poetic functions to consider. On many levels, the poetry in *The Story of the Stone* holds the key to the novel as the Stone himself wished it to be read, as "a true record of real events" (*yi zhi shi shilu qi shi*) (SS I.1.51, HLM I.1.3). This function of poetry links the artist's intention with the canonical function of poetry, namely, "expressing individual intent" (*yanzhi*).[2] In the context of a masterwork of prose fiction, this dictum becomes even more complex than it is in the everyday life of a poetry critic because the poetry is composed, declaimed, recalled, and quoted in a fictional world. The conventional association of *zhi* ("intent") with *qing* ("emotion" or, as rendered in this study, "attachment"), and the fact that poetry is the accepted medium of both, invests every line of poetry in *The Story of the Stone* with the potential to represent disillusionment and transcendence.[3]

On the expository level, poetry is also a vehicle for the revelation of character and fate. The poetry of social gatherings can be just as revealing as the most intimate cri de coeur. As often as not, however, the composers of public poetry, and their readers or listeners, are unaware of its real significance. Private poetry, by contrast, is overinvested with significance. The solitary poet assumes the clichéd persona of one in the grip of lyric transcendence. When the poet is a confused adolescent, it can be difficult to tell what is cliché and what is genuine insight. Furthermore, a poet's peak experience is not, traditionally, solitary; rather, the poet requires a "perfect listener" (*zhiyin*), who instinctively understands the emotion of the poet without mediation.[4] The real significance of a poem in *The Story of the Stone* may be revealed only when it is overheard, but the question of whether the listener can understand the reciter's feelings, or whether only the reader can understand them while the listener remains in a fog, is part of the complexity of the relation of poetry to the novel as a whole.

Even if we are alert to poetry's role as a key to the allegorical structure of the novel, it can still be difficult to grasp the import of any given poem. Each poem must be read through the multiple veils of social and literary convention as well as the emotional vagaries of the individuals involved. A reader's difficulty in understanding poetry's intimations of disillusionment is just a shadow of the difficulties for those fictional characters living the life whose vanity is revealed. The author must have hoped that readers would be able to appreciate the poetry in all its avatars. He quotes and alludes to the entire tradition. He contributes original examples of poems of every genre, which, depending upon their context, range from fine poems in their own right (in his descriptions, or in representing the work of such poetic talents as Dai-yu and Bao-chai) to commendable efforts by earnest aspirants to lyric transcendence to crude lampoons by crude buffoons.[5] Nevertheless, in *The Story of the Stone* the appreciation and practice of poetry are objects of nostalgia and manifestations of social ideals that, even within the novel itself, are lamented as slipping away. It is not just the poetic view of life but the practice of poetry that is essential to this elegy for traditional Chinese society.[6]

Bao-yu's first encounter with poetry in all its potential is in his dream in chapter 5, in the hypersensuous and luxurious bedchamber of his niece, Qin Ke-qing. The fairy Disenchantment herself is described in a rhapsodic verse in the *fu* ("rhymeprose" or "rhapsody") form. This genre had been favored since the Han dynasty for lavish descriptions, and Disenchantment comes from a noble lineage of beautiful women celebrated in poetry. Indeed, when Bao-yu views fine images of women, he appreciates them by recalling Disenchantment's literary ancestor, the Goddess of the River Luo from a poem in the same genre by the Wei dynasty poet Cao Zhi (192–232).[7] Touched by the urgent plea of the spirits of Bao-yu's ducal ancestors, Disenchantment has agreed to plant in the boy the seeds of his awakening to the vanity of his existence. The first vehicle of this intended awakening is poetry, in a set of riddles in the Celestial Registers that reveal the fates of the girls in his life. The rebuses and dense symbolism of the short verses contained in the Registers are beyond him, especially since he cannot conceive what the poems have to do with him. Disenchantment then presents her pageant of poetry and music—"The Dream of Golden Days" (*honglou meng*)—twelve songs spelling out the messages of the registers even more plainly.[8] Again Bao-yu does not understand their specific prophecies of the tragic loves and marriages of the women in his life: Dai-yu will die in despair, Bao-chai will be frozen in a loveless marriage, Xiang-yun's bliss in marriage will be cut short by her husband's fatal consumption, Ying-chun's sadistic husband will batter her to death— even Qin Ke-qing, in whose chamber he dreams, will hang herself when her adultery with her father-in-law is discovered. If he cannot understand the particulars, the final chorus carries explicit warning:

The Birds Into the Wood Have Flown

The office jack's career is blighted,
The rich man's fortune now all vanished,
The kind with life have been requited,
The cruel exemplarily punished;
The one who owed a life is dead,
The tears one owed have all been shed.
Wrongs suffered have the wrongs done expiated;
The couplings and the sunderings were fated.
Untimely death sin in some past life shows,
But only luck a blest old age bestows.
The disillusioned to their convents fly,

The still deluded miserably die.
Like birds who, having fed, to the woods repair,
They leave the landscape desolate and bare.

(*SS* I.5.144, *HLM* I.5.53)

This poem comments on the futility of attachment in both the mundane and fictional worlds. The workings of fate are inexorable; yet, even when all fates are justly fulfilled, we are mired in attachment to the characters and feel loss when this pageant of actors rings down the curtain. Unless Bao-yu can awaken to the dangers and delusions of his existence, he is doomed to slow disillusionment in the world of the red dust, instead of the complete revelation the pageant offers. Bao-yu, unfortunately, is attuned only to the color and noise of such entertainments. Even as he seeks lyrical transcendence through poetic expression, it has never occurred to him to appreciate poetry as a document of truth: intellectual, emotional, or spiritual. It is not just the feelings of the words, but their literal content that is essential to their appreciation. Until Bao-yu learns to appreciate what poetry *says*, he cannot understand what it *means*, even in his own compositions. The evolution of Bao-yu's poetry appreciation is actually the history of his self-awareness. As his appreciation matures, so does his worldview. Since he cannot recognize the significance of the "Dream of Golden Days," he must plod on through a comprehensive sentimental education that gradually awakens him to the fact that even his poetic view of life cannot mitigate the necessary suffering of a mortal existence.

Part of this education comes at the hands of his father, through attempts to inculcate in the boy the skills and knowledge expected of the sons of the gentry class. Certain kinds of social occasions are regarded as training grounds for later careers in public service. Chinese boys with these aspirations would be called upon to recite texts for cultivated guests or to compose poetry to celebrate special events.[9] Bao-yu's progress in such polite accomplishments is often tested and harshly criticized. In chapter 17, egged on by his pseudo-intellectual hangers-on (the "literary gentlemen" [*qingke*] who assiduously pay court to their patron), Jia Zheng tests Bao-yu's talent for composition by conducting him on a tour of the extraordinary garden, really a separate imperial residence, built to honor the imperial concubine. An essential part of such a garden's design would be the titles and poetic inscriptions bestowed on its significant sites. Jia Zheng himself insists that the garden will be incomplete without poetry:

"These inscriptions are going to be difficult. . . . Her Grace should have the privilege of doing them herself; but she can scarcely be expected to make them up out of her head without having seen any of the views which they are to describe. On the other hand, if we wait until she has already visited the garden before asking her, half the pleasure of the visit will be lost. All those prospects and pavilions—even the rocks and trees and flowers will seem somehow incomplete without that touch of poetry which only the written word can lend a scene."

(*SS* I.17.324–325, *HLM* I.17.154)

The test of versifying on command requires that Bao-yu concentrate fully upon his task, which includes both evocative inscriptions for various sites and couplets to accompany them. He must exercise his powers of observation to extract the essence of the scenes to be celebrated, capture their unique qualities in his inscriptions, with appropriate allusions to sites, events, and poems from the tradition at large. This is an important social attainment in traditional Chinese gentry culture, whose significance for professional success should not be slighted, even though a talent for poetry alone is not enough for an illustrious public career.

Jia Zheng is ill disposed because, according to the schoolmaster, poetastering is the only area in which the boy is making any progress. So Bao-yu is on the line to show his father that his talent is genuine. Jia Zheng's personal prestige is also on the line, however: to prove to his enthusiastic toadies not only that his son's promise is being fulfilled but that he can exercise authority over him. Jia Zheng can make Bao-yu's life a misery, but Bao-yu can disgrace him in public with a flabby performance. The conflict between the two is the central tension of this poetry ordeal, with the disdainful father balancing anger and pride, the adolescent son dread, inspiration, and a sassy desire to show off.

That the occasion becomes an ordeal shows how far the family has deviated not just from ideal authority patterns but also from the solidarity patterns proper authority is supposed to establish. If Jia Zheng and Bao-yu's relations conformed to ideal patterns, the son would be anxious to earn his father's approval, the son's success would reflect well on the father, and the father's pleasure in the son's accomplishment would enhance the son's feelings of affection and gratitude toward him. Because of the estrangement of father and son, even if Bao-yu distinguishes himself, his father has no way of showing his approval positively. Bao-yu's most skillful titles and couplets Jia Zheng can only praise with faint damns; for his lesser efforts, his father has sharp words and even threats of physical punishment. The Garden of Total Vision is thus the scene of the explicit revelation of the erosion of the Jia family's sense of priorities. The boy does have talent, and his position as Jia Zheng's sole surviving son by his primary wife makes him the object of great hopes. When asked to demonstrate his abilities to his father's entourage, however, he must struggle with his resentment at being the object of his father's contempt and despair. Indeed, when Yuan-chun visits the garden we are surprised to discover that, in spite of his father's scorn, Bao-yu's contributions have been used after all. The Stone as narrator goes out of his way to explain, in a special note to the reader, that this is out of deference to the imperial concubine's affection for her little brother; however, Jia Zheng could not have relented had he found Bao-yu's work truly beneath the family's literary standards.[10]

This power struggle takes place in a setting so beautiful that conflict should be forgotten, for never was there a man-made paradise so conducive to spontaneous celebration. The Garden of Total Vision (*Daguan yuan*) is not yet named at this point in the narrative, but as we tour it for the first time we get a vivid sense of its scope.[11] Its title is the inspiration of the imperial concubine herself. Her commemorative verse honors the designer (a hired professional) as much as the family whose wealth could purchase such perfection:

> Embracing hills and streams, with skill they
>   wrought:
> Their work at last is to perfection brought.
> Earth's fairest prospects all are here installed,
> So "Prospect Garden" let its name be called!
>   (*SS* I.18.365, *HLM* I.18.173)

The phrase *daguan* literally means "grand view," embracing the many brilliant prospects contained in a garden covering altogether about an acre of land. The phrase is also a Buddhist metaphor for spiritual insight. The "grand view" in spiritual terms is profound insight or complete grasp of the nature of existence; Plaks renders it as spiritual and metaphorical "total vision." Is Yuan-chun merely honoring the genius of the designer? Or can she have an inkling of what the garden will be to her beloved younger brother when, by her express order, he is sent to live there along with his female relations?

Although Yuan-chun's name for the garden is literally inspired, what the family sees is the best that money can buy for a daughter elevated to the emperor's favor. For all their highbrow pretensions, the senior Jias see the garden as a practical work of craft. An important aspect of this particular garden is that its various prospects and sites evoke as many different styles and environments as possible, from imperial style (Hall of Reunion, *Xingqin bieshu*) to a simple rural farmhouse (Sweet-Rice Village, *Daoxiang cun*), from luxurious prosperity (House of Green Delights, *Yihong yuan*) to a secluded hermitage (All-Spice Court, *Hengwu yuan*).[12] The garden, however, is a work of art within the larger work of art—the novel. What the adults see as a site for a unique formal occasion the children will regard as a universe. In literary terms, it *is* a universe, not least because the description of the buildings, promenades, waterways and pools, hills and dales, and most abundantly the plants, symbolically represent all the elements of the environment of a vastly wealthy and privileged gentry family.[13]

The garden, therefore, invites "that touch of poetry" which is so essential to the pleasure of its beauty, but the different generations have different notions of what is to be celebrated. This is also a struggle between the father's inflexibly orthodox interpretation of the natural world and the son's romantic one. The range of poems that Bao-yu must compose reflects this, along with the range of historical and textual allusions he calls upon to justify himself. The literary gentlemen are there to promote Jia Zheng's happiness, and so they are bound to encourage their patron's son to excel. Their contributions are insignificant: The real exchange is between the talented boy and his harshest critic. Bao-yu must check both his desire to one-up his elders and betters in knowledge and poetic talent and his impulse to express his own feelings, which are not what Jia Zheng wants in his home, his son, or the inscriptions in his garden.

Bao-yu does best when he combines his romantic approach with orthodox references to classic texts. When he names the small artificial mountain at the gate of the garden "Pathway to Mysteries" (*Qujing tongyou*), he gratifies not only his father's desire for a dignified and evocative reference but his own as-yet unformed anticipation of the possibilities of life for him. Unknown to him yet, the heart of Bao-yu's experience will take place in this garden, and in that light the title alludes to the novel's allegorical frame as well as the boy's potential liberation.

As long as they refer to sites of "natural" beauty, Bao-yu's titles and couplets pass muster. But at Sweet-Rice Village, a miniature farm plunked down in a corner complete with vegetables, livestock, and reed-thatched cottages, Bao-yu unwisely shows his antipathy to his father's orthodoxy. When Jia Zheng rhapsodizes on its evocation of rural simplicity, Bao-yu obstinately challenges him at the philosophical level:

"I have never really understood what the ancients *meant* by 'natural.'. . ."

"Why, fancy not knowing what 'natural' means—you who have such a good understanding of so much else! 'Natural' is that which is *of nature*, that is to say, that which is produced by nature as opposed to that which is produced by human artifice."

"There you are, you see!" said Bao-yu. "A farm set down in the middle of a place like this is obviously the product of human artifice. . . . It sticks up out of nowhere, in total isolation from everything else. It isn't even a particularly remarkable view—not nearly so 'natural' in either form or spirit as those other places we have seen. The bamboos in those other places may have been planted by human hands and the streams diverted out of their natural courses, but there was no *appearance* of artifice. That's why, when the ancients use the term 'natural' I have my doubts about what they really meant. For example, when they speak of a 'natural painting,' I can't help wondering if they are not referring to precisely that forcible interference with the landscape to which I object: putting hills where they are not meant to be, and that sort of thing. However great the skill with which this is done, the results are never quite . . ."

(*SS* I.17.336–337, *HLM* I.17.159–160)

Jia Zheng explodes at this point. Although Bao-yu is certainly out of line with his top-lofty disquisition, the parent/adolescent conflict is underscored by the essential conflict of their two worldviews. Jia Zheng's is firmly rooted in his social and political context. Bao-yu's comes from his essential nature as determined by his origin in the Land of Illusion—he even uses the phrase *daguan* (here rendered by Hawkes as a "remarkable view") to describe precisely what this part of the garden lacks. These two planes of existence can never be fully reconciled. But in common-sense terms, Bao-yu's critique is also justified—how could there be a farm in such a place? Here the boy's lack of experience, or his lack of patience with conventional modes of social and aesthetic discourse, shows through. His interpretation of Sweet-Rice Village cannot prevail against a system of philosophical and artistic conventions that reads simplicity and naturalness into a thoroughly artificial image of rustic life.

Bao-yu nearly comes to grief again when they reach the main reception hall of the imperial concubine's separate residence. Jia Zheng deprecates the showiness of the building, while accepting that his daughter's exalted position now demands it. Bao-yu is struck dumb, in the grips of an overpowering sense of déjà vu. The place he cannot remember is the palace of the fairy Disenchantment. During the imperial concubine's visit, we find that this hall has been given the temporary title "Precinct of the Celestial Visitant" (*Tianxian baojing*), which Yuanchun changes to "the Hall of Reunion." Both titles refer to aspects of the evocative hall that Bao-yu cannot access: the first a reference to Disenchantment herself, the second to the reunion that will take place after Bao-yu and Dai-yu have fulfilled their worldly karma. For the moment, in his confusion, Bao-yu is quite unable to respond to his father's demand for a name and couplet for the arch. Indeed, if he could recall the correct name, his trials as a mortal would be over, and he would not need to fear his father's displeasure. But the mortal boy cannot recall his dream into conscious memory. Fearing possible repercussions from Grandmother Jia for overtaxing her darling grandson, Jia Zheng takes advantage of this lapse to let him off. What Bao-yu cannot recall on his own he will have to realize through experience.

As they wind their way out of the garden, Bao-yu recovers enough to show that he has more poetic insight into the other sites of the garden than do his elders, favoring names that stress youth and transcendence. A slightly malicious jibe is aimed at Jia Zheng when they come to the building that will later become Bao-yu's residence. The building that Yuan-chun will name the "House of Green Delights" (*Yihong yuan*, literally, "the house of the pleasures of youth"; *hong*, "red," conventionally referring to youth) is a maze of corridors and partitions, with no regular rooms at all. Jia Zheng actually loses himself in the maze, dodging a huge mirror to confront a bewildering array of doorways. Cousin Zhen, who has acted as overseer to the landscaping, considerately leads him out the back. These passages and choices are for Bao-yu, not for him.

At Yuan-chun's behest, to keep him from dissipating himself outside the home, Bao-yu moves into the Garden of Total Vision with his female relatives. It is a new world: enclosed and self-contained. Since this is to be *their* world, it makes sense that most of Bao-yu's names and couplets are kept. After all, the garden has been created by the author of *The Story of the Stone* for Bao-yu's emancipation. Consistent with the Jia family's faulty household management, the children conduct their affairs in the garden either with no supervision or with too much of the wrong kind. The domestics vie to pamper their charges and to avoid work as much as possible. The elder Jias regard the garden as a place for pleasure themselves, to escape everyday cares in parties and festivals. The garden is a world of romantic release for all generations, and the fact that the children come of age there makes their initiation into the world of adult affairs that much more abrupt and traumatic. They are not just living in an ideal world, doubly protected from the realities of life beyond the red walls of the Ning-guo and Rong-guo Houses. They are integrated into a world created by artifice and self-consciously resonant with poetic allusions. The isolation of this ideal world encourages its residents to take their roles from poetic references and aspirations, and, as they assume these roles, they are deluded into thinking that they have a chance of fulfilling their dreams.

Each residence in the garden, in name and style, evokes the character of the person who settles in it. Li Wan, whose wealthy family enforced ignorance and industry on women as a matter of principle, is installed at the artificially rustic "Sweet-Rice Village" to act as chaperone for the adolescents. Dai-yu takes the "Naiad's House" (*Xiaoxiang guan*), secluded in a green thicket of bamboos. Bao-chai is allotted "All-Spice Court," as she is the only member of the family thoroughly versed in the properties of the myriad useful plants at that site. Level-headed and bookish Tan-chun chooses the "Autumn Studio" (*Qiushuang shuzhai;* literally, a library study).[14] Bao-yu, of course, has the House of Green Delights. These residences, in turn, will provide the inspiration for the artistic and social personae that their inhabitants will assume in their exclusive society.

In the garden Bao-yu comes to appreciate, as far as he can, the poetic view of life. Poetry is no frivolous pastime here: It is a mode of existence and a way to prepare for life in practical and intellectual terms. The residents of the Garden of Total Vision use poetry as a means of self-expression and as a way to practice adult-style social behavior, testing and enforcing their internal loyalties and hierarchy without overt interference from the outside world.[15] It is also functions as a tool for developing mutual awareness and understanding. Although Bao-yu's poetic gifts may make a small lion of him in his father's world, in the inner quarters they are consistently overshadowed by those of his female cousins. But here he has a chance to find out what poetry can be, both in the semiprivate context of the frequent poetic gatherings in the garden and in the intimate context of truly private expression.

The Crab-Flower Club (*Haitang shishe*) founded in chapter 37 is the inspiration of Tan-chun. Her flowery invitation to celebrate their exclusive society in poetry meets with universal enthusiasm. Their only previous opportunity to compose together was at the request of the imperial concubine, who requested poems to celebrate her favorite sites in the garden. There the emphasis was on Bao-yu, whose success depended on help from Dai-yu. Although his quatrains were appropriate to the occasion and pleasantly turned, the situation demanded formality and decorum before inspiration.

Not only does the club give focus to a set of talents hitherto without purpose, but it reinforces the boundaries of their wonderful world against the outside world, while expanding its possibilities within. There is much more to a poetry club than writing poems. Their first activity is to give one another pen names. This is a time-honored activity of literary aspirants—after all, even Cao Xueqin's own commentators are known to us only by their sobriquets. Part of the purpose of these pennames is to break down the hierarchies of family relationships—sisters, cousins, in-laws—to which they are bound outside the garden and by which they are supposed to address one another. Part of the purpose is symbolic, as each name evokes some essential aspect of their characters and the dwellings they selected: "River Queen" (*Xiaoxiang feizi*) for the perpetually weeping Dai-yu alludes to the speckled bamboos that screen the Naiad's House, said to be flecked with the tears of the two queens of the emperor Shun after his death; "Lady All-Spice" (*Hengwu jun*) for the pharmacologically learned Bao-chai; "Green Boy" (*Yihong gongzi*; literally, "lord of the pleasures of youth") for the boy who lives in the House of Green Delights, and so forth. Even the cousin who visits frequently from outside, Grandmother Jia's great-niece Shi Xiang-yun, is given a pen name, "Cloud Maiden" (*Zhenxia jiuyou*), to evoke the imaginary residence she would have chosen, had she lived in the garden.[16]

Li Wan, as arbiter of decorum and nominal overseer of their activities, appoints herself president. The children are soon deep in a structured performance of literary conventions: part pleasure, part earnest competition. The first meeting of the Crab-Flower Club meticulously details conventions of poetry composition as a social activity. Even in play, there are rules to be followed. The procedures for selecting the subjects, genres and rhymes to be used are half arbitrary, half formal. "White Crab-Flower" (*baihaitang*; in this case, the pendulous, white blossom of the autumn flowering crabapple) is the first subject because Li Wan has seen the gardeners bringing in two pots of the lovely "Maiden's crab" to Bao-yu's apartment. The fact that she is the only one who has actually seen the plants is not really a problem:

> "How are they going to write poems about it if they haven't seen it?"
>
> "We all know what white crab-blossom looks like," said Bao-chai. "I don't see why we necessarily have to look at it in order to be able to write a poem about it. The ancients used a poetic theme as a vehicle for whatever feelings they happened to want to express at that particular moment. If they'd waited until they'd *seen* the objects they were supposed to be writing about, the poems would never have got written!"
>
> (*SS* II.37.221, *HLM* I.37.374)

Bao-chai speaks explicitly to the strength of conventions of composition and, incidentally, allows the author to take a sly poke at the biographical fallacy—the assumption that every poem is on some level a true record of events in a poet's life and therefore a potential source of authentic biographical information. The notion that an individual's writing is a key to his or her experience is attributed to Mencius, who in speaking of the writings of the ancients declared, "If we chant their poems and read their books, how could we fail to know them as people? By these means we can speak of their world."[17] *The Story of the Stone* itself has been mined exhaustively for information about the author and his world.[18] Here Bao-chai, with typical practicality, insists on the use of the imagination.

Ying-chun sets the genre for their poems at random from a book in Tan-chun's shelves; an octet in regulated verse (*lüshi*). She then asks a maid for two words to determine the end of the first line and the rhyme word in the second line. Matching rhymes for lines four and six are drawn from the set of "rhyme cards" (*yunpai xiazi*), which would be at hand in any well-appointed young lady's room. These cards were practical aids to aspiring poets, identifying appropriate rhymes and tones for correct composition. Lastly, the maid is asked to draw a card for a word to turn the final couplet.[19] The participants work against the clock (a short stick of incense is lit to act as a timer), each in his or her own style. The poems produced, while all adhering to these strict conditions, reflect the personalities of the poets, as do their processes of composition.

Tan-chun applies herself to the task at hand and writes a workmanlike hymn to the radiant fragility of the autumn blossoms. Bao-chai admits that she has come up with something, but deprecates her contribution—her poem is a perfect mirror of her own preferences for plain colors and autumnal imagery. Bao-yu paces up and down, working up a sense of pressure as he listens to the others, then writes his in a fluster, indiscreetly comparing the chaste blossoms to the notorious Yang Gui-fei rising naked from her bath. Dai-yu appears unconcerned, sauntering in at the end and knocking off a poem that conveys the ethereal scent and grace of the autumn crab blossoms.

From the first, Dai-yu and Bao-chai jockey for first place, while Bao-yu's contribution goes to the bottom of the ranks. Bao-chai and Dai-yu represent two opposite but complementary styles of creativity, just as they represent opposite but complementary styles of women. Li Wan, as befits the dignity of the chaperone of the garden, is ex-officio arbiter of taste and decorum, and although she herself does not compose, the members of the Crab-Flower Club respect her judgment of poetry. Sometimes Bao-chai will take first place, sometimes Dai-yu. Dai-yu leads in "elegance and originality" (*fengliu biezhi*), Bao-chai in "character and depth" (*hanxu hunhou*).[20] Together the girls represent great genius *and* brilliant execution, the two irreconcilable yet complementary approaches to poetry composition in the Chinese tradition.

This alliance of rivals is just one aspect of their relationship. Bao-chai's attitude toward poetry is fraught with conflict. On the one hand, she has great talent for composition and tremendous knowledge of poetry and poetic theory. On the other hand, she is painfully aware that the transcendence of poetry is virtually unavailable to women in her society. Poetry is not a woman's "proper business," and women's poetry is not for public display; it is usually only chance that preserves a woman's poems and carries them beyond the intimate family context. But even within the family, which is a woman's proper sphere, Bao-chai apprehends the irony and frustration of personal expression without the prospect of an audience. The more restricted the potential audience, the less likely a poet will find that "perfect listener" to know her heart.

Dai-yu and Bao-chai are the two great talents of the garden, but there are several others, newcomers or outsiders, with talent to illuminate certain features of the garden's society. The Crab-Flower Club's wild-card talent is Shi Xiang-yun. As Grandmother Jia's great-niece, she has been an intimate of the Jias since babyhood, but, as she lives outside the garden with her uncle, she is forgotten in the first rush of enthusiasm. Her hurt is soothed by a chance to write on the original topic of crab blossoms, at which she excels with two poems, and the opportunity to invite the others to a session the following day. Xiang-yun's enthusiasm is briefly damped when Bao-chai, with whom she spends the night, reminds her that she lacks the wherewithal to manage and pay for such a party. Bao-chai offers her support in arranging a cassia-viewing party for the Crab-Flower Club and Grandmother Jia as well. Xiang-yun is grateful; both girls know how the happiness of the garden depends on the patronage of Grandmother Jia.

As part of the next day's entertainment, they together select the subject and form of the poems. Bao-chai's sense of the occasion is linked directly to her sense of the mainstream poetic tradition:

> "About the theme for tomorrow's poems . . . we don't want anything too outlandish. If you look at the works of the great poets, you find that *they* didn't go in for the weird and wonderful titles and 'daring' rhymes that people nowadays are so fond of. Outlandish themes and daring rhymes do not produce good poetry. They merely show up the poverty of the writer's ideas. Certainly one wants to avoid clichés; but one can easily go too far in the pursuit of novelty. If one has fresh ideas, one does not need to worry about clichés: the words take care of themselves! But what am I saying all this for? Spinning and sewing is the proper occupation for girls like us. Any time we have left over from that should be spent in reading a few pages of some improving book—not on this sort of thing!"
>
> (SS II.37.235, HLM I.37.382)

Bao-chai's speech, in spite of its feminine disclaimer, is a fair echo of the Stone's denunciation of hackneyed and meretricious poetry. But the girls do find a way to carry out Bai-chai's critical imperatives. Their choice of subject is chrysanthemums, and the next question is how to infuse with it with originality. Bao-chai continues:

> "[If] you somehow involved the *poet* in the theme . . . You could do that by making up verb-object or concrete-abstract titles in which 'chrysanthemums' was the concrete noun or the object of the verb as the case might be. Then your poem would be both a celebration of chrysanthemums and at the same time a description of some action or situation. Such a treatment of the subject *has* been tried in the past, but it is a much less hackneyed one. The com-

bining of narrative and lyrical elements in a single treatment makes for freshness and greater freedom."

(SS II.37.236, HLM I.37.383)

The result is a plan for a poem sequence whose twelve topics will produce a unified work of art: "All three months of autumn condensed into a single sequence of a dozen poems!" (*SS* II.37.238, *HLM* I.37.384).[21] The Chrysanthemum Suite is the Crab-Flower Club's most polished exercise in the social practice of poetry. The process of selection of topics, as well as the execution of the exercise at the next day's entertainment, provide insight into poetic practice as a rite of passage into maturity in Chinese gentry society and further insight into the relations among the inhabitants of the garden. Although the young people's contributions are again uneven, overall this is the most uniform, and unified, work the garden will produce.

Bao-chai's introductory verse, "Remembering the Chrysanthemums," sets the flowers in their seasonal and cyclical context. She also writes of "Painting the Chrysanthemums" in black ink, to keep their image alive after they have faded. Bao-chai eschews color in her own domain—when Grandmother Jia brings Grannie Liu to see her room, she is shocked by its complete austerity. Her reproach to her granddaughter suggests that such apparent self-effacement is not only unfeminine but arrogant. In fact, her taste is an unfeigned expression of her way of seeing and imagining. As we know from her remarks about not needing to see the autumn crab blossoms to write about them, for Bao-chai evocation of the object suffices, and a black ink painting would still bring out the chrysanthemums' bright colors.

Bao-yu's poems are all action: "Seeking the Chrysanthemums" and "Planting the Chrysanthemums." Xiang-yun "admires" and "arranges" them, then intensifies her image of "The Shadow of the Chrysanthemums" by mingling scent with evening shadow. Tan-chun writes of "Wearing the Chrysanthemums" and finishes the suite with "The Death of the Chrysanthemums," which refuses to mourn but looks forward to meeting them the next autumn. Dai-yu's poems, which triumph in this contest, treat the chrysanthemums as personifications of autumn inspiration—she "celebrates," "questions," and "dreams" of them, as sentient beings in perfect sympathy with her autumn feelings.

Again, the poets' contributions mirror their personalities and preoccupations. Bao-chai and Tan-chun are grounded in appreciation of seasonal rituals. Xiang-yun has an intense sense of the inspiration of a unique moment. Bao-yu distracts himself with fussy actions and misses a more profound appreciation. Dai-yu evokes the awareness that plants are in harmony with human beings, yet her symbolic communion with the flowers comments rather pathetically on her difficulties with human communion. Considering Dai-yu's origin as the Crimson Pearl Flower, this mode of self-presentation should not surprise us.

There are many other such events, though none quite so crisply structured. Some are deliberately informal, as with the riot of poems on the subject of eating crabs (crustaceans, not apples) at Xiang-yun's party following the composition of the Chrysanthemum suite. Later that winter, the members of the poetry club try their hands at a long linked-verse composition celebrating a magnificent snowfall (chapter 50). The garden's society has by now been swelled by the arrival of several more female cousins, including Bao-chai's cousin Xue Bao-qin. All the new arrivals are competent poets, and Bao-qin, whose beauty and personality make her a possible compromise between Bao-chai and Dai-yu, is almost as gifted as the two girls she closely resembles. The party begins with the girls broiling kebobs of venison over an open fire, and the poets carry their high spirits into their couplets. Even Xi-feng participates: She provides the first line and introduces the snowstorm as the subject of the poem. The participants start out taking turns, but as the most agile poets quickly get carried away the others are elbowed out of the poem. Xiang-yun, Dai-yu, Bao-chai, and Bao-qin end up in a free-for-all.[22] Xiang-yun collapses with laughter, saying, "This isn't verse-making. . . . It's more like a duel to the death!" (*SS* II.50.494, *HLM* II.50.522). Xiang-yun's capacity for living in the moment as well as her inventive intellect give her poems a special energy that sets her apart from Bao-chai and Dai-yu, as indeed her level of sheer physical energy does. Her particular life-force has a distinctive voice in the Crab-Flower Club.

Xue Bao-qin's poetry also has a distinctive voice, although her compositions tend to be ingenious rather than inspired. She acquits herself well in every exercise, but her most ambitious effort is a set of riddles on historical sites that she claims to have visited with her father. Her older cousin Bao-chai protests that two of her sites celebrate characters from plays, rather than strictly historical figures—the monastery at Pu-dong from the *Romance of the Western Chamber* and the Plum-Tree Shrine from *The Peony Pavilion* (*Mudan ting Huanhun ji*; also known as *The Return of the Soul*).[23] Even Li Wan finds Bao-chai a bit priggish here and rules that the very fame of the stories lends the sites imaginatively associated with them authenticity (rather like associating Verona with

Romeo and Juliet). With the garden's chaperone arguing for the palpable existence of fictional creations, how can the young poets expect to distinguish fiction from truth?[24]

That is precisely why Bao-chai regards, or affects to regard, such poems as a threat to the innocence of the garden. It is not so much that she feels that poetry and plays undermine authority—she is well aware that the authority patterns in the household are already far from ideal. But she understands, with regret, that the wish fulfillment so gratifying in literature is not to be found in everyday life, even in such a privileged household as this. Her critiques of poetry as an enterprise, therefore, are both ironic and self-ironizing. She can be hilariously pedantic:

> "*I* shall call the next meeting," said Bao-chai brightly. "There will be four themes for poems in Regular Verse and four for poems in other metres and everyone will have to do all eight of them. The first will be a three-hundred-line poem in pentasyllabics exhausting the rhyme 'first.' Its subject will be 'On the Diagram of the Supreme Ultimate.'"
>
> Bao-qin laughed.
>
> "One can see that it isn't really poetry you are interested in but in making things difficult for others."
>
> (*SS* II.52.539, *HLM* II.52.546)

Here Bao-chai is satirizing her own tendency to pedantic disquisitions, not just on poetry but on the futility of poetry as social exercise. She is far more generous with her chief rival, Dai-yu, whose genius in wit and poetic originality she readily acknowledges. When Dai-yu lampoons Grannie Liu's visit to the garden in chapter 42, Bao-chai deadpans the role of commentator:

> "The secret of [Dai-yu's] sarcastic tongue is that she uses the method adopted by Confucius when he edited the *Spring and Autumn Annals*, that is to say, she extracts the essentials from vulgar speech and polishes and refines them, so that when she uses them to illustrate a point, each word or phrase is given its maximum possible effectiveness. The mere name 'Old Mother Locust,' for example, is sufficient to evoke the whole scene of yesterday's party and everything that happened at it. What's more, she is able to do this sort of thing almost without thinking."
>
> (*SS* II.42.335, *HLM* II.42.435)

Bao-chai's attitude toward women's poetry is one of self-doubting elitism, while Dai-yu's, though just as elite, is far more optimistic about the role of poetry in women's education. When Xue Pan's concubine, Caltrop, begs to be taught to write poetry while her master is away on a long trading mission, Bao-chai laughs, but Dai-yu readily agrees to teach her. In order to refine Caltrop's middlebrow tastes, Dai-yu sets her to reading the poetry of the Tang dynasty greats and admonishing her to learn from their example. Caltrop devours their poems and spends day and night reading and trying to write poetry. When Caltrop worries that she will never write good poetry, Tan-chun reminds her:

> "Good heavens! *we* only write for the fun of it ourselves. . . . You surely don't imagine that what we write is good poetry? If we set ourselves up to be real poets, people outside this Garden who got to hear of it would laugh so loud that their teeth would drop out!"
>
> (*SS* II.48.461, *HLM* II.48.502)

Tan-chun echoes Bao-chai, but Bao-yu reproves the girls for their general self-depreciation:

> "That's what Mencius calls 'throwing yourself away' . . . You shouldn't do that. The other day . . . [some of Father's gentlemen] told me they had heard about our poetry club and asked if they could see some of our poems, so I wrote a few out for them from memory. I assure you, they were genuinely impressed. In fact, they have calligraphed them for blocks to have them printed." . . .
>
> "You really are the limit! Quite apart from the fact that the poems aren't good enough, you have no business to go showing our stuff to people outside."
>
> "What's the harm?" said Bao-yu. "If those famous poems written by poetesses in days gone by had never been taken outside the women's quarters, we shouldn't know about them today."
>
> (*SS* II.48.461, *HLM* II.48.502)

Actually, all the poems by the garden's female inhabitants are known to the outside world, by grace of the author of *The Story of the Stone*. The reader has access to works that might otherwise be lost, the chance to admire the authors and know their hearts, to appreciate their talent and receive instruction from their compositions; keeping in mind, of course, that these carefully preserved examples of women's poetry are as much fictional creations as their authors are. It is part of the fulfillment of the vow Cao Xueqin made in the introduction to the novel to cherish and preserve the memory of the women he loved during his childhood: "however unsightly my own shortcomings might be, I must not, for the sake of keeping them hid, allow those wonderful girls to pass into oblivion without a memorial."[25] *The Story of the Stone* may not preserve their actual poems, but it recreates a world in which such exceptional women could express themselves to the fullest and be understood.

Dai-yu's "Songs for Five Fair Women" (*Wumei yin*) take as their subject the heroic resolve of five notorious beauties of Chinese history (*SS* III.64.257–258, *HLM* II.64.696–697). Dai-yu gives their tales a tragic dimension, emphasizing not their roles as *femmes d'histoire* bringing ruin upon households and kingdoms, but on their unflinching confrontations with the disasters brought down around them. Xi Shi, Yu Ji, Wang Zhaojun, Green Pearl, and Red Duster are all portrayed as remaining true to themselves, refusing to compromise in their drive to find someone to understand their true worth or perish in the attempt. Dai-yu's treatment of their careers provides a sharp contrast to the treatment of the women associated with the objects in Qin Ke-qing's bedchamber, where their sensuality and its dangers overwhelm sense and senses. The chastity and integrity of Dai-yu's character shine through in her original treatment of these archetypes and suggest that these figures are not well served in other hands. Although Dai-yu may not know what her destiny is, it is certain that her resolve will carry her through without compromise to her essential nature. Cao Xueqin records Dai-yu's sympathy and insight and, in so doing, reinforces the purity of her character. He, at least, will not allow her to "throw herself away."

Dai-yu's leadership of the garden's poetry society is confirmed in chapter 70 when the others read her ballad "The Flower of the Peach" (*Taohua xing*). This is a long poem whose title, in addition to the association of peach blossoms with the essence of spring beauty and vitality, also evokes the ancient utopian theme of the Peach Blossom Spring (*Taohua yuan*). According to the legend, a fisherman following an unknown stream forgot himself, space, and time in contemplation of the beauty of flowering peach trees on the edge of the stream. At the end of the grove he found himself in a village cut off from the outside world, where everyone lived in harmony and no one suffered from envy or want. Happy as he was there, the fisherman grew homesick and departed. When he later tried to retrace his path, he could not find the stream, the trees, or the passage into the hidden village.[26]

Bao-chai has already praised Dai-yu's originality in her treatment of the easily hackneyed themes of the five beauties. In "The Flower of the Peach" Dai-yu once again displays an unconventional imagination. While the title of the poem fixes the theme, Dai-yu's rendition transforms the archetype.[27] In this her achievement goes beyond any of her rivals', and the author demonstrates his unique gift of characterization; that is, not only in depicting a character truly capable of artistic innovation but in providing her with the credible fruits of poetic inspiration. Although Dai-yu is a fictional creation, her artistic excellence is genuine.

In "The Flower of the Peach," Dai-yu breaks down the barrier between the flowering trees and the seeker, a maiden as lovely and fragile as the blossoms themselves. Indeed, she is a flower among the others, subject to the same short cycle of bloom, with this exception—she is sentient, and the flowers are not. She confers awareness upon them through the pathetic fallacy, but ultimately she knows that the trees do not share her melancholy or sense of doom. The flowers fade and die in due season, but if she follows them her season would be cut short.

Dai-yu does not hope for another spring, another chance to discover the lost secret of the peach blossoms. Instead of taking comfort in the prospect of a longer life, the girl who was the Crimson Pearl Flower in her previous existence is ineluctably drawn to melancholy contemplation of her flower-nature. In one sense she is right. Because of her illness, Dai-yu is indeed not long for *this* world. What she cannot know is that death, for her, will be a release from illusion and a return to her true state of being, the immortal Crimson Pearl Flower. In that avatar, she will embody the essence of the flowers more completely than any earthly flower could. Dai-yu's experience of mortality, however poetically transcendent, is still only a matter of illusion. When she compares the present evanescence but ultimate recurrence of the peach blossoms to her own evanescence (which she does not realize will bring her to her proper home in the cosmos), she emphasizes the very delusion from which her present life is supposed to liberate her. Dai-yu's glimpse of the nature of the peach blossoms, in that sense, is like Bao-yu's frisson of inaccessible memory when he first views the Hall of Reunion in the garden (chapter 17). Even her powers of intuition cannot lead Dai-yu to this realization because the only person with knowledge of all aspects of her being is the author himself. Cao Xueqin has created a convincing portrait of poetic genius, complete with worthy if minor works from "her" hands, but uses her lyrical insight to point to the inadequacy of lyrical insight. Is his only purpose to emphasize the necessity of her return to the Realm of the Void, or is it an admonition to the reader, to remember that his own book, however brilliant and illuminating, still operates within the limits of human consciousness?

Fired with enthusiasm for Dai-yu's piece, the members of the Crab-Flower Club, which has not met for more than a year, vote to revive their society and change its name to the Peach-Flower Club (*Taohua she*). It is spring, a chance for a new beginning. The former idealized state of the poetry club, however, like the location of the Peach Blossom Spring, is not easily recovered.

When Bao-yu reads "The Flower of the Peach," he has not been told who the author is. He recognizes Dai-yu's voice immediately, just as immediately understands her intent, and is moved to tears. When teased by Bao-qin about his certainty, he explains: "Cousin Lin writes like this because she has actual experience of grief" (*SS* III.70.380, *HLM* II.70.764). He cannot mean that the others have never experienced grief: Both Bao-qin's parents are dead, Bao-chai's father died long ago, and Xiang-yun has been an orphan since infancy. It is as if Bao-yu has an intuitive sense of the debt of tears. Others experience grief, but eventually heal. Dai-yu never recovers from any loss or hurt. While she suffers from a serious illness, her spiritual suffering is also a fundamental part of her being, necessary to her loveliness and loveableness, even as it is fatal to herself and those who love her.

Indeed, most of Dai-yu's poems are preoccupied, if not with death, with the passing of the seasons, loss, and decay. Later in the same chapter, Xiang-yun suggests trying another genre, *ci* (song lyrics), which are usually on informal, even light-hearted themes. The theme is willow floss—light enough. Dai-yu focuses exclusively on the catkins' demise, at the mercy of the uncaring wind. All admire the poem, but remark on its pessimism. Dai-yu's vivid imagination always has darkness at its heart.

In addition to writing poems at the poetry meetings, members of the garden's society pair off to compose, enriching our insight into their relationships. Bao-chai and Xiang-yun's collaboration on the titles for the Chrysanthemum Suite is an example of this. Indeed, Xiang-yun is often one of a pair and is crucial to these special intimacies. Notably, Bao-yu never exchanges poems or composes à deux. Xiang-yun is essentially remote, even though she is her cousins' equal in talent. Dai-yu actually recognizes her as an equal but unthreatening talent, perhaps because Xiang-yun's style, while often brilliant, never diminishes her own. In another sense, Xiang-yun is Dai-yu's most compatible partner because she is a plausible substitute for Bao-yu. She is often described as a Bao-yu look-alike, and her brand of spontaneity and sympathy is a feminized version of Bao-yu's own style—so inappropriate in a boy, but within the bounds of decorum in a tomboyish girl.[28]

In one of the last beautiful moments in the garden, Xiang-yun and Dai-yu compose linked pentameters. The poetry club is in decline; Dai-yu's attempt to resuscitate it with "The Flower of the Peach" has fallen flat, in part because Bao-yu is under renewed pressure from his father to devote his time to serious study. But the girls have one last chance. Under a brilliant moon, Xiang-yun rallies her cousin's spirits:

> "All that talk about spending Mid-Autumn night enjoying the moon together and using the occasion to revive the Poetry Club with another linked couplets session—and then, when the time comes, they leave us in the lurch and go off to enjoy the moon by themselves! No Poetry Club, no linked couplets, nothing! . . . Never mind. Since the others haven't come, we'll make up some linked couplets ourselves and take them along tomorrow to shame them with."
>
> (*SS* III.76.513–514, *HLM* II.76.836)

Linked couplets balance cooperation and competition, a perfect medium for these two.[28] Although she sometimes has extravagant notions, Xiang-yun knows the meaning of compromise and is able to find happiness in less than ideal circumstances. She is an appropriate and effective substitute for Bao-yu in moments of intimacy that would not be possible for two people of opposite sex. Xiang-yun's capacity for reflection and equanimity can fortify and encourage Dai-yu. Here, they bring out the best in each other. Standing under a radiant moon in a water pavilion, Dai-yu is comforted, and when Xiang-yun wishes for a boat and wine to complete her happiness, Dai-yu reminds her of the old saying, "Who seeks perfection must abandon joy" (*SS* III.76.515, *HLM* II.76.837). They then compose a poem celebrating the present moment, even as its melancholy tone acknowledges the end of their childhood. In a sense, the Concave Pavilion (*Aojing guan*) in which they stand recalls their best days, when the children could reach out to the limits of their fancies to name all the sites in their artificial paradise, and their world was full of promise. They celebrate the Mid-Autumn Feast with images of companionship and the poetry games that did not take place that night. The couplets then turn to the overwhelming night, as the music dies, the toadstools sprout, and a stork flashes over the water in the darkness. The rhyme is difficult, and Dai-yu seems to exhaust it by turning to an image of herself: "Where, moon-embalmed, a dead muse lies in state" (*Lengyue zang shi hun*) (*SS* III.76.522, *HLM* II.76.842). Xiang-yun is admiring, but rueful:

> "Excellent! Couldn't be better! I love your 'dead muse'!" She sighed. "I mean excellent from a purely poetic point of view, because it's so original. It's a bit morbid, though." . . .
>   "With you to compete against, how else could I keep my end up?" said Dai-yu.
>
> (*SS* III.76.522, *HLM* II.842)

At this point, the redoubtable Adamantina, the unshorn nun who has taken up residence at the Jia family's Green Bower Hermitage, a secluded retreat within the garden, surprises them. Adamantina is a symbolic twin of Dai-yu, a glimpse of what Dai-yu might have been had her parents heeded the monk's warning and taken steps to shelter her from contact with anyone but her mother and father. Like Dai-yu, Adamantina is a young woman of the most exquisite taste, with considerable poetic talent, but she takes it for granted that her position as a privileged Buddhist practitioner has set her apart from the lesser mortals who populate the world. Actually, Adamantina has taken only "half-vows"—she has cut her hair, but not shaved her head, signs of her parents' attempt to compromise with her destiny: A wandering monk (yes, Impervioso) warned them that if she did not take vows she would meet a tragic fate. Her presence as the Jias' pet religious in the garden indicates her underlying ambivalence. Her obsession with the forms of purity and refinement point to her equivocal state of existence; the appearance of being above the red dust is not the same as being free from it.

Adamantina praises the girls' exercise in pure refinement, but admonishes them to stop: "There were lines which, in spite of their excellence, contained a note of almost decadent melancholy, lines which made me fearful for the person uttering them" (522, 842). She takes them back to her hermitage for tea, then undertakes to bring the poem back to the "proper aspect" (*zhenqing zhenshi*). Adamantina adds thirteen couplets of her own (the original number from which they derived the rhyme word), brings the poem and the poets to the light of morning, and reminds them of the evanescence of poetry:

Why should this rapt enjoyment end in sorrow,
Or timid cares our conscience irritate?
Poets ought in themselves to find their pleasure,
Not in the message they communicate.
(*SS* III.76.525, *HLM* II.76.843)

Adamantina is a creature of absurdly self-conscious fastidiousness, but is apparently oblivious to the irony of her implicit chastisement of the girls, particularly Dai-yu, for their unfeminine behavior in overinvesting their poetry with personal significance. Dai-yu's poetry, at least, is more significant than Adamantina can ever imagine. Dai-yu creates images of self in her poetry that, on the one hand, foreshadow, and, on the other, precipitate her own destruction. Her obsession with poetry as the ultimate form of communication and self-expression, especially with Bao-yu, will provoke Dai-yu's last great grief, the last spurt of tears before her debt is paid.

The poems written in the garden are idealized celebrations of a place that is already an ideal. In order to survive their necessary departure from the garden, the children must heed the potential of poetry as a vehicle for the development of self-awareness, if not awareness of the vanity of existence. After his dream of the palace of the fairy Disenchantment in chapter 5, Bao-yu learns his first important lesson in the significance of poetry for life at the hands of Bao-chai. Exasperated by the noise level of the theatrical entertainments at a birthday party, Bao-yu demands to know why a cultivated girl like his cousin keeps selecting rackety scenes like *Zhi-shen at the Monastery Gate* instead of the quieter, more sentimental scenes that he himself favors. Tactfully not mentioning the fact that Grandmother Jia, the hostess, has a preference for the more vigorous style, Bao-chai points out that Bao-yu is neither hearing the music nor listening to the words, which contain deep emotion and transcendence. When Bao-chai recites a "Clinging Vine" aria from the play in a low voice, just for his benefit, he can focus on its quality. The aria is the lament of the disgraced monk Lu Zhi-shen, who has been dismissed from his monastery for wreaking drunken havoc, knocking down a pavilion, and smashing the guardian gods at the monastery gate. When he bids farewell to his abbot, however, he expresses genuine commitment and regret:

"I dash aside the manly tear
And take leave of my monkish home.

A word of thanks to you, my Master dear,
Who tonsured me before the Lotus Throne:
'Twas not my luck to stay with you,
And in a short while I must say adieu,
Naked and friendless through the world to roam.
I ask no goods, no gear to take away,
Only straw sandals and a broken bowl,
To beg from place to place as best I may."
                                 (SS I.22.435, HLM I.22.211)

Although Lu Zhi-shen had entered the monastery unwillingly, on the run from the law and without vocation, his genuine calling to the Buddhist faith begins with his exile from its community. After Bao-yu is "enlightened" by Bao-chai, he wreaks havoc in his own community. Trying to avoid a quarrel, he offends both Dai-yu and Xiang-yun and has the door shut in his face by the one and is told off by the other. Recalling the aria, he experiences the self-pity ("Naked and friendless through the world to roam") without the self-realization. He even goes so far as to write a callow imitation of a Buddhist *gāthā* and his own "Clinging Vine" style verse to accompany it:

I swear, you swear,
With heart and mind declare;
But our protest
Is no true test.
It would be best
Words unexpressed
To understand,
And on that ground
To take our stand.

. . .

You would have been at fault, if not for me;
But why should I care if they disagree?
Free come, free go, let nothing bar or hold me!
                                 (SS I.22.440–441, HLM I.22.214)

When Dai-yu discovers this doggerel she shows it to Bao-chai and Xiang-yun, and all three go to his room to untangle his inadequate paradox. This is the first of many non-enlightenments for Bao-yu:

Bao-yu *had* in fact believed that he had attained an Enlightenment. . . . He consoled himself with the reflection that if they,
whose understanding was so superior, were manifestly still so
far from Enlightenment, it was obviously a waste of time for *him*
to go on pursuing it.

(*SS* I.22.443, *HLM* I.22.215)

Bao-yu may make light of the transcendent powers of poetry from
plays, but Dai-yu responds very differently. In chapter 23, she overhears
the Jia family's troupe of actresses practicing their arias and has an
epiphany of the verses' power to speak to her mood. The lines, from an
exchange between the lovers in *The Return of the Soul*, are of love and
hopeless longing. The actresses' voices bring a revelation of the beauty
of the play, and an overwhelming feeling of identity and hopelessness:

> "And the bright air, the brilliant morn
> Feed my despair.
> Joy and gladness have withdrawn
> To other gardens, other halls—" . . .

"It's true," she thought, "there is good poetry even in plays.
What a pity most people think of them only as entertainment. A
lot of the real beauty in them must go unappreciated." . . .
She listened again . . .

> "Because for you, my flowerlike fair,
> The swift years like the water flow—"

The words moved her to the depths of her being.

> "I have sought you everywhere,
> And at last I find you here,
> In a dark room full of woe—"

(*SS* I.23.466, *HLM* I.23.227)

Dai-yu goes into a virtual fugue of recalled lines of poetry, all al-
luding to the death of the flowers, the relentless passing of spring, the
inevitable death of youth and beauty blighted without romantic love.
She even has some awareness of the effect this power has on her, as il-
lustrated by a line from *Romance of the Western Chamber*: "As flowers fall

and flowing stream runs red, / A thousand sickly fancies crowd the mind" (*SS* I.23.467, *HLM* I.23.227). Instead of illuminating her mind to the fact that her situation is by no means unique, she gives herself over to the moment completely, and, were it not for the arrival of the solicitous Caltrop, she might have wept for hours.

Although the children must have watched scenes from these plays dozens of times, their language does not become part of Bao-yu and Dai-yu's intimate dialect until they have *read* the original texts in their entirety. Bao-yu, unfortunately, tends to offend his cousin when he cites them, going straight to the heart of a matter she finds mortifyingly delicate. This is a core feature of their relationship: When Bao-yu finally brings himself to speak of his affection, or alludes to it carelessly (as something so thoroughly understood between them that it needs no delicate indirectness), Dai-yu rebuffs and upbraids him. She takes his carelessness as a sign of trivializing her feelings. For a boy like Bao-yu the opposite is true: His attachment to Dai-yu is so complete that it is an unself-conscious part of his being. It is only through the constant discipline of her oversensitivity that he learns to restrain his direct expression of emotion, ultimately to the detriment of both of them.

In chapter 26, Bao-yu overhears Dai-yu quoting from *Romance of the Western Chamber*: "Each day in a drowsy waking dream of love" (*SS* I.26.516, *HLM* I.26.256). Bao-yu laughs, recognizing "their" play—to whom could the lines refer but to himself? Dai-yu is terribly embarrassed and pretends still to be asleep. Bao-yu is touched by her sleep-flushed face and lets it go, then immediately missteps by thanking Nightingale for tea with another quote from the same play: "If with your amorous mistress I should wed, / 'Tis you, sweet maid, must make our bridal bed" (*SS* I.26.517, *HLM* I.26.257). Bao-yu is speaking too directly, and this offends both Dai-yu's maidenly modesty and her agonizing insecurity. Accusing him of dredging up coarse expressions to make fun of her, she flings back at him the enhanced communion the play affords them. It is a source of endless frustration to Bao-yu that, although he and Dai-yu are fluent in the same secret language, she refuses to speak to him in it.

Dai-yu is right to be cautious up to a point. The poetry in plays is beautiful, but plays are dangerous territory precisely because they are associated with romantic release. Bao-chai is able to appreciate their poetry well enough to teach its power to others, but she is also ready to warn of its dangers. During a drinking game in honor of Grannie Liu (chapter 40), Dai-yu thoughtlessly quotes from *The Return of the Soul* and *Romance of the Western Chamber* to keep up her end of the game. Fortunately for her, only Bao-chai notices. It is one thing to listen to these plays during a family party, but quite another to reveal detailed familiarity with the texts. These are forbidden books, and knowledge of them is not to be revealed in a public context. The next day, Bao-chai summons Dai-yu to an inquisition.

> "*What* were those things I heard you saying yesterday? Come now, the truth!" . . .
> Dai-yu cast her mind back and remembered, blushing, that the day before, when stumped for an answer, she had got through her turn by citing passages from *The Return of the Soul* and *The Western Chamber*. She hugged Bao-chai imploringly.
> "Dear coz! I really don't know. I just said them without thinking. If you tell me not to, I promise not to say them again."
> (*SS* II.42.332, *HLM* II.42.434)

Bao-chai then proceeds to give Dai-yu a good deal of sisterly advice on the dangers of poetry and plays for young people in general, young women in particular. Although the homily suggests acquiescence in social norms, her words imply no quiet resignation:

> "So, you see, in the case of us girls it would probably be better for us if we never learned to read in the first place. Even boys, if they gain no understanding from their reading, would do better not to read at all; and if that is true of boys, it certainly holds good for girls like you and me. The little poetry-writing and calligraphy we indulge in is not really our proper business. Come to that, it isn't a boy's proper business either. . . . And unfortunately, it isn't merely a case of their being led astray by what they read. The books, too, are spoiled by the false interpretations they put upon them. . . . What do we need to be able to read for? But since we *can* read, let us confine ourselves to good, improving books; let us avoid like the plague those pernicious works of fiction, which so undermine the character that in the end it is past reclaiming."
> (*SS* II.42.333–334, *HLM* II.42.435)

This is not just a pompous disquisition on the dangers of art by an officious young woman anxious to one-up her brilliant cousin. Bao-chai echoes the Stone himself, deploring the false interpretations encouraged by meretricious romancers. More unhappily, Bao-chai's professed views on women's education are ambivalent because she has already resigned herself to limited expectations for intellectual and emotional fulfillment in adulthood. Her speech is an ironic commentary on the opportunities for self-discovery and self-expression by women, however talented and educated.[30] Since the world affords them so little scope for fulfillment in these areas—not just in the realm of literary achievement but in all the social realms they can encounter through poetry, plays, and fiction, including emotional and romantic fulfillment—they might indeed be happier if they never had their horizons of possibility broadened. If a girl seeks fulfillment in the mundane world, she must make the best of what will be hers. If Bao-chai's is the voice of reason, it is certainly tinged with irony, if not outright regret.

Dai-yu not only acknowledges the truth in Bao-chai's pronouncements, she is grateful for her cousin's concern and discretion. She admits that if *she* had been the one to catch Bao-chai, she would not have been able to resist exposing her in public. This encounter becomes the basis of a rapprochement between the two rivals. We could see their opposition, cosmologically and temperamentally, in their previous relationship, but from this point their cosmic complementarity is translated into a mutually supportive friendship.[31] Bao-chai and Dai-yu are not just the two essential halves of Bao-yu's ideal woman; they exemplify two approaches to the possibilities of life for women of gentry families. Neither could find happiness or fulfillment without the other. The artistic temperament must find a grounding in social necessity; the perfect, dutiful woman will wither without dreams and sense awareness. When these two are separated, both are diminished. When Bao-chai marries Bao-yu, she loses her friend as grievously as Bao-yu loses his love.

Some time later, Bao-yu manages to quote from *Romance of the Western Chamber* without offending Dai-yu. Puzzled by Dai-yu's rapprochement with Bao-chai, he asks: " 'Since when did Meng Guang accept Liang Hong's tray?' " (SS II.49.477, HLM II.49.510). In this case, there is no romantic insinuation, and Dai-yu explains the incident in full. Freed from the threat of romance, Dai-yu can safely reveal her knowledge.

Imagining themselves cast in their favorite dramatic works is one of the most dangerous games the lovers play. The penalty for forgetting the distinction between the roles they adore and their own lives is literally death, at least for Dai-yu. In *The Return of the Soul*, the heroine dies of longing, then is resurrected by the power of her lover's devotion. That is magic and fiction. Dai-yu cannot be revived by Bao-yu after her death; she does not even visit his dreams. *Romance of the Western Chamber* is a reworking of the Tang dynasty short story by Yuan Zhen (779–861) , "The Story of Ying-ying." The original story is tragic: Ying-ying is a brilliant, spirited, and contrary beauty; her lover is an opportunistic cad.[32] In the dramas based on this story, the lover is reformed and returns to his beleaguered fiancée covered with honors. Dai-yu's touchy and passionate temperament evokes Ying-ying's, but she makes a mistake in clinging to the play and forgetting that the original. Bao-yu is no cad. Dai-yu dies without knowing that he is faithful to her. If she regards herself as the living heiress of Ying-ying's archetype, she should have recalled into conscious memory the original from which the happily-ever-after version was transformed.[33]

The play that most evokes Dai-yu's destiny is one that is obscure to almost all the guests at an entertainment arranged by Jia Zheng's in-laws to celebrate his promotion to the rank of permanent secretary, in chapter 85. The selection is "The Transfiguration" ("Ming sheng") from *The Palace of Pearls* (*Ruizhu gong*).[34] The play explores the relationship between the mortal and immortal realms through the story of the moon goddess, Chang E, and her love for a mortal man. So great is her passion that she leaves her heavenly abode to pursue a mortal life with her lover. At the moment of fulfillment, the boddhisattva Guanyin enlightens her as to the vanity of attachment. She dies before her marriage can take place and returns to her proper place in the heavens. None of the members of the Jia household know this play, but they should recognize its main character. The day of the party is Dai-yu's birthday, and she arrives at the festivities looking "exactly like the Goddess of the Moon descending to Earth" (*SS* IV.85.131, *HLM* III.85.948–949). Like Chang E, the Crimson Pearl Flower is a being of celestial origin whose love of a mortal clouds her perception of the emptiness of mortal attachment, but whose awakening to that emptiness can be achieved only through experiencing the pain of love and loss. Dai-yu's career on earth is destined to follow that of the archetype in *this* play, and no other.

There are others in the garden who act as if the world of plays were real. In chapter 58, Bao-yu rescues one of the resident actresses, Nenuphar (Ou-guan), from punishment when she is caught in the garden burning an offering to a deceased friend who used to play opposite her in romantic roles. The elder Jias deplore such superstitious manifestations, but Bao-yu is deeply moved by the girl's gesture. Nenuphar keeps her friend's memory alive by mourning her as if they really had been lovers. The actress can be seen either as utterly deluded by plays or as potentially participating in the process of awakening to the vanity of existence propounded by the Stone for the readers of *his* book; namely, entering the realm of form and attachment through the role she plays, awakening to passion, then realizing its vanity—it's only a play!—and reaching spiritual liberation. Several of the actresses, in fact, resolve their disillusionment with the world and the vanity of their enterprise by entering a convent in all sincerity. They awaken to the vanity of existence through the experience of plays. Or is it the shock of realization that life is not like art? They have always known that they had no social prospects because of their class and trade, but they find that they have vast spiritual prospects by virtue of their practice of that trade.

There are many occasions when the significance of poetry is clear to the reader yet most of the characters remain oblivious. Poetry composition and appreciation play a major role at the festive gatherings associated with seasonal holidays or family celebrations and often illuminate feelings of emotional attachment that otherwise go unexpressed and unacknowledged. In chapter 22, Bao-yu's father shows an unwonted sensitivity when Bao-yu, his sisters, and female cousins compose a set of systematically foreshadowing riddles in poetic form. These riddles are conceived in the tradition of *yongwu* poetry (poems about objects). This thematic subgenre of poetry uses an object to build up a central image, which is both intrinsically and metaphorically appropriate to the author's expressive purpose. Such poems may have political significance (a politician becomes a parrot in a gold cage or a giant dead tree), but not necessarily (a wild goose embodies the poet's longing for home, a peony a woman of marriageable age).[35] The occasion is a party that takes place during the Lantern Festival, inspired by an exchange of riddles with the imperial concubine, Bao-yu's elder sister Yuan-chun. The festivities begin with the contribution of Bao-yu's strait-laced father Jia Zheng, whose riddle of a plain inkstone is a fair image of his own limited talent and inflexibility. The children then, one after another, unself-consciously compose riddles about objects that are metaphors for themselves.[36]

Yuan-chun's firework embodies her flashy rise and rapid extinction as "an object of amusement" (*wanwu*, the clue she sends with the riddle) for the emperor. Tan-chun's kite (her leitmotif), Dai-yu's self-consuming incense clock, Bao-chai's poignant "bamboo wife" (*zhufuren*, a wicker cylinder that helps keep the sheets from sticking to a sleeper during the summer but is discarded when the season changes)—all are apt metaphors, and all are foreboding. Curiously enough, only Jia Zheng seems to understand them, and the unsympathetic fellow is plunged into dejection. It is the first intimation that anyone on the mundane level can catch a glimpse of the future, or the truth.

Bao-yu's self-revealing riddle is perhaps the most apt, as it exemplifies both the boy's susceptibility and his inability to find release from it:

> Southward you stare
> He'll northward glare.
> Grieve, and he's sad.
> Laugh, and he's glad.
>
> (SS I.22.449, HLM I.22.218)

Bao-yu's extraordinary sympathy with the girls is what makes his enlightenment possible, by virtue of the suffering it inflicts on both himself and his loved ones. At this stage, of course, he is incapable of understanding it. As a "mirror," he reflects the emotion of anyone with whom he is in contact, but it is just a reflection.[37] To an adolescent, perfect reflection may seem like perfect sympathy, but an adult knows all too well the limited possibilities of such a response. There is something terribly unchildlike about all the riddles. Jia Zheng is unable to speak his feelings, but inwardly he is quite overcome:

> "Enough is enough!" he thought. "What can it be that makes these innocent young creatures *all* produce language that is so tragic and inauspicious? It is almost as if they were all destined to be unfortunate and short-lived and were unconsciously foretelling their destiny."
>
> (SS I.22.450, HLM I.22.218)

A drinking game in chapter 63 contains another set of poetic prophecies for the girls and Bao-yu. In honor of Bao-yu's birthday, his maids organize a late-night party and invite the young ladies over for a game of "Choosing the Flower" (*zhanhua ming'er*). This game is played with a set of ivory tiles, each painted with a different flower and including ingenious directions on whom, and how, each player should toast and be toasted. The flowers are labeled with captions and a line of poetry capturing their symbolic essence, and, incidentally, the essence of the young lady who has chosen the tile. In this way, the girls all unwittingly tell their fortunes again, many echoing the prophecies of chapter 5.

The first to choose is Bao-chai, who selects the peony (*mudan*), titled "Empress of the Garden" (*yanguan qunfang*), with an inscription by the Tang poet Luo Yin: "Yourself lack passion, yet can others move" (*SS* III.63.224, *HLM* II.63.680). While the merry company carries out the instructions for drinking and singing on the back of the tile, Bao-yu picks up Bao-chai's tile and muses abstractedly on Luo Yin's line, so perfect an expression of the effect of Bao-chai's beauty and deportment. The implicit text, however, is even more important.[38] This is *Book of Songs* (*Shi jing*) 95, "Qin Wei." The poem is a betrothal song in which a young lady and a young lord participate in a spring festival. Enjoying the beauty of the landscape, the lady invites the lord to walk with her and presents him with a peony:

> When the Chen and Wei
> Are running in full flood
> Is the time for knights and ladies
> To fill their arms with scented herbs.
> The lady says, "Have you looked?"
> The knight says, "Yes, I have finished looking;
> Shall we go and look a little more?
> Beyond the Wei
> It is very open and pleasant."
> That knight and lady
> Merrily they sport.
> Then she gives him a peony.[39]

By picking up the tile with the peony, Bao-yu symbolically betrothes himself to Bao-chai.[40]

When it is Dai-yu's turn, she draws the hibiscus (*furong hua*; "Mourner of the Autumn Mere"). The tile instructs "Hibiscus" to take a cup of wine with "Peony," and the cousins drink together. The accompanying line of poetry on the tile is by the Song poet Ou-yang Xiu: "Your own self, not the East Wind, is your undoing" (*SS* III.63.228, *HLM* II.63.682). The meaning of the line of poetry on Dai-yu's tile is clear enough, but her association with the hibiscus flower becomes clear only after the death of Skybright (Qing-wen), Bao-yu's clever but fatally beautiful and outspoken maid. In looks, sensitivity, and wit, Skybright is Dai-yu translated into the status of a purchased body servant. Also like Dai-yu, Skybright is infected with tuberculosis. Skybright's agony does not last long, as she is driven from the garden during Lady Wang's puritanical raid in chapter 77. Tossed into the squalor of her callous cousin's house, she bids farewell to her master and succumbs to her disease. Desperate for consolation, Bao-yu persuades himself that she has not died but, rather, returned to the realm of the immortals from which she came, to resume her duties as the spirit of the hibiscus. He composes and declaims an ode to her in that persona. As he finishes, he is approached by a young woman who appears to be Skybright herself. It is Dai-yu, who, overhearing the ode, is moved to praise it and offer some suggestions. She focuses especially on the lines:

> The young man in his crimson-curtained bed
> must seem most cruelly afflicted;
> And the maiden beneath the yellow earth must
> seem most cruelly ill-fated.
> (*SS* III.79.582, *HLM* II.79.875)

Dai-yu, however, points out that the image of the "crimson-curtained bed" and the phrases "young man" and "maiden" seem too clichéd. Bao-yu hits on something much more direct in his revision:

> I by my rosy-misted casement seem most cruelly
> afflicted;
> And you beneath the yellow earth seem most cru-
> elly ill-fated
> (*SS* III.79.584, *HLM* II.79.876)

Bao-yu is oblivious, but Dai-yu is struck with a horrid premonition as these lines, merely pathetic before, speak to her deepest and most justified fears. Dai-yu drew the hibiscus before Skybright was assimilated to it, but Skybright's death and translation to a flower spirit, however fanciful, presage Dai-yu's destiny as well. Bao-yu's ode mourns them both.[41]

After the death of Dai-yu, Bao-yu realizes the insufficiency of poetry either to express his feelings or to recall what he has lost. Recalled lines of poetry bring him no comfort. Musing on lines from one of the greatest romances in the tradition, the "Song of Everlasting Sorrow" (*Changhen ge*, also translated as Song of Enduring Grief), by the Tang poet Bo Juyi (772–846), he lights on the eternity of loss that attends such an abiding love: "Since death's parting, slow and sad the year has been; / Even in my dreams, her soul has not been seen" (*SS* V.109.174, *HLM* III.109.1188). Nothing he can do can recall Dai-yu's spirit to comfort him. His own poetic inspiration seems to have dried up completely. He is quite unable to compose an ode to honor her life or her spirit. Is it because he has lost his jade? Or is his acceptance of her loss the beginning of his awakening to the jade's true significance?

Bao-yu, unable to invoke her by any volitional means, must wait for a transmission from the Land of Illusion. When his lost jade is unexpectedly returned to him in chapter 115 by Impervioso, in spirit form Bao-yu follows the monk back to the Land of Illusion. Here he is struck by the resemblance of the Paradise of Truth to his own Garden of Total Vision. Over the doorway of the chamber of the Celestial Registers is an inscription he is finally ready to read: "Awaken from Love's Folly" (*Yinjue qingchi*).

This is Bao-yu's extraordinary second chance to examine the Registers and learn, once and for all, the fates of the girls he cherishes. He is not distracted this time by the sensual stimuli of the court of the fairy Disenchantment, and when he reads the Registers a second time he understands their contents at once. Even then, Bao-yu has not arrived at the point of full awakening to the vanity of attachment. Denied more than a glimpse of a fairy lady whom he thinks must be Dai-yu, the still worldly young man is crushed to be cut off without a word. The monk admonishes him that all he needs to know is in the Registers, whose poems he has been granted the privilege of seeing *twice*. Those riddling poems read so long ago were indeed the key to the illusion that Bao-yu, and the reader, have played with for so long. Could words from the mundane world, however inspired, have such significance? Perhaps they could, but no revelation could result in awakening until the moment was right.

THE CHIMING OF THE VOID

Poetry as a Vehicle to Enlightenment

The Story of the Stone consistently holds out to characters and readers alike the possibility of liberation, while at the same time attesting to the extraordinary difficulty of seizing the opportunity if it should come. Again and again, beings with superior insight expose benighted mortals to the workings of destiny and the vanity of attachment to the mundane world but, unless they are ready—unless the mortals are already at the point in their karmic careers where destiny can be fulfilled—they cannot receive this grace. Even Bao-yu's particular case, as the Stone-turned-jade-boy for a single lifetime, seems to hang in the balance. Despite the heavenly hosts and their earthly auxiliaries hovering over him, even at the last possible moment Impervioso has to spell it out for him after he has seen the Registers for the second time in chapter 115:

> "You have seen the Registers themselves and are *still* blind! Now listen to me carefully: predestined attachments of the human heart are all of them mere illusion, they are obstacles blocking our spiritual path."
>
> (*SS* V.116.293, *HLM* III.116.1269)

For Bao-yu, the fix is in and has been from the first chapter, and yet, even with the entire apparatus of *The Story of the Stone* in place for his enlightenment, things still look touch and go. Should we readers, mere mortals all, expect to do half as well? Our passionate attachment to the novel's fictional characters is the least of our delusions. According to the Stone and Brother Amor, they are actually our best chance.

Buddhist enlightenment is by definition beyond words or reason. But even among Buddhist schools of thought and practice, Chan (Zen) stands out for its emphasis on spontaneous, arational leaps of intuition. Practitioners recognize many ways of preparing for the all-important leap, in the sense of both making it possible and being ready to take advantage of illumination when it comes. The systematic study of, and meditation on, Buddhist religious writings is a privileged path in all schools, but scriptures and koans are by no means the only vehicle to enlightenment. Monks, nuns, and lay practitioners have traditionally availed themselves of a variety of intellectual, artistic, and even physical disciplines, all of which, undertaken in the right spirit, were accepted as valid paths to the insight that would supersede them.[1]

Although Chan's teaching rejects language on the most radical level, poetry is in part exempt among the artifacts of language because the nature of inspiration in traditional Chinese poetics has a strong affinity to Chan intuition. The Chan emphasis on spontaneity was aesthetic as well as religious, and this formed the bridge between Buddhist thought and Chinese poetics.[2] The Song dynasty critic Yan Yu (c. 1180–1235) equated poetic inspiration with Chan intuition in a way that made language a vehicle for spiritual awakening: "One should speak of poetry as one speaks of Chan. . . . Just as the essence of Chan is arational illumination, the essence of poetry is likewise arational illumination."[3]

Poetry, then, contains a potential for enlightenment that, while different from immersion in Chan practice, is a legitimate vehicle in its own right. This kind of illumination comes suddenly and completely, through a direct verbal communication that opens the mind to complete insight rather than the tortuous winding stair of arcane study. Every human being has the potential to receive enlightenment by this means, but only when the conditions are right.

The author of *The Story of the Stone* explicitly holds out poetry as a vehicle of enlightenment for both characters and readers. His fictional world is exhaustively detailed with all the distractions, potentials, and pitfalls of a lifetime spent seeking awakening to the emptiness of the mundane world. Ironically, as readers follow his fictional creations to see whether they will achieve liberation, attachment to these characters leads readers to insight even as it impedes them on their way. As characters and readers alike puzzle to construe the obscure meanings of riddles, prophecies, divine pageants, and poems, the truth inherent in the mundane world slips by even as it is revealed. This is doubly ironic when we consider the origin of the main characters as celestial beings in need of a refresher course in the nature of emptiness. Although detachment from worldly concerns is the heart of Buddhist enlightenment, this is a dynamic process, driven by emotion. Of what value is the bliss of the Land of Illusion without an understanding of its nature?[4]

Hence the process followed actually by the Stone and Crimson Pearl Flower, vicariously by Vanitas, and hypervicariously by readers. The text is the Stone's unadorned experience. Vanitas reads the text and through its epiphany recreates himself as Brother Amor, the monk who approached enlightenment by way of passion. And the readers? Are we reading for this kind of liberation, or are we so deluded that we are enmeshed in finding out what happens?

If we consider poetry as an expedient to enlightenment, there is absolutely no need to read the entire *Story of the Stone* to find out "what happens." As the author laments:

> Pages full of idle words
> Penned with hot and bitter tears:
> All men call the author fool;
> None his secret message hears.
>
> (*SS* I.1.51, *HLM* I.1.3)

The most explicit vehicle for the author's "secret message" (*qizhongwei*; literally, "innermost flavor, essence") is the poetry that forms an integral part of the narrative.[5] Throughout *The Story of the Stone*, poetry is used in myriad ways to point to levels of meaning beyond the literal record of events. This technique allows the author to integrate the possibility of poetic transcendence with prosaic existence, even if that prosaic existence takes place in a social and economic milieu beyond the wildest dreams of most of his readers.

Poetry in *The Story of the Stone* comes from two different sources: from the Land of Illusion where the Stone originated and the "world of red dust" in which the Stone's beleaguered incarnation finds himself. Poetry from the supramundane realm, either encountered there or transmitted by one of its agents (i.e., the Taoist or the Buddhist monk) invariably points to truth—if the listener can understand it. Poetry from Bao-yu's world *can* point to truth and *can* lead to enlightenment, but is more liable to be misread than to lead to revelation. Ontologically and allegorically speaking, there is no distinction between the poems of the Land of Illusion and those of the mundane world; but, like the hero, we are preoccupied by the wonders of everyday experience and may miss the constant chiming of the void.

Bao-yu is introduced in chapter 3 with several accompanying poems. The first descriptive passage, actually in parallel prose, describes his physical appearance in the eyes of his newly arrived cousin, Dai-yu. Although his beauty is extraordinary, for her the key image is of his eyes

> that even in anger seemed to smile,
> and, as they glared, beamed tenderness the while.
>
> (*SS* I.3.101, *HLM* I.3.29)

Here the eyes are certainly the windows of the soul. Dai-yu sees the essential sympathy of her cousin's unusual character, which the rest of the world regards as impossibly eccentric.[6] The narrator immediately counters Dai-yu's impression with this jeering verse:

> Oft-times he sought out what would make him sad;
> Sometimes an idiot seemed and sometimes mad.
> Though outwardly a handsome sausage-skin,
> He proved to have but sorry meat within.
>
> (SS I.3.102, HLM I.3.30)[7]

The narrator presents these poems as a "more accurate" appraisal than Dai-yu's, condemning the boy for his failure to conform to the ideal patterns of family convention and social aspiration. But this must be ironic, since we already know that this is simply not Bao-yu's purpose in life. From the boy's first introduction in the mundane world, we feel the split between what society expects of such a promising lad and what the Stone's incarnation truly is.

Bao-yu himself knows that he is different from other boys, not least because of his fascination with *materia feminea* and disinclination to emulate any of the males in his family. It is not an obsession with sex, although sex can cloud the issue. Rather, it is his susceptibility to women's feelings and his assimilation of their emotional worlds that block his path both to conventional achievement and to spiritual liberation. During his dream in chapter 5, Bao-yu reads poems in the Celestial Registers and is treated to a pageant, both of which are explicit expositions of the fates of all the girls he loves. When he is unable to absorb the poetry, which would lead directly to enlightenment, Disenchantment tries sending him down a different path to detachment, through sexual initiation. This rapturous lesson backfires so completely that, when Bao-yu wakes, he remembers only the intended vehicle of his disillusionment, not the lesson that vehicle should have taught. Since it is necessary for Bao-yu to achieve enlightenment through passion, he is bound to encounter disillusionment through the stuff of everyday existence. He must plod on regardless of his visit to the Land of Illusion and plunge fully into the world of experience and delusion. His dream is so thoroughly forgotten that he must learn from the ground up not just that the experience of poetry can be *compared* to Buddhist enlightenment but that it can *be* enlightenment. The experience of poetry as epiphany is intuitive as well as aesthetic. But it can be difficult to recognize this in the mundane world, even when encountering poetry from a different dimension. Enmeshed as Bao-yu is in that world, he does not recognize that the poetry that is so vital a part of his everyday life is just as significant for the revelation of the illusory nature of experience as the poems originating in the Land of Illusion itself. And since Dai-yu is the primary object of his passion, delusion, and self-delusion, her poems are his best chance for insight, short of another chance at the poems from the Land of Illusion itself.

It is not surprising that Bao-yu should have trouble understanding the transcendent messages in poetry composed in a party game, or even poetry straight from the Land of Illusion. But the messages in poetry composed to express innermost feeling are also missed repeatedly, even when they reveal the truth of the vanity of existence and point the way to emptiness. Sometimes the characters may fortuitously encounter poetry that suits their mood, but, rather than use it as a path to transcendence, they arrogate their insights to their individual emotional needs only. For a poet to achieve full self-expression, however, he or she must have a "perfect listener" (*zhiyin*) to appreciate the utterance. For Dai-yu, that person *should* be Bao-yu, but he never gets it. In part this is because Bao-yu can be thoughtless and miss Dai-yu's cues, but Dai-yu often most perversely seems to escalate their misunderstandings in her exacting demands for his exclusive affection.

The most self-revealing poems—those most likely to contain intimations of the true nature of emptiness—are not intended for other ears. Of these poems, Dai-yu's are the most important, and the most numerous. While others among the girls are talented poets, Dai-yu is uniquely gifted when it comes to putting her deepest feelings into poetic form. In a social gathering, Dai-yu competes for acclaim, but her best work is spontaneous and intimate. Moreover, it is not just the reader who is privy to it because as often as not her poems are surreptitiously read or overheard while she is declaiming them to herself.

In chapter 27, Bao-yu seeks Dai-yu at the site of her burial mound for flowers. As he approaches, he overhears a sobbing recitation. Dai-yu is declaiming a long lyric on the death of the flowers, which overwhelms her even as the flowers are at the height of their bloom. She is also in the poem, rake and muslin bag in hand, attempting to rescue the flowers from defilement as they fall by burying them in the earth. Her heart is filled with sorrow for the end of spring even as it comes to its fullest:

I know not why my heart's so strangely sad,
Half grieving for the spring and yet half glad:
Glad that it came, grieved it so soon was spent.
So soft it came, so silently it went!

(*SS* II.27.39, *HLM* I.27.271)

The more burgeoning the powers of nature around her, the more she senses their futility. The spring is her season in every sense of the word. Her surname, Lin, means "forest," which associates her with wood, the element of spring. Her poem is filled with the colors of spring—not only green by any means.[8] Her own delicate beauty is of a kind not destined to fruit, and she reveals the flowers' metaphor to her listener:

Can I, that these flowers' obsequies attend,
Divine how soon or late *my* life will end?
Let others laugh flower-burial to see:
Another year who will be burying me?

(*SS* II.27.39, *HLM* I.27.271)

Bao-yu flings himself weeping on the ground. Her poem has stricken him to the core, but his active sympathy soon turns to self-pity:

Lin Dai-yu dead! A world from which that delicate, flower-like countenance had irrevocably departed! It was unutterable anguish to think of it. Yet his sensitized imagination *did* now consider it—went on, indeed, to consider a world from which the others, too—Bao-chai, Caltrop, Aroma and the rest—had also irrevocably departed. Where would *he* be then? What would have become of him? And what of the Garden, the rocks, the flowers, the trees? To whom would they belong when he and the girls were no longer there to enjoy them? Passing from loss to loss in his imagination, he plunged deeper and deeper into a grief that seemed inconsolable. As the poet says:

Flowers in my eyes and bird-song in my ears
Augment my loss and mock my bitter tears.

(*SS* II.28.41–42, *HLM* I.28.272)

In a sense, this nonencounter illustrates the power of poetry to mislead, as Bao-chai is so fond of explaining. Poetry can indeed lead to truth, but only if the hearer is able to divine it. Instead of gaining insight into the transitory nature of existence, Bao-yu is overwhelmed by his powerlessness to stop time, hold the moment, even ignoring the capacity of the lyric he hears to do so. Locked in their adolescent self-absorption, Dai-yu and Bao-yu use poetry as a means of self-definition and self-affirmation. By expressing the feeling stirred within them through poetry, either spontaneously composed (as per Dai-yu) or overheard and recalled (as per Bao-yu), they valorize their self-absorption. While both are moved by the poetry, this shared emotion does not bring them closer together; rather, it enforces their separation. If this were one of the romantic comedies these two are so fond of reading, the scene would resolve in a new level of intimacy. But the terrifying and alienating nature of adolescent self-awareness causes the potential communion to backfire. Seeing Bao-yu weeping on the ground, Dai-yu walks off in disgust. Bao-yu follows her and, in a hyperbolic paean to their early days of companionship, draws Dai-yu into his self-pitying need for centrality in her life. They make up, but the moment of poetic transcendence that they have shared is translated into neither enhanced self nor mutual awareness, much less detachment.

Much later, in response to a set of mournful stanzas sent to her by Bao-chai, Dai-yu composes a suite of poems set to the music of the *qin*, which Bao-yu overhears.[9] This time he is not alone: He is in the company of the fastidious unshorn nun Adamantina. Here Bao-yu is caught between the devil and the deep blue sea. Adamantina herself is attracted to Bao-yu, a susceptibility that gives rise to demons of temptation in her meditations (which ultimately take physical form when she is kidnapped by bandits in chapter 112). While the nun senses the danger of temptation, she accepts Bao-yu's offer to escort her back to her hermitage after a late-night game of Go with his cousin Xi-chun. Along the way, they overhear Dai-yu's *qin*. Poor Dai-yu! Although the ideals of Chinese artistic culture should afford her a *zhiyin*, a perfect listener to overhear her lament,[10] Bao-yu shows his obtuseness to Dai-yu's strange double:

"Shall we go and watch?" he suggested.

"You mean listen, I suppose?" said Adamantina. "One listens to the Qin. One never watches."

"There you are!" said Bao-yu with a grin. "I said I was a common sort of mortal."

(*SS* IV.87.171, *HLM* III.87.970)

Although Dai-yu's poems are intended to respond to Bao-chai's lament, they are actually directed at her imperfect listener:

"Fate denies you freedom,
holds you bound;
Inflicting on me too
a heavy wound.
In closest harmony
Our hearts resound;
In contemplation of the Ancients
Is solace to be found."

(*SS* IV.87.172, *HLM* III.87.970)

While Adamantina sighs with sympathy, Bao-yu seems not to comprehend the words and is only able to respond to the *way* she sings, which he finds "terribly sad" (*guobei*). In the final stanza, Dai-yu reveals her futile attempt to attain transcendence:

"Alas! This particle of dust,
the human soul,
Is only playing out
a predetermined role.
Why grieve to watch
The Wheel of Karma turn?
A moonlike purity remains
My constant goal."

As she listened, Adamantina turned pale with horror. "Just listen to the way she suddenly uses a sharpened fourth there! Her intonation is enough to shatter bronze and stone! It's much too sharp!"

"What do you mean, too sharp?" asked Bao-yu.

"It will never take the strain."

As they were talking, they heard a sudden twang and the tonic string snapped. Adamantina stood up at once and began to walk away.

"What's the matter?" asked Bao-yu.

"You will find out in time. Please don't say anything about this."

(*SS* IV.87.173, *HLM* III.87.971)

What is Adamantina responding to? It could simply be that she, as Dai-yu's double and therefore an almost perfect listener, understands that the great technical risks Dai-yu takes with her *qin* are a direct reflection of her emotional extremity. Or perhaps, as an accomplished Chan practitioner, she does have some insight into "the wheel of karma." If so, in this moment she could have had a sudden strong epiphany of the *power* of karma, yet without knowing what it means or where it leads. When Adamantina voices the emotion Dai-yu's poem and music arouse in her, she literally says that Dai-yu's tone is "enough to shatter *gold and stone*" (*jin/shi*). These two characters (which mean literally "metal and stone") are an idiomatic expression for inscriptions made on metal and stone monuments to record great deeds and events from the past. *Jinshi* is therefore a metonymy for writing as eternal monument, something that the inscription on the Stone, the text we are reading, certainly aspires to be.[11] Here, however, the two individual characters "mix" the affinities of Bao-yu's two existences—the flower and stone (*shi*) from the previous life, the bond of gold (*jin*) and jade from this one. The power of Dai-yu's art is such that it might even break the power of karmic destiny, if only her real perfect listener, Bao-yu, could "hear" it. Indeed, her music, if he understood it, would shatter the text itself, and the universe of form it represents.

But there is a counterpower at work: Bao-yu in this life is the *incarnation* of the stone, not the Stone himself. And Bao-yu, for all his aestheticism and romantic sensibility, is a very human adolescent. The Crimson Pearl Flower has been incarnated not to achieve emotional transcendence through romantic love but to pay her debt of tears. To this end, it is essential that her efforts at self-realization be futile. Dai-yu can never express herself, either in direct speech or in art, in such a way as to make her love for Bao-yu explicit. If she did so, her suffering would be done with and she would disrupt the destiny that theoretically will bring her a greater good than romantic fulfillment. Therefore even her greatest works of self-expression, her breakthroughs in lyrical transcendence, go unappreciated. Dai-yu's woes are the legacy of her previous existence, and her suite of poems seems to refer more to her origin as the Crimson Pearl Flower than to her aspirations in her present life. Ultimately, Bao-yu will understand. He *will* be Dai-yu's perfect listener, but only after he understands her place in the necessary suffering of his whole life. By that time, Dai-yu will have returned to the Land of Illusion and her life's pain will be over.

The only poems for Bao-yu that the boy has never seen are three quatrains, which Dai-yu wrote on the pair of everyday handkerchiefs that he sent her after the near-fatal beating inflicted by his father. This strange gift was meant to allay her fears for Bao-yu: fears for his health, naturally, but also for his intentions—would such a traumatic experience set him on another course, turn him into another person? The gift of the handkerchiefs shows that Bao-yu understands the source of Dai-yu's emotional woes. When he sends Skybright to her with these tokens, the maid protests, but Bao-yu is absolutely confident:

> "What's she going to do with a pair of your old handkerchiefs? Most likely she'll think you're making fun of her and get upset again."
>   "No she won't," said Bao-yu. "She'll understand."
>
> (166, 344)

In the original Chinese, Bao-yu's reply is: "she will *naturally* (*ziran*) understand." Bao-yu is speaking casually, out of his confidence in the perfection of their communion. Although the maid who brings the gift is mystified, Dai-yu's initial bafflement is replaced with a flash of understanding:

> "I feel so happy . . . that in the midst of his own affliction he has been able to grasp the cause of all *my* trouble. . . . Oh, and I feel so ashamed when I think how I am forever crying and quarreling . . . and all the time he has understood! '.' . .
>   And her thoughts carried her this way and that, until the ferment of excitement within her cried out to be expressed. Careless of what the maids might think, she called for a lamp, sat herself down at her desk, ground some ink, softened her brush, and proceeded to compose the following quatrains, using the handkerchiefs themselves to write on.
>
> (*SS* II.34.167–168, *HLM* I.34.344)

Because of her sudden insight, Dai-yu is flooded with emotion, which, in accordance with conventional notions of the process of poetic inspiration and expression, must find an outlet in poetry.[12] The quatrains plainly express her attachment to Bao-yu, but he will never see them. Can the fact that she accepted his odd gift in the first place be enough to ensure that he understands her feelings for him? On a deeper level, can her use of his gift lead either of them to insight into the futility of their attachment? All three poems evoke the destiny of which they have no conscious knowledge. In her first quatrain, Dai-yu writes that, for a gift of handkerchiefs, tears are the appropriate payment, and indeed tears are the decreed currency to fulfill the bond of the previous existence. Although she may treasure the handkerchiefs and use them as they were intended to be used, her tears will still be shed in secret and dry without a trace (poems 2 and 3). Her plentiful tears are preserved only symbolically, transferred to the speckled bamboos that surround her garden pavilion (poem 3). Bao-yu's confidence that Dai-yu would appreciate his odd gift unwittingly evoked Dai-yu's original nature and the karmic source of Dai-yu's trouble. She is fully aware that she seems always to be "crying and quarreling," but neither she nor Bao-yu can know why in anything more than a local sense. The cosmic significance of her actions is inaccessible.

When Dai-yu learns that Bao-yu is indeed to marry Bao-chai, she allows the illness that has plagued her all her life to finish its course. Even as her body is consumed, her mind remains clear, and she destroys all her manuscripts (chapter 97), including the handkerchiefs. She cannot know that Bao-yu is faithful to her. Reconciliation or comfort of any kind in her agony would default upon Dai-yu's debt of tears. Certain that there is not, has never been, a heart to understand her heart's expression, she destroys all traces of her emotion on her deathbed to signal the end of her folly.

There are several instances of poems from the spiritual realm offered to mortals as quick, explicit expedients to salvation, but they are efficacious only when the object of their instruction is sufficiently aware to receive their instruction. The first person to achieve liberation, in chapter 1, is Zhen Shi-yin. As mentioned in chapter 1 of this book, this unambitious scholar leads an uneventful life until he encounters the Stone's ubiquitous sponsors, the Taoist and the Buddhist, in a dream. The immortals are discussing the plans for the incarnation of the Stone and the contract with the Crimson Pearl Flower for her debt of tears. In fact, this conversation is the reader's source of knowledge about the ultimate relationship of Bao-yu and Dai-yu. Zhen Shi-yin greets them and asks for further instruction in the operations of karma. Although they decline to enlighten him, they give him a glimpse of the Stone and leave him under the archway to the Land of Illusion, where the novel's signature couplet is inscribed:

> Truth becomes fiction when the fiction's true;
> Real becomes not-real where the unreal's real.
>
> (SS I.1.55, HLM I.1.5)

Awakening to a great clap of thunder, he forgets his dream as soon as he holds his only daughter, Ying-lian, in his arms. But, carrying her out to the street, he sees the crazy pair again. They warn him of his impending disaster, all because of his attachment to the child:

> Fond man, your pampered child to cherish so—
> That caltrop-glass which shines on melting snow!
> Beware the high feast of the fifteenth day,
> When all in smoke and fire shall pass away!
>
> (SSI.1.56, HLM I.1.6)

Zhen Shi-yin is disconcerted, but the men vanish before he can ask for elucidation: "There must have been something behind all this. . . . I really ought to have asked him what he meant, but now it is too late" (SS I.1.56, HLM I.1.6). While there is no way that he can understand the allusion to his daughter's fate, he could heed the warning about the Fifteenth Night festival. How could Zhen Shi-yin be inducted into the higher mysteries when he is obtuse about the significance of his everyday existence? When the Fifteenth Night comes around, his daughter is sent out with a servant named "Calamity" (Huo-qi) to watch the fun, and she is kidnapped. The distraught parents soon lose their home in a fire and are further reduced to humiliating poverty by Zhen Shi-yin's own father-in-law. In this extremity, Zhen Shi-yin's mind is finally ready to listen to the wisdom of the limping Taoist when he reappears, chanting these verses:

> Men all know salvation should be won,
> But with ambition won't have done, have done.
> Where are the famous ones of days gone by?
> In grassy graves they lie now, every one.
>
> Men all know that salvation should be won,
> But with their riches won't have done, have done.
> Each day they grumble they've not made enough.
> When they've enough, it's goodnight everyone!
>
> Men all know that salvation should be won,
> But with their loving wives they won't have done.
> The darlings every day protest their love,
> But once you're dead, they're off with another one.

Men all know that salvation should be won,
But with their children won't have done, have done.
Yet though of parents fond there is no lack,
Of grateful children saw I ne'er a one.

(SS I.1.63–64, HLM I.1.10)

Zhen Shi-yin requests instruction from the Taoist, who assures him that:

"If you can make out 'won' and 'done' . . . you may be said to have understood; for in all the affairs of the world what is won is done, and what is done is won; for whoever has not yet done has not yet won, and in order to have won, one must first have done. I shall call my song the 'Won-done Song.' "

(SS I.1.64, HLM I.1.10)

Zhen Shi-yin finally gets it: In order to "win" (*hao*), one must give up the notion of attempting to "achieve" (*liao*) anything. Striving for any result only leads to disappointment. Red Inkstone praises the "Won-done Song" (*Haoliao ge*) for its lack of highbrow language, which allows even unsophisticated readers to understand it.[13] This seems rather ironic since the listener, Zhen Shi-yin, is identified as a Confucian scholar and intellectual whose main shortcoming is lack of ambition rather than of learning. His training serves him well at last, however, as he provides the "Won-done Song" with a commentary:

Mean hovels and abandoned halls
Where courtiers once paid daily calls:
Bleak haunts where weeds and willows scarcely
 thrive
Were once with mirth and revelry alive.
Whilst cobwebs shroud the mansion's gilded
 beams,
The cottage casement with choice muslin gleams.
Would you of perfumed elegance recite?
Even as you speak, the raven locks turn white.
Who yesterday her lord's bones laid in clay,
On silken bridal-bed shall lie today.
Coffers with gold and silver filled:
Now, in a trice, a tramp by all reviled.

One at some other's short life gives a sigh,
Not knowing that he, too, goes home—to die!
The sheltered and well-educated lad,
In spite of all your care, may turn out bad;
And the delicate, fastidious maid
End in a foul stews, plying a shameful trade.
The judge whose hat is too small for his head
Wears, in the end, a convict's cangue instead.
Who shivering once in rags bemoaned his fate,
Today finds fault with scarlet robes of state.
In such commotion does the world's theatre rage:
As each one leaves, another takes the stage.
In vain we roam:
Each in the end must call a strange land home.
Each of us with that poor girl may compare,
Who sews a wedding-gown for another bride
      to wear.

          (*SS* I.1. 64–65, *HLM* I.1.10–11)

The commentary, which the Taoist praises for its accuracy, shows complete knowledge of the entire inscription on the Stone. It is also an explicit exposition of the conflict between ideal and actual in the "real" world. Evoking the rhythm of waxing and waning characteristic of traditional interpretations of the patterns of Chinese imperial history, Zhen Shi-yin outlines the former glory of the Jias and foreshadows their decline, while others may then come into their own. The young men of good family, defying every advantage, turn to their own and their family's destruction; the young ladies exploit their beauty and in the end are exploited. The ambitious boy from a poor family may rise, then guarantee his own fall through disdain for his origins. To assume that one's situation is unique is to be deluded. The pageant of mundane existence depends on no single individual: The flow is not stayed for anyone. The will to seek fulfillment deludes us, and salvation lies only in recognizing its emptiness and futility.

    Strictly speaking, this is not a *spiritual* insight, in the sense that recognizing that "reality" is an illusion is a spiritual insight. What is otherworldly about these concrete manifestations of retribution for arrogance, greed, and overweening ambition? The spiritual dimension is not the inevitability of these patterns, but the recognition of the futility of *all* striving, for compassion or personal gain, good or ill. All striving is a sign of attachment to the world. Zhen Shi-yin is able to draw on his Confucian discipline to compose an accurate commentary on the "Won-done Song," but Confucianism will only lead him back to the illusory world of his present existence. Once he has seen through the vanity of attachment, he has no reason to stay in his present existence, and off with the Taoist he goes. He does not even need to affect reincarnation: Having seen through the vanity not just of his particular existence but of all possible existences, Zhen Shi-yin is freed from all ties that make existence a necessity.[14] He has indeed achieved liberation.

The "Won-done Song" receives a second commentary, although the commentator is unaware of it. This is from Bao-chai's brother, Xue Pan, during a highbrow drinking game with Bao-yu and a couple of other young men of some refinement. Xue Pan, incidentally, is Zhen Shi-yin's unwitting "son-in-law"—his purchased concubine, the girl named "Caltrop," is none other than Zhen Shi-yin's lost daughter, as foretold in the line "That caltrop-glass that shines on melting snow!"[15] There is nothing refined about Xue Pan: He is as coarse as his sister is cultivated, a regular one-man *Animal House*. The game requires that the player compose four matching rhymes, sing a popular song, and quote a line of poetry that refers to one of the objects on the laden table. Xue Pan plows through the matching rhymes, disgusting the others with his crude images. He then offers up a tuneless ditty that he calls the "Hum-bum Song" (*Heng-heng yun*):

> One little gnat went hum hum hum . . .
> Two little flies went bum bum bum . . .
> (*SS* II.28.59, *HLM* I.28.281)

When the others shout at him to stop, he responds with indignation: "This is the very latest new hit. *If you can't be bothered to listen to it . . .*" (italics added).

Xue Pan is a completely thick expedient to enlightenment, but he has a point. The clue to the correspondence between the "Won-done Song" and the "Hum-bum Song" is not so much in the similarity of the titles: In fact, Hawkes's translation makes the titles sound much more similar than they do in Chinese, almost like puns. The link is in the *listening*. Zhen Shi-yin is bewildered because, with a bona fide, scruffy, and limping Taoist adept before him, he is convinced that he is in the presence of mysteries, and all he can make out is "a lot of won [*hao*] and done [*liao*]." All Xue Pan's listeners can make out is a lot of "hum" (*heng*) and "bum" (*weng*). *Heng* and *weng* are onomotopoeic words for insect noises—we don't expect them to mean anything. But the insistence on sense is the single most insuperable obstacle to understanding the emptiness of existence. Those who hear *and* listen to the direct transmissions from the Land of Illusion are few. Once they understand that the words say exactly what they mean—that there is in fact no gap between the words and the allegory—they can understand that the words are empty. In this ultimate perspective, the "Won-done Song" has no more meaning than does the "Hum-bum Song."

In effect, the "Hum-bum Song" validates the "Won-done Song" as a guide to transcendence by destroying it. The "Won-done Song" is practical, not metaphysical, in its admonitions; and that is true for Zhen Shi-yin's commentary as well.[16] They reveal the vanity of life and its attachments, not in the sense of its ultimate unreality, but in the sense of its futility and evanescence. If Xue Pan's "very latest hit" is also a commentary, its purpose is to dissolve the still rather prissy and goal-oriented liberation of the two earlier poems. If there is no gap between words and allegory, then the words are empty by definition since the subject of their allegory is emptiness itself. So long as the "serious" poems are taken seriously, liberation must be incomplete. Word and allegory are equivalent only when the words have been reduced to absurdity by parody, or (which amounts to the same thing) shown to be ontologically equivalent to nonsense.

This seems paradoxical because we expect the epiphany of the equivalence of words and allegory to give insight into *something*. That *something* may be the understanding that "something" is really *nothing*, but that still satisfies our inclination to follow a chain of inference and insight to a rational conclusion. No one in the novel is prepared to grasp a revelation denying the chain of inference itself, and that is just what the "Hum-bum Song" does. Instead of ending up with "nothing," it *starts* with nothing. The equation is the same (by definition), but the unfamiliar form is much more disorienting, and correspondingly more efficacious, because it short-circuits the instinct to pursue insight systematically. There is less opportunity for self-satisfied intellection and false insight, but only if we are prepared to catch the revelation. In *The Story of the Stone* it must come in a flash or not at all.[17]

We should remember that, of all the great religions, only Taoism and Buddhism have established traditions of using nonsense to induce enlightenment. Xue Pan's commentary on the "Won-done Song" is just as valid, just as insightful, as Zhen Shi-yin's, but falling as it does in a party of the blind leading the blind, no light is shed. The "Hum-bum Song" is further explicit evidence that the author has indeed filled his text with clues, especially poetic clues, which the reader may have a chance of understanding even though the characters do not. The fact that the source of the clue is one of the most clueless characters in *The Story of the Stone* is more than ironic.

Starting with the magical, mystical frame of chapter 1, Cao Xueqin laid out the didactic purpose of his novel explicitly. It is not every day that we have direct access to heavenly mysteries, but in *The Story of the Stone* the admonitions of the Stone himself are always near the surface. More often than not, the poems pervading the text can be the means of breaking through that surface to the realm of truth. As is the case with all good allegorical structures, the clues are in plain sight. The fact that we resist understanding or accepting them is a measure of our participation in the delusion that is the world—in the double delusion of a fictional world!

That is the final paradox of *The Story of the Stone*—how can the author expect his readers to accept what he himself never could? Intellectually, author and reader may be secure in the understanding that there is no ontological distinction between mundane and transcendent, "real" and "not-real," sense and nonsense. Poetry in *The Story of the Stone* is an opening between these realms, and since poetry is everywhere, there is always a window of opportunity for awakening. Distinction among *kinds* of experience is irrelevant. But no matter how well we know this, the fascination of the story confirms our inability to reject the form and passion of a "fictional" world. The text must be read through to the end, and even then, we are left lonely rather than liberated. As the final *envoi* says:

> When grief for fiction's idle words
> More real than human life appears,
> Reflect that life itself's a dream
> And do not mock the reader's tears.
> (*SS* V.120.376, *HLM* III.120.1324)

This is the difference between a work of fiction and a religious tract. The metaphysical framework of *The Story of the Stone* is Buddhist, but Buddhism itself is neither the answer nor the goal. The real goal is wisdom. To this end, the author has created a fictional world in which the social, psychological, literary, and religious realms are inseparable. Not only does each shed light on the others, but none can finally be understood without the others. The fact that the Buddhist vision of time and human nature, in all its grandeur, is neither more nor less than a metaphor for the kind of wisdom Cao Xueqin brings to bear on his fictional universe is a measure of the encompassing character of his fiction and his creative genius.

INTRODUCTION

1. The novel is better known, in China and the West, as *The Dream of the Red Chamber* (*Honglou meng*), a title mentioned by the author in the first chapter and used by the editor Gao E in his 120-chapter edition printed in 1792. I have followed David Hawkes to key readers of this study to the complete translation of the novel: David Hawkes, ed. and trans., *The Story of the Stone*, vols. 1 (London: Penguin, 1973), 2 (London: Penguin, 1977), and 3 (London: Penguin, 1980); and John Minford, *The Story of the Stone*, vols. 4 (London: Penguin, 1982) and 5 (London: Penguin, 1986). Unless otherwise noted, all translations of *The Story of the Stone* are from this version. It should be noted that Hawkes and Minford do not absolutely follow any single Chinese edition of the novel but, rather, draw on all available editions and commentaries to create what amounts to an edition of their own, with a view to providing the most complete and consistent text possible to the English-speaking reader. See Hawkes, I, Introduction, 45–46. The Chinese text I have cited is Cao Xueqin, Zhao Cong, ed., *Honglou meng* (Hong Kong: Youlian, 1960). These will henceforward be cited in the text as *SS* and *HLM*, respectively. Citations include volume, chapter, and page numbers. I have also followed the version edited by Wang Yunwu, *Shitou ji* (Shanghai: Shangwu, 1931).

2. I have dealt with the characteristics of these two modes at length in my earlier study, *Chinese Narrative Poetry: The Late Han Through T'ang Dynasties* (Durham: Duke University Press, 1988), 1–19, 104–120, and passim.

3. Kao Yu-kung, "The Aesthetics of Regulated Verse," in Shuen-fu Lin and Stephen Owen, eds., *The Vitality of the Lyric Voice: Shih Poetry from the Late Han to the T'ang* (Princeton: Princeton University Press, 1986), 332–385.

4. Yu-kung Kao, "Lyric Vision in the Chinese Narrative Tradition: A Reading of *Hung-lou Meng* and *Ju-lin Wai-shih*," in Andrew H. Plaks, ed., *Chinese Narrative: Critical and Theoretical Essays* (Princeton: Princeton University Press, 1977), 227–243.

5. Levy, *Chinese Narrative Poetry*, 2–7, 113–114.

6. I borrow the term "equipollent" from the visual arts, where it connotes a principle of organization in which distinct units are intimately con-

nected in a single composition yet bound by no formal hierarchy. See James Trilling, "Medieval Interlace Ornament: The Making of a Cross-cultural Idiom," *Arte Medievale*, 2d series, 9.2 (1995): 59–86, esp. 66–67.

7. Andrew H. Plaks, "Towards a Critical Theory of Chinese Narrative," in Plaks, ed., *Chinese Narrative*, 309–352.

I. IDEAL AND ACTUAL, REAL AND NOT-REAL

1. There are several overviews of what is known about Cao Xueqin and his two main editors: see *SS*, Introduction, 32–38; Wu Shih-Ch'ang, *On the Red Chamber Dream* (Oxford: Clarendon Press, 1961), 103–130; Zhao Gang and Chen Zhongyi, *Honglou meng xintan* (Hong Kong: Wenyi, 1970), vol. 1, 143–177; Zhou Ruchang, *Honglou meng xinzheng* (Beijing: Renmin, 1976) vol. 2, 785–801, 833–868.

2. In this I agree with C. T. Hsia, Anthony C. Yu, and John Minford, among others. The two translators of *The Story of the Stone* themselves seem to diverge on this matter, with Minford more inclined to accept Gao E's role as an editor than as a fabricator of the last third of the novel. This divergence presumably affected their division of labor in the translation. See David Hawkes, "*The Story of the Stone*: A Symbolist Novel," *Renditions* 25 (spring 1986): 11–12; and *SS* I, Introduction, 15–18, 41. Minford provides an explicit apologia for the last forty chapters. See his preface, *SS* IV.22–30, and, in the greatest depth, his original dissertation, "The Last Forty Chapters of *The Story of the Stone*: A Literary Appraisal" (Ph.D. diss., Australian National University, 1980). See also C. T. Hsia, *The Classic Chinese Novel: A Critical Introduction* (New York: Columbia University Press, 1968), 250–257; Anthony C. Yu, *Rereading the Stone: Desire and the Making of Fiction in "Dream of the Red Chamber"* (Princeton: Princeton University Press, 1997), preface; and idem, "The Quest of Brother Amor: Buddhist Intimations in SS," *HJAS* 49.1 (June 1989): 70–71. For recent studies of the novel's language, diction, and style to evaluate the authenticity of the later chapters, see Bing C. Chan, "A Computerized Stylostatistical Approach to the Disputed Authorship of The Dream of the Red Chamber," *Tamkang Review* 16.3 (1986): 247–278; and idem, *The Authorship of "The Dream of the Red Chamber": Based on a Computerized Statistical Study of Its Vocabulary* (Hong Kong: Joint Publishing, 1986).

3. For discussions of the characteristics of historiography as narrative in the Chinese tradition, see Andrew H. Plaks, "Towards a Critical Theory of Chinese Narrative," in Plaks, ed. *Chinese Narrative*, 309–352; and, in the same volume, John C.Y. Wang, "Early Chinese Narrative: The *Tso-chuan* as Example," 3–20.

4. Andrew H. Plaks, *Archetype and Allegory in "The Dream of the Red Chamber"* (Princeton: Princeton University Press, 1976), 11.

5. For an introduction to these *realia*, see Susan Naquin and Evelyn S. Rawski, *Chinese Society in the Eighteenth Century* (New Haven: Yale University Press, 1987).

6. For a historical study of the rise and fall of Cao Xueqin's own family, which inspired the story of the Jias, see Jonathan Spence, *Ts'ao Yin and the Kang-hsi Emperor: Bondservant and Master* (New Haven: Yale University Press, 1966).

7. *SS* I, Introduction, 24; Weijun Cheng, "The Politics of the Queue," in Alf Hiltebeitel and Barbara D. Miller, eds., *Hair: Its Power and Meaning in Asian Cultures* (Albany: State University of New York Press, 1998)..

8. On the nature and condition of Chinese bondservants, see Spence, *Ts'ao Yin and the Kang-hsi Emperor*, 1–18.

9. Yu, *Rereading the Stone*, esp. chap. 2, "Desire," 53–109.

10. For a study of the inevitable dynamism of "desire" in Western culture: see Catherine Belsey, *Desire: Love Stories in Western Culture* (Oxford: Blackwell, 1994). I am indebted to Siu-leung Li for this reference. Wai-yee Li translates *qing* variously as "attachment," "desire," or "passion," emphasizing romantic love as the primary vehicle to disillusionment. See *Enchantment and Disenchantment: Love and Illusion in Chinese Literature* (Princeton: Princeton University Press, 1993), passim.

11. Arthur F. Wright describes the process of mutual appropriations of Taoism and Buddhism in late imperial China from a historical perspective: see *Buddhism in Chinese History* (Stanford: Stanford University Press, 1959), 86–107. A survey of the accompanying issues of doctrine and the contributions of Buddhism to Chinese culture is in Kenneth Ch'en, *Buddhism in China: A Historical Survey* (Princeton: Princeton University Press, 1964), 434–454, 471–486.

12. *Qinggen* actually is rendered by Wai-yee Li as "roots of desire," *Enchantment and Disenchantment*, 170. I use the rendering "greensickness" for its association with concepts of lovesickness; see chapter 3.

13. The sense of identity with the creative process and experience of literature is actually an interpretative process, but, because of the intuitive nature of lyrical experience, the reader participates in the illusion of recreating the author's experience. See Levy, *Chinese Narrative Poetry*, 4.

14. David Hawkes explains Vanitas's conversion by suggesting that Brother Amor is Bao-yu himself. See his *"The Story of the Stone*: A Symbolist Novel," 6–17.

15. Yu, *Rereading the Stone*, 149–150, 169–171; see also his "The Quest of Brother Amor," 55–92.

16. Wendy Doniger O'Flaherty, *Dreams, Illusions and Other Realities* (Chicago: University of Chicago Press, 1984), 225–227.

17. For Bao-yu's hopes for a "match" for his jade, see Shuen-fu Lin, "Chia Pao-yü's First Visit to the Land of Illusion: An Analysis of a Literary Dream in an Interdisciplinary Perspective," *CLEAR* 14 (1991): 101.

18. Plaks, *Archetype and Allegory*, 65. While the "affinity of gold and jade" (*jinyu yinyuan*) has been exhaustively discussed, rather less attention has been given to the "jade" relationship between Bao-yu and Dai-yu; see Jing Wang, *The Story of Stone: Intertextuality, Ancient Chinese Stone Lore, and the Stone Symbolism of "Dream of the Red Chamber," "Water Margin," and "The Journey to the West"* (Durham: Duke University Press, 1992), 123–124.

19. The Western rationalist tradition rejects this understanding. Physical laws underscore that action is random, so coincidence is not only possible but powerful. On the emotional level, however, it is unacceptable that such powerful consequences could result from random causes, and so one feels justified in assigning causes as great as the consequences. This is part of the attraction of the theory of reincarnation; it contradicts the randomness of events and assigns sufficient (if unknown) cause for any event without the immediate responsibility of present, conscious action. The notion of karma does not explain the inexplicable, but allows acceptance of experience to have, if not overarching logic, at least some sense, if only on the cosmic level. Whether there is much comfort on the cosmic level is another matter.

20. Yu, *Rereading the Stone*, 110–121; and idem, "The Stone of Fiction and the Fiction of Stone: Reflexivity and Religious Symbolism in *Hung-lou Meng*," *Studies in Language and Literature* 4 (1990): 1–30; Li, *Enchantment and Disenchantment*, 181–182.

21. Yu, *Rereading the Stone*, xii.

22. See, for example, Huo Guoling and Huo Jiping, *Honglou jiemeng*, 2 vols. (Beijing: Yanshan, 1995), which seeks to identify and explicate the true historical background of all the events detailed in the novel. See also Wu, *On the Red Chamber Dream*, 103–144.

23. Yü Ying-shih , *Honglou meng de liangge shijie* (Taipei: Lianjing, 1978), esp. 2–3, 39–41.

24. Marion J.Levy, Jr., *The Family Revolution in Modern China* (Cambridge: Harvard University Press, 1949), Introduction ("General Concepts"), 3–40, 45; and idem, *Modernization and the Structure of Society* (Princeton: Princeton University Press, 1966), 26–32, 426–435.

25. Marion J. Levy, Jr., "Some Aspects of the Analysis of Family Structure," in Ansley J. Coale, Lloyd A. Fallers, Marion J. Levy, Jr., David M. Schneider, and Silvan Tompkins, ed., *Aspects of the Analysis of Family Structure* (Princeton: Princeton University Press, 1965), 7–8.

26. The model is particularly oriented toward demographic analysis, focusing on questions of family size and structure. See Levy, "Some Aspects of the Analysis of Family Structure," 9 ff. See also Francis L.K. Hsu, "The Myth of Chinese Family Size," *American Journal of Sociology* 48.5 (March 1943): 555–562.

27. Quoted by Grannie Liu when she names Xi-feng's daughter Qiao-jie in chapter 42 (*SS* II.42.325, *HLM* II.42.430).

28. Wong Kam-ming describes the disorientation of Bao-yu's personal aesthetics: see his "Point of View, Norms, and Structure: *Hung-lou Meng* and Lyrical Fiction," in Plaks, ed., *Chinese Narrative*, pp. 214–216.

29. For a discussion of the various types of sensuality in *The Story of the Stone*, see Jiang Shunyi, "Du *Honglou meng* zaji," in *Honglou meng juan* (Taipei: Qihai, 1981), 206.

30. For a discussion of the relation of the mythic-fantastic elements of chapters 1 and 5, see Li, *Enchantment and Disenchantment*, 190–193. Emphasizing the spiritual symbolism of the kingdom of the fairy Disenchantment, Li translates *Taixu huanjing* as "the Illusory Realm of the Great Void."

31. For a detailed explication of the significance of the poems of the registers and the pageant, see *SS* I, Appendix, 527–534.

32. Lin, "Chia Pao-yü's First Visit to the Land of Illusion," 106. The theme of discovery of sexual passion as an instrument of self-knowledge and awakening to the emptiness of desire (hence a vehicle of liberation) is common in both fiction and drama; see Giovanni Vitiello, "The Fantastic Journey of an Ugly Boy: Homosexuality and Salvation in Late Ming Pornography," *positions: east asia cultures critique* 4.2 (fall 1996): 291–320. On dreams in Buddhist soteriology, see Bernard Fauré, *The Rhetoric of Immediacy: A Cultural Critique of Chan/Zen Buddhism* (Princeton: Princeton University Press, 1991), chap. 10.

33. Qin Ke-qing herself will admit to this aspect of her personality. See chapter 3.

34. Wai-yee Li analyses in detail the relation of "lust of the mind," self-reflexivity and the lyrical ideal; see *Enchantment and Disenchantment*, 203–210.

35. Ping-leung Chan describes Zhen Bao-yu as Jia Bao-yu's "manifest double," a character overtly resembling another, as opposed to a "latent double," a character sharing crucial tendencies but not overt resemblance. See his "Myth and Psyche in *Hung-lou Meng*," in Winston L.Y. Yang and Curtis P. Atkins, eds., *Critical Essays on Chinese Fiction* (Hong Kong: Chinese University Press, 1980), 169.

36. For an analysis of this dream as a sign of Bao-yu's self-objectification, see Li, *Enchantment and Disenchantment*, 226–227.

37. Plaks, *Archetype and Allegory*, 68.

38. See, for example, the *dufa* of Zhang Xinzhi (fl. 1828–1850), translated by Andrew H. Plaks in David L. Rolston, ed., *How to Read the Chinese Novel* (Princeton: Princeton University Press, 1990), 331: "As for the depiction of Tai-yü, she constantly causes injury to others with her sharp tongue. She is a person who is extremely unadept at getting along with other people, extremely lacking in concern for protecting herself even to the point that she unwittingly treads right on the trigger of destruction [*sha-chi*]. As for the depiction of Pao-ch'ai, she constantly uses material possessions to ingratiate herself with other people. She is a person who keeps her own counsel and is extremely practiced in the ways of the world."

39. On the cosmic relation of Dai-yu and Bao-chai, both in terms of the seasonal sequence of the five elements and complementary bipolarity, see Plaks, *Archetype and Allegory*, 58–64.

2. "FAMILY TOGETHERNESS"
Patterns of Authority and the Subversion of Family Structure

1. Translated by Andrew H. Plaks in Rolston, ed., *How to Read the Chinese Novel*, 326. Zhang's essay, "How to Read the *Dream of the Red Chamber*" (*Honglou meng dufa*), goes on to describe the novel as a literal compendium of the essential moral instruction of many of the classics of philosophy, especially the *Yi jing*, the narrative style of the *Zhanguo ce*, *Shi ji*, and the three members of the Su family (Su Xun [1009–1066] and his two sons Su Shi [1037–1101] and Su Che [1039–1112]), brilliant prose stylists of the Song Dynasty, and many of the great works of prose fiction, including *Journey to the West* (*Xiyou ji*), *The Plum in the Golden Vase* (*Jin Ping Mei*), and *Water Margin* (*Shuihu zhuan*). Zhang's analysis emphasizes the function of these texts as bedrock for the moral structure of *The Story of the Stone*. *How to Read the Chinese Novel* contains a complete translation of Zhang Xin-zhi's *dufa* (a "how-to-read" essay) with extensive annotation by both Plaks and Rolston, 323–340.

Plaks has also written his own *dufa* for *The Story of the Stone*, as yet unpublished, which promises to be one of the most comprehensive.

2. The phrase, *shijiao* in pinyin romanization, is used in the *Zuo zhuan*, first year of the duke of Yin, to explain the tactic used by the duke of Zhuang to set his feckless younger brother on the road to defeat. In this case, the duke refrained from correcting his brother, whose arrogance brought about his own disaster. See Rolston, *How to Read the Chinese Novel*, 326; James Legge, *The Chinese Classics*, vol. 5, *The Ch'un Ts'ew with the Tso Chuen*, rev. ed. (Shanghai: Mer Sang Press, 1935), 1–7.

3. The first two lines quoted here more literally read: "The failure to carry on the family profession originated with [Jia] Jing/The slide into ruin of the household's affairs had its first fault in the Ning-guo House." The phrase *jiqiu* is more fully quoted as *keshao jiqiu* ("continuing the family trade") and alludes to a passage from *The Book of Rites (Li ji)*: "The son of a good bowmaker first needs to learn how to make a basket; the son of a good foundry-man first needs to learn how to make fur garments." In other words, to learn the skills of their fathers, sons must be dedicated apprentices, practicing simple tasks on the way to learning harder ones. (The connection between foundry-work and the making of fur garments is closer than it seems, once we understand that the reference is not to casting but to working with metal and rivets. Leather-work provides training in shaping and fastening flat, tough materials to make complex three-dimensional shapes.) In the Appendix to volume I, Hawkes remarks that, although the text is uncertain, "I think it means no more than that Jia Jing was to blame for the shocking state of affairs in the Ning-guo household because of his refusal to shoulder his responsibilities as head of the family" (534).

4. For the application of this principle under the Qing, see Naquin and Rawski, *Chinese Society in the Eighteenth Century*, 34.

5. Spence, *Ts'ao Yin and the K'ang-hsi Emperor*, 282–292. The fascination with kinship, marriage, and the family as a microcosm of the state continued well into the twentieth century. See Ai-li S. Chin, "Family Relations in Modern Chinese Fiction," in Maurice Freedman, ed., *Family and Kinship in Chinese Society* (Stanford: Stanford University Press, 1970), 87–120.

6. Hugh D. Baker comments: "The ultimate extended family was the ideal family" (*Chinese Family and Kinship* [London: Macmillan, 1979], 3). See also Levy, *The Family Revolution in Modern China*, 48–60; and Mai Huiting, *Zhongguo jiating gaizao wenti* (Problems of Chinese Family Reconstruction)(Shanghai: Commercial Press, 1930).

7. Lawrence Stone, *Family and Fortune: Studies in Aristocratic Finance in the Sixteenth and Seventeenth Centuries* (Oxford: Clarendon Press, 1973), 44–46; Michelle Perot, ed., Georges Duby and Philippe Ariès, gen. eds., *A History of Private Life*, vol. 4, *From the Fires of Revolution to the Great War* (Cambridge: Belknap Press of Harvard University Press, 1987), 77.

8. SS I.4.123, HLM I.4.40. For a discussion of the structure and dynamics of the joint family system, see Maurice Freedman, *Lineage Organization in Southeastern China* (London: Athalone Press, 1958; rev. ed. 1965).

9. "Father-in-law pokes in the ashes" (*pahui de pahui*) refers to incest with a daughter-in-law, by means of a pun on two words pronounced *xi*, one meaning "to kneel" and the other "daughter-in-law." Thus a man who "[kneels] to poke in the ashes" is debauching his daughter-in-law.

10. See Levy, *The Family Revolution in Modern China*, 109, 129–130; also Ping-chen Hsiung, "Constructed Emotions: the Bond Between Mothers and Sons in Late Imperial China," *Late Imperial China* 15.1 (1994): 87–117.

11. Susan Mann points out that, if his older brother had survived, Bao-yu might well have been released from this pressure: see her *Precious Records: Women in China's Long Eighteenth Century* (Stanford: Stanford University Press, 1997), 51 and n. 19.

12. For a discussion of Bao-yu's eccentric notions of the superiority of females as a possible indication of bisexuality, see Louise P. Edwards, *Men and Women in Qing China: Gender in the Red Chamber Dream* (Leiden: Sinica Leidensica [Brill], 1994), 33–49.

13. For customs of sexual segregation of children in Bao-yu's age cohort, see Levy, *The Family Revolution in Modern China*, 75–84; and Patricia Buckley Ebrey, *The Inner Quarters: Marriage and the Lives of Chinese Women in the Sung Period* (Berkeley: University of California Press, 1993), 21–44.

14. For the conflicts between generations as a result of disrupted authority patterns, see Margery Wolf, "Child Training and the Chinese Family," in Freedman, ed., *Family and Kinship in Chinese Society*, 37–62.

15. For a description of this custom, see Mann, *Precious Records*, 51.

16. Bao-yu's difficulty with his father's erratic oversight has an organic dimension; see chapter 3.

17. Besides their spontaneous mutual attraction, Jiang Yu-han has further affinities with Bao-yu in both his personal name ("jade-enveloping") and his stage name (Qi Guan-er— another way of saying "Master Jade"; *qi* is a piece of jade, usually white in color). This close affinity may allude only to the fact that Jiang will marry Bao-yu's principal maid, Aroma, after Bao-yu leaves the world, but the actor's brilliant talent in roles demanding romantic feeling and erotic tenderness speaks to an important aspect of Bao-yu's personality.

18. For a discussion of concubinage as an institution and its vicissitudes, see Ebrey, *The Inner Quarters*, 217–234. For the ramifications of the institution for domestic structure, see Francesca Bray, *Technology and Gender: Fabrics of Power in Late Imperial China* (Berkeley: University of California Press, 1997), 335–368.

19. As per Mencius, 4A.26: "There are three unfilial acts, of which the greatest is to lack posterity" (*Buxiao you san, wuhou wei da*). Grandmother Jia herself accuses Jia Zheng of willfully cutting off the family line, but, technically speaking, Bao-yu is not the only surviving son. Why is Jia Huan not regarded as a full member of the family? In the ideal patterns of traditional Chinese society, "[the concubine's] children had equal legitimacy with those of [the principal] wife and assumed regular places in the relative

age precedence picture with their half brothers and sisters" (Levy, *The Family Revolution in Modern China*, 201). Huan's biological sister, Tan-chun, confidently takes her appropriate place and is treated as the full equal, according to age precedent, of the other children of the house. Yet Jia Zheng himself muses, when considering how best to arrest an apparently fatal decline in Bao-yu's health, "If anything were to happen to Bao-yu, I should be left without an heir in my old age. I have a grandson, but that is not the same" (*SS* IV.96.326, *HLM* III.96.1057) because that would skip a generation. It may be just be a matter of Huan's unsavory character, but his systematic exclusion may point to some question of his paternity, never alluded to by any member of the family. There are indirect clues: the fact that Aunt Zhao is always called Huan's "mother," rather than his "aunt," and that he continues to live with her and be in her care throughout the novel, is most unusual. Tan-chun refers to Lady Wang as "Mother" and calls her biological mother "Aunt." The only remotely explicit clue to another possible father is given when Aunt Zhao has been felled by a seizure during Grandmother Jia's funeral. She babbles that Jia She had "tried all manner of tricks to lay his hands on me" (*SS* V.112.237, *HLM* III.112.1220), which is taken as a sign that the spirit of Faithful has possessed her. All the rest of her speech is consistent with her own known actions, however, so perhaps this accusation suggests more than meets the eye.

20. Levy, *The Family Revolution in Modern China*, 94, 168. Ming legal codes concerned with internal family matters apparently were taken over wholesale by the Qing. "Family murder" and "stranger murder" were two different crimes, and the worst punishment a father could receive for killing his son was 100 strokes with the heavy bamboo and a year of penal servitude. See Ann Waltner, "Breaking the Law: Family Violence, Gender and Hierarchy in the Legal Code of the Ming Dynasty," *Ming Studies* 36 (1996): 30–31.

21. Literally, "How did *your* father teach you?" (*ni fuqin zenme zhaoxun ni lai zhe?*). She is referring not just to physical discipline but the whole social complex of standards of conduct and deportment set by her husband, which she still represents in the household. Jia Zheng's failure of control is his own and shames him in his father's memory.

22. See Olga Lang, *Chinese Family and Society* (New Haven: Yale University Press, 1946), 33ff.; and Levy, *The Family Revolution in Modern China*, 88. Even Grandmother Jia sees the family's deviation from ideal patterns, although she only admits to this long after the damage (both to the family's reputation and to the individuals involved) is done: " 'Bao-yu and Miss Lin have been together since they were little, and this had never troubled me, as I have always thought of them as children' " (*SS* IV.90.217, *HLM* III.90.996).

23. On the separation of male and female realms, see Dorothy Ko, *Teachings of the Inner Chambers: Women and Culture in Seventeenth Century China* (Stanford: Stanford University Press, 1994), 179–217.

24. For the complex spiritual and social web of Dai-yu's relationship with Bao-yu, see Yu, *Rereading the Stone*, chap. 5, 219–255.

25. Ebrey, *The Inner Quarters*, 99–113; Bray, *Technology and Gender*, 118.

26. Glen Bowersock has made a study of the independent life and reality of fictional objects in late antiquity; see his *Fiction as History, Nero to Julian* (Berkeley: University of California Press, 1994).

27. For a discussion of Qin Ke-qing's illness, see chapter 3.

28. Odd Tablet is said to have precipitated the substitution of illness for hanging because he found the description of the suicide too upsetting: see Hawkes, *SS*, Introduction, 42–43; Chen Qinghao, ed., *Xinbian Shitou ji Zhiyan zhai pingyu jijiao* (Taipei: Lianjing, 1986), 240; and Yu Pingbo, "*Honglou meng bian*," in *Yu Pingbo lun "Honglou meng"* (Shanghai: Guji, 1988), 264–272.

29. The expression *femme d'histoire* is used to describe Helen of Troy in Jean Giraudoux's *La Guerre de Troie n'aura pas lieu* (Paris: L'Illustration, 1935). See also Robert Cohen, *Giraudoux: Three Faces of Destiny* (Chicago: University of Chicago Press, 1968).

30. A special section of *Honglou meng yanjiu jikan 6* (August 1981) is dedicated to the investigation of the inconsistencies of the story of Qin Ke-qing, 89–142.

31. I am indebted to Chieh-fang Ou Lee for this insight. Incest in legal terms would be considered a crime that destroys essential social bonds, *yijue* (literally, "to break [the bonds of] righteousness"). It was one of the few grounds on which a wife could divorce her husband. In this case, You-shi simply disappears from the scene for several chapters, but the possibility of a pitched internal struggle is there. See Waltner, "Breaking the Law," 34–35.

32. See Levy, *The Family Revolution in Modern China*, 117; and Andrew C. K. Hsieh and Jonathan Spence, "Suicide and the Family in Pre-modern Chinese Society," in Arthur Kleinman and Tsung-yi Lin, eds., *Normal and Abnormal Behavior in Chinese Culture* (Dordrecht, Netherlands: D. Reidel, 1981), 29–47.

33. For the nature of a gentry wife's duties as household manager, see Ebrey, *The Inner Quarters*, 114–130.

34. For a discussion of Xi-feng as exemplar of young women and power, see Angelina Yee, "Counterpoise in *Honglou meng*," *HJAS* 50.2 (December 1990): 636–648; and Edwards, *Men and Women in Qing China*, 68–86.

35. Praising Tan-chun's ability, Xi-feng explains to her maid, Patience, that the prospects for a concubine's daughter can be shaky: "I know being

a wife's or a concubine's child isn't *supposed* to make any difference, and in a boy's case perhaps it doesn't; but I'm afraid with girls, when the time comes to start finding husbands for them, it often does. Nowadays you get a very shallow class of person who will ask about that before anything else and often, if they hear that the girl is a concubine's child, will have nothing further to do with her" (*SS* III.55.62, *HLM* II.55.588). See Ebrey, *The Inner Quarters*, 217–234.

36. Bao-chai, unlike her brother, the loutish Xue Pan, is the picture of proper deportment and sense of duty. From her first appearance, Bao-chai has represented the epitome of feminine decorum, and she is the ideal candidate for marriage in a gentry family. See Susan Mann, "Grooming a Daughter for Marriage: Brides and Wives in the Mid-Ch'ing Period," in Rubie Watson and Patricia Ebrey, eds., *Marriage and Inequality in Chinese Society* (Berkeley: University of California Press, 1991), 204–230.

37. For a discussion of Tan-chun's foresight, see Yee, "Counterpoise in *Honglou meng*," 636.

38. On the workings of time in the novel, as it affects both readers and characters, see Kao, "Lyric Vision in the Chinese Narrative Tradition," 241.

39. Girls from gentry families were often all too aware of the dangers of the end of childhood: see Mann, *Precious Records*, 54–75.

40. Mai Huiting, *Zhongguo jiating*, 63; Baker, *Chinese Family and Kinship*, 32–37.

41. Female fertility as the bedrock of domestic structure in traditional Chinese society is a unifying theme in Bray, *Technology and Gender*, passim. For a detailed discussion of Dai-yu's illness in both clinical and karmic terms, see chapter 3, 79–85.

42. Even in contemporary Chinese society, marriage between first cousins is acceptable *provided the cousins have different surnames*. See Francis L. K. Hsu, "Observations on Cross-Cousin Marriage in China," *American Anthropologist* 47.1 (1945): 83–103; Bernard Gallin, "Cousin Marriage in China," *Ethnology* 2 (1963): 104–108; and Eugene Cooper and Meng Zhang, "Patterns of Cousin Marriage in Rural Zhejiang and in *The Dream of the Red Chamber*," *Journal of Asian Studies*, 52.1 (1993): 90–106.

43. This aphorism ("*Bu shi yuanjia bu jutou*") turns on the phrase *yuan-jia*, which can mean both "enemies" and "lovers." Here it refers not only to outright love and enmity but to people in "love-hate" relationships or to those who show their affection by affecting displeasure.

44. Louise P. Edwards suggests that Xi-chun's guardians are distraught with her decision not only because the outside world will assume that they drove her to a nunnery or even because it would deprive the family of a potentially lucrative marriage alliance, but because of a popular notion of the

secret lewdness of religious communities, especially nunneries, whether Taoist or Buddhist: *Men and Women in Qing China*, 66. In *The Story of the Stone* the sexual self-restraint of nuns is presented as a measure of the sincerity of their vocation. There are several examples of girls without vocation, who have been sent to nunneries because they are orphans or their parents cannot provide for them, who fall into passionate love affairs that lead to their ruin. But there are also some whose vocation is sincere and who seem to find genuine refuge in the cloister — the actress Parfumée (Fang-guan), once she takes vows, is as single-mindedly insensible to sensuality as she was once dedicated to self-dramatization. Because of her strange history and her transcendent fastidiousness, the nun Adamantina's (Miao-yu) vocation is equivocal from the start. The fact that her end is unknown — did she submit to her ravisher? or did she resist and meet her death? — is not really an escape, because in chapter 5 the poems in the registers and in the pageant describe her as a "jade sunk in the mud" (*baiyu zaoni xian*). For a discussion of Adamantina's relationship with Bao-yu, see chapter 5.

45. In a lecture titled "The Emperor as Collector: Taste and Terror in Eighteenth-Century China" (Princeton University, October 1997), Jonathan Spence outlined the role of confiscations, which could be ordered by the emperor alone, as modes of political control and means of bringing valuable artistic and cultural properties into imperial hands. Chinese emperors were not alone in using political persecution as a means of getting their hands on fabulous art collections. When the Roman writer and courtier Petronius fell afoul of the emperor Nero, he luxuriously smashed his priceless collection of stone utensils, greatly coveted by his enemy, before he committed suicide. See Pliny, *Natural History*, 37.7.20. For an analysis of the power of the emperor to control cultural production through censorship in China, focused primarily on literary inquisitions, see R. Kent Guy, *The Emperor's Four Treasuries: Scholars and the State in the Late Ch'ien-lung Era* (Cambridge: Council on East Asian Studies, Harvard University, 1987), 166–190.

46. In the conduct of an imperial confiscation, the faults of one family member could involve the entire household. See Brian E. McKnight, *Law and Order in Sung China* (Cambridge: Cambridge University Press, 1992), 53 ff.

47. Fêng Han-yi, "The Chinese Kinship System," *HJAS* 2 (1937): 141–275; Maurice Freedman, *The Study of Chinese Society: Essays of Maurice Freedman* (Stanford: Stanford University Press, 1979); Patricia Buckley Ebrey and James Watson, eds., *Kinship Organization in Late Imperial China* (Berkeley: University of California Press, 1986).

48. Literally: "All of these affairs originally got started up *outside* [wai-

tou]," "outside" referring to the men's realm; the women would have charge of the "inside" (*neishi* or *neiwu*).

49. Liu Xu, ed., *Jiu Tang shu* (Beijing: Zhonghua, 1975), *zhuan* 188 (vol. 15), 4920. Zhang Gongyi enjoyed a popular reputation as an archetype of filial piety. There is even a play about his career, *Jiushi tongju* (*Nine Generations of Family Togetherness*) from the Yuan dynasty. I owe this reference to Chieh-fang Ou Lee. See also Lang, *Chinese Family and Society*, 31; and Levy, *The Family Revolution in Modern China*, 48.

50. Kao Yu-kung, "Lyric Vision in Chinese Narrative Tradition," 228–233; Levy, *Chinese Narrative Poetry*, 3–10.

51. For a detailed examination of Bao-chai's homilies, given in the guise of aesthetic disquisitions, see chapter 4.

52. *SS* V.119.350–351, *HLM* III.119.309. For a study of national amnesties, see Brian E. McKnight, *The Quality of Mercy: Amnesties and Traditional Chinese Justice* (Honolulu: University of Hawaii Press, 1981).

3. PREEXISTING CONDITIONS
Retributory Illness and the Limits of Medicine

1. See chapter 1 in this volume, p. 11.

2. Helen King, "Green Sickness: Hippocrates, Galen and the Origins of the 'Disease of Virgins,' " *International Journal of the Classical Tradition* 2.3 (winter 1996): 372–387.

3. J. J. Brumberg, "Chlorotic Girls, 1870–1920: A Historical Perspective on Female Adolescence," *Child Development* 53 (1982): 1468–1477; and Thomas Sydenham, *The Entire Works* (London: 1753), 658, as cited in King, "Green Sickness," 374.

4. Manfred Porkert with Christian Ullmann, trans. and adapted by Mark Howson, *Chinese Medicine* (New York: William Morrow, 1982), 148; see also Judith Farquhar, *Knowing Practice: The Clinical Encounter in Chinese Medicine* (Boulder, CO: Westview Press, 1994).

5. Porkert, *Chinese Medicine*, 142.

6. Ibid., 58.

7. Xu Zhenjun, *Xinzeng buhui tuxuan ze wanbao Yuxia ji quanshu* (facsimile of the 1684 edition).

8. Cf. Susan Sontag, *Illness as Metaphor* (New York: Farrar, Straus and Giroux, 1978).

9. W. S. Gilbert and Arthur Sullivan, *The Mikado* (1885), act 2, scene 1.

10. Cf. the work of Oliver Sacks, whose profiles of patients with obscure neurological disorders bring out both the unique character of each in-

dividual sufferer and their overriding universal humanity. See, for example, *The Man Who Mistook His Wife for a Hat and Other Clinical Tales* (New York: Summit Books, 1988), *An Anthropologist on Mars: Seven Paradoxical Tales* (New York: Knopf, 1995), and *The Island of the Colorblind* (New York: Knopf, 1996). For a literary study of illness as characterization, see Athena Vrettos, *Somatic Fictions: Imagining Illness in Victorian Culture* (Stanford: Stanford University Press, 1995).

11. For a discussion of the impact of Qin Ke-qing's illness and death on the family, see chapter 2, 45–46, chapter 3, 73.

12. For the main areas of investigation for diagnosis, see Bray, *Technology and Gender*, 297–318. For the procedures of reading the pulse, see Giovanni Macioccia, *The Foundations of Chinese Medicine: A Comprehensive Text for Acupuncturists and Herbalists* (Edinburgh and London: Churchill Livingstone, 1989), 167–171, 181–185.

13. Macioccia, *The Foundations of Chinese Medicine*, 77–78; see also Charlotte Furth, "Blood, Body and Gender: Medical Images of the Female Condition in China, 1600–1850," *Chinese Science* 7 (1986): 43–66. For a discussion of the role of regulating the menses and the implication of amenorrhea see Bray, *Technology and Gender*, 328–334.

14. A handy source for the identification and properties of Chinese pharmaceuticals is available on CD-ROM: *Traditional Chinese Medicine and Pharmacology* (Hopkins, MN: Hopkins Technology, 1996).

15. Louise Edwards analyzes Jia Rui's fatal attraction to Xi-feng as it illuminates her inappropriate power in the household and her own casual relations with the opposite sex: see *Men and Women in Qing China*, 63, 76.

16. Literally: "the toad wishing to eat the swan."

17. *Traditional Chinese Medicine and Pharmacology*.

18. This episode is cited as the emblem of one of the five titles, *A Mirror for the Romantic*, given to the novel in chapter 1. Monika Motsch offers an explanation in terms of the aesthetics of mirror symbolism. See her "The Mirror and Chinese Aesthetics: A Study of the *Honglou meng*," *Ming Qing Yanjiu* (1996): 117–136, esp. 119–123.

19. For the spiritual symbolism of the mirror, and its crossover to Taoist rhetoric, see Paul Demiéville, "Le miroir spirituel," *Sinologica* 1 (1948): 112–137; updated and trans. by Neal Donner as "The Mirror of the Mind," in Paul Gregory, ed., *Sudden and Gradual: Approaches to Enlightenment in Chinese Thought* (Honolulu: University Press of Hawaii, 1987), 13–40.

20. Mario Praz, *La carne, la morte et il diavolo nella letteratura romantica* (Milan and Rome: La Cultura, 1930); trans. by Angus Davidson as *The Romantic Agony* (London: Oxford University Press, 1970); Sontag, *Illness as Metaphor*, 28.

21. For the topos of beauty linked with illness in *The Story of the Stone*, see Wu Xinlei, "Lun Lin Daiyu xingxiang di meixue jingjie ji qi wenxue yuanyuan" (A Discussion of Lin Dai-yu's Appearance and Its Literary Sources), *"Honglou meng" yanjiu jikan* 14 (1989): 210–228; Ebrey, *The Inner Quarters*, 41–42; and Bray, *Technology and Gender*, 350–351.

22. W. W. Stead and J. H. Bates, "Evidence of a 'Silent' Bacillema in Primary Tuberculosis," *Annals of Internal Medicine* 74 (1971): 559; Herbert French, *French's Index of Differential Diagnosis*, F. Dudley Hart, ed., 12th ed. (Bristol: Wright, 1985); Harvey B. Simon, *Scientific American Medicine*, vol. 3 (New York: Scientific American, 1980), chap. 7, sec. 8, pp. 1–21.

23. Simon, *Scientific American Medicine*, chap. 7, sec. 8, pp. 1–3.

24. On the relation of malnutrition and the progress of the disease, see Joseph A. Johnston, M.D., *Nutritional Studies in Adolescent Girls and Their Relation to Tuberculosis* (Springfield, IL: Charles C. Thomas, 1953).

25. On the possibility of tuberculosis as the underlying cause of these seasonal afflictions, see W. W. Stead, "Pathogenesis of the Sporadic Case of Tuberculosis," *New England Journal of Medicine* 277 (1967): 1008.

26. *SS* I, Introduction, 32.

27. This analysis first appeared in my article "Why Bao-yu Can't Concentrate: Attention Deficit Disorder in *The Story of the Stone*," *Literature and Medicine* 13.2 (fall 1994): 257–273. I follow the terminology of Edward M. Hallowell and John J. Ratey, *Driven to Distraction: Coping with Attention Deficit Disorder from Childhood Through Adulthood* (New York: Pantheon, 1994). It is also called "Attention Deficit Hyperactivity Disorder," or A.D.H.D.; cf. Russell Barkley, *Attention Deficit Hyperactivity Disorder: A Handbook for Diagnosis and Treatment* (New York: Guilford, 1990). Bao-yu meets all the diagnostic criteria for A.D.D. in the American Psychological Association's *Diagnostic and Statistical Manual of Mental Disorders*, 3d ed., rev. (Washington DC: American Psychiatric Association, 1980), 50–53.

A far more comprehensive diagnostic test appears in Hallowell and Ratey, *Driven to Distraction*, 209–214. The authors do not claim to have established norms for the questionnaire, describing it as an informal gauge. The more questions answered "yes," the more likely it is that A.D.D. may be present. Of the 100 questions, 15 do not apply to Bao-yu's situation because they presuppose a modern society. Of the eighty-five remaining questions, three could not be answered because of lack of information, twenty-one were answered "no," and sixty-one were answered "yes" — a whopping 74 percent and, according to the test, a virtually decisive diagnosis.

28. Wu, *On the Red Chamber Dream*, 103–130; Zhao and Chen, *Honglou meng xintan*, vol. 1, 143–177; Zhou, *Honglou meng xinzheng*, 785–801, 833–868.

29. See George F. Still, "Some Abnormal Psychical Conditions in Chil-

dren," *Lancet* (April 1902): 1008–1012, 1077–1082, 1163–1168. Charles Bradley pioneered the paradoxically effective use of stimulants to treat the disorder. See his "The Behavior of Children Receiving Benzadrine," *American Journal of Psychiatry* 94 (1937): 577–585, and "Benzadrine and Dexadrine in the Treatment of Children's Behavior Disorders," *Pediatrics* 5 (1950): 24–36. For a detailed history of the understanding of the nature and diagnosis of A.D.D. see Barkley, *Attention Deficit Hyperactivity Disorder*, 3–38. Recent descriptions and studies of the disorder intended for a popular audience include Frank Wolkenberg, "Out of a Darkness," *New York Times Magazine*, October 11, 1987, 62 ff.; and Robert A. Moss, with Helen Huff Dunlap, *Why Johnny Can't Concentrate: Coping with Attention Deficit Problems* (New York and Toronto: Bantam, 1990).

An alternative approach to the analysis of children with A.D.D. is suggested in C. Janet Newman, Cynthia Fox Dember, and Othilda Krug, " 'He Can But He Won't': A Psychodynamic Study of So-Called 'Gifted Underachievers,' " *Psychoanalytic Study of the Child* 28 (1973): 83–129. This article profiles underachieving boys with high I.Q. scores who seem clearly to be afflicted with A.D.D.; however, the authors discuss the cases in strictly psychoanalytical terms, summing up the manifestations of emotional development with the following *sloka*:

"I can, but I won't."

"I won't, so I don't."

"I don't, so I can't."

"I can't, but I'll say I won't."

The article is frustrating because the authors have brought considerable powers of observation and analysis to bear on their cases, while ignoring studies of the organic aspects of the disorder.

30. Stella Chess, "Diagnosis and Treatment of the Hyperactive Child," *New York Journal of Medicine* 60 (1959): 2379–2385; Hallowell and Ratey, *Driven to Distraction*, 97, 278–285.

31. The lectures by Still published in *The Lancet* contain an eloquent description of the behavioral characteristics of children with A.D.D. For detailed cases of the disorder in children and adults see Hallowell and Ratey, *Driven to Distraction*, chaps. 1–3 and 6. For a study of children with the disorder in their social context, see Lauren Braswell and Michael L. Bloomquist, *Cognitive-Behavioral Therapy with A.D.H.D. Children: Child, Family and School Interventions* (New York: Guilford Press, 1991), 11–48. For a description of A.D.D. from a more strictly neurological perspective, see Paul H. Wender, *Minimal Brain Dysfunction in Children* (New York: John Wiley, 1971), 135–154. The term "minimal brain dysfunction" is now no longer used because it included disorders caused by brain damage and

covered too broad a spectrum of disabilities. For a more recent study see idem, *The Hyperactive Child, Adolescent, and Adult* (New York and London: Oxford University Press, 1987).

32. See Xue-rong Li, Lin-yan Su, Brenda D. Townes and Christopher K. Varley, "Diagnosis of Attention Deficit Disorder with Hyperactivity in Chinese Boys," *Journal of the American Academy of Child and Adolescent Psychiatry* 28.4 (1989): 497–500; X. R. Li, "Duodong zonghe zheng" (Hyperactivity Syndrome), in Li Xuerong, ed., *Ertongzhong de zhengchang yu fanchang xingwei* (Normal and Abnormal Behavior in Children) (Changsha: Human Science and Technology Press, 1983), 15–44; and S. L. Zhu, L. Y. Su et al., "Ertongzhong de duodung zhonghe zheng: 814 lie linchuang yu xinli yanjiu" (Hyperactivity Syndrome in Children: A Clinical and Psychological Study of 814 cases), *Zhongguo shenjing yu jingshen bing xuebao* (Chinese Journal of Neurology and Psychiatry) 18 (1985): 382–385. Until recently, A.D.D. was referred to in Chinese research as "minimal brain dysfunction" (*naoshi tiao*). See W. O. Shekim, Y. F. Wang, and L. Yang, "Ruozhi zheng" (Minimal Brain Dysfunction), *Zhongguo shenjing yu jingshen bing xuebao* 18 (1985): 29–32.

33. See Y. I. Zhang, W. Z. Sang, and H. G. Cui, "Ertong xinli teyan yu jiating zhijian de guanxi" (The Relationship Between Children's Psychological Assessments and Their Family), *Xinlixue nianjian* 18 (1986): 371–375.

34. Moss, *Why Johnny Can't Concentrate*, 22–23.

35. *SS* II. 45.391–392, *HLM* II.45.549–550.

36. Wai-yee Li has discussed these terms as they relate to desire's preexistence to the object of desire in *The Story of the Stone*; see *Enchantment and Disenchantment*, 203–204 ff.

37. Plaks, *Archetype and Allegory in The Dream of the Red Chamber*, 59–60.

38. See Li-li Ch'en, trans., *Master Tung's Western Chamber Romance (Tung Hsi-hsiang chu-kung-tiao): A Chinese Chantfable* (Cambridge: Cambridge University Press, 1976); Stephen H. West and Wilt Idema, eds. and trans., *Wang Shifu: The Moon and the Zither: The Story of the Western Wing, With a Study of Its Woodblock Illustrations by Yao Daijun* (Berkeley: University of California Press, 1991). For the role of *Xixiang ji* in Bao-yu and Dai-yu's private language, see chapter 3. See also Ann Waltner, "On Not Becoming a Heroine: Lin Dai-yu and Cui Ying-ying," *Signs* 15 (1989): 61–78.

39. Hallowell and Ratey, *Driven to Distraction*, 283.

40. Again, the fatal dynamics of this father/son relationship are typical of the effects of the disorder in many family contexts: see Barkley, *Attention Deficit Hyperactivity Disorder*, 130–168.

41. For the necessity of structure to the amelioration of A.D.D., see Barkley, *Attention Deficit Hyperactivity Disorder*, 499–505; Hallowell and Ratey, *Driven to Distraction*, 221–225.

42. The question of whether traditional Chinese medicine had the resources to treat hyperactivity will have to await another study. For the use of stimulants to treat the disorder in the West, see n. 27. Typical of many A.D.D. profiles is an attempt to self-medicate, often through drug or alcohol abuse (see Hallowell and Ratey, *Driven to Distraction*, 17–18, 172–174). Bao-yu does ingest some bizarre substances; in particular, his maids despair of breaking him of the habit of eating their lipstick and other cosmetics. This is interpreted as part of his obsession with things feminine; however, it is possible that these elaborate mixtures contained chemicals that had an ameliorating effect on his A.D.D.

43. There are several overviews of what is known about Cao Xueqin and his two main editors: see *SS* Introduction, esp. 32–38; Wu, *On the Red Chamber Dream*, 73–102; Zhao and Chen, *Honglou meng xintan*, vol. 1, 173–182, 785–801; and Zhou, *Honglou meng xinzheng*.

44. *SS* I, Introduction, 34–43, and III, Preface, 13–17; Cao Xueqin, *Zhiyan zhai chongping "Shitou ji"* (Beijing: Wenxue guji kanxingshe, 1955), vol. 1, 15.

4. A WORLD APART
Poetry and Society in the Garden of Total Vision

1. See *SS* I, Appendix, 527–534; III, Appendices I and II, 614–619. David Hawkes and John Minford provide interpretations of Cao Xueqin's creative process and the relation of the "original" text to the version edited by Gao E and Cheng Wei-yuan. See *SS* I, Introduction, 15–48; IV, Introduction, 20–30.

2. This has been the canonical function of poetry from time immemorial, the phrase occurring in the *Classic of History (Shu jing)* perhaps as early as the eleventh century A.D. See Chow Tze-tsung, "The Early History of the Chinese Word *Shih* (Poetry)," in Chow Tze-tsung, ed., *Wen-lin: Studies in the Chinese Humanities* (Madison: University of Wisconsin Press, 1968), 151–152. As an explicitly literary critical concept, it first appears in Wei Hung's "Great Preface" (*Shi daxu*) to the *Book of Songs (Shi jing)*, probably first century A.D. See James J. Y. Liu, *Chinese Theories of Literature* (Chicago: University of Chicago Press, 1975), 118–120.

3. Xu Shen, "Shuowen jiezi," in Ding Fubao, ed., *Shuowen jiezi gulin*, 12 vols. (Taipei: Shangwu, 1966), 968a–b. Although the late Ming novelist and playwright Feng Menglong (1574–1646) was a connoisseur of love in all its aspects, he objected to limiting the meaning of *qing* to sexual love, extending its meaning to include empathy, or dedicated sympathy for the feelings of others. See Patrick Hanan, *The Chinese Vernacular Story* (Cambridge: Harvard University Press, 1981), 96–97.

4. The ideal of the "perfect listener" (*zhiyin*) derives not from poetry but from music. Its locus classicus is the story of the lutenist Bo Ya and his friend Zhong Ziqi (cf. "Liezi," in Yang Bojun, ed., *Liezi jishi* [Hong Kong: Taiping, 1954], 5.111; trans. by A. C. Graham as *The Book of Lieh-tzu* [New York: Columbia University Press, 1960], 109–110). Whatever Bo Ya played, Zhong Ziqi instantly divined his meaning; when Zhong Ziqi died, Bo Ya broke his lute in two. See Peter H. Lee, *Celebration of Continuity: Themes in Classic East Asian Poetry* (Cambridge: Harvard University Press, 1979), 170–171; James J. Y. Liu, *The Interlingual Critic* (Bloomington: Indiana University Press, 1982), 90; Stephen Owen, *Traditional Chinese Poetry and Poetics: Omen of the World* (Madison: University of Wisconsin Press, 1985), 59, 73, 234.

5. On Cao's skills as a poet, see Li, *Enchantment and Disenchantment*, 183.

6. Kao, "Lyric Vision in Chinese Narrative," 227–243; Martin W. Huang, "The Dilemma of Chinese Lyricism and the Qing Literati Novel " (Ph.D. dissertation, Stanford University, 1991).

7. On the relationship of Disenchantment to Cao Zhi's goddess of the Luo and the intervening tradition of rhapsodies on beautiful women, see Li, "The Genealogy of Disenchantment," in *Enchantment and Disenchantment*, 3–46. Cai Yijiang provides a detailed commentary on the language and poetics of *fu* in *The Story of the Stone*: On Bao-yu's sense of the "*Luoshen fu*," see "*Honglou meng*" shici qufu pingzhu (Beijing: Xinhua, 1991), 35.

8. For a discussion of the pages of the registers as they relate to conventions of representation of beautiful women in the visual arts, see Wu Hung, "Beyond Stereotypes: The Twelve Beauties in Qing Court Art and the *Dream of the Red Chamber*," in Ellen Widmer and Kang-i Sun Chang, eds., *Writing Women in Late Imperial China* (Stanford: Stanford University Press, 1997), 306–365.

9. Arthur Waley, *Yuan Mei: Eighteenth Century Chinese Poet* (London: George Allen and Unwin, 1956), paints a vivid picture of the function of poetry as both polite accomplishment and political tool for the Chinese literati: see also Naquin and Rawski, *Chinese Society in the Eighteenth Century*, 71. For a more explicitly political biography, see F. W. Mote, *The Poet Kao Ch'i* (Princeton: Princeton University Press, 1962).

10. SS I.18.357–358, HLM I.18.169–170.

11. In Hawkes's translation, "Prospect Garden." Here I am following Andrew H. Plaks, whose translation evokes the complex allegory of the garden as a microcosm of the universe. See Plaks, *Archetype and Allegory*, 178–211.

12. On the Chinese garden as craft and art, see Maggie Keswick, *The Chinese Garden: History, Art and Architecture* (New York: Rizzoli, 1978), and Han Pao-teh, trans. Carl Shen, *External Forms and Internal Visions: The Story of Chinese Landscape Design* (Taipei: Youth Cultural Enterprise, 1992). This

work contains an appendix on the relation of the garden to literature, "The Garden in the Novel *Dream of the Red Chamber*," 244–259. On the garden as social construction, see Craig Clunas, *Fruitful Sites: Garden Culture in Ming Dynasty China* (Durham: Duke University Press, 1996). For discussions of the site of the garden that may have inspired the Garden of Total Vision, see Wu, *On the Red Chamber Dream*, 137–144; Spence, *Ts'ao Yin and the K'ang-hsi Emperor*, 205–209; and Minford, *SS* IV, Preface, 15–20.

13. The catalogue of plants in the Garden bears investigation. *Caomu tu*, the Qing botanical encyclopedia, contains descriptions and illustrations of the trees and plants mentioned in *The Story of the Stone*, which would be items of luxury and status. The work is part of Chen Menglei, comp., *Gujin tushu jicheng* (Beijing, ca. 1728; reprint, Taipei: Wenxing, 1964).

14. The apartment's name is written with a different character, *Qiuyan shuzhai*, in chapter 33.

15. Mary Scott, "The Image of the Garden in *Jin Ping Mei* and *Honglou meng*," *CLEAR* 8 (1986): 83–94.

16. Xiang-yun is literally the "old friend of the colored-cloud-pillowing water pavilion," the name of a garden structure remembered from her family home by Grandmother Jia, née Shi. Xiang-yun is thus the rightful heir ("old friend") of the memory of this vanished pavilion.

17. Mencius 5B.8: "*Song qi shi, du qi shu, buzhi chi ren, ke hu, shi yi lun qi shi.*" See also Stephen Owen, *Readings in Chinese Literary Thought* (Cambridge: Council on East Asian Studies, Harvard University, 1992), 22–23.

18. Huo Guoling and Huo Jiping, *Honglou jiemeng*, seeks to identify and explicate the true historical background of as many events detailed in the novel as possible. See also Wu, *On the Red Chamber Dream*, 103–144.

19. *SS* II.37.221, *HLM* I.37.374–375.

20. *SS* II.37.224, *HLM* I.37.376.

21. On poem sequences as unified works, combining narrative and lyrical elements, see Levy, *Chinese Narrative Poetry*, 104–113.

22. For a discussion of this occasion as it lampoons conventions of linked verse composition see David Pollack, "Linked-Verse Poetry in China: A Study of Associative Linking in *Lien-chü* Poetry with Emphasis on the Poems of Han Yü and His Circle" (Ph.D. dissertation, University of California at Berkeley, 1976), 326–337.

23. For a complete translation of this version of the play, see West and Idema, *Wang Shifu: The Moon and the Zither*.

Cyril Birch has edited and translated the complete text of *The Peony Pavilion* (Bloomington: Indiana University Press, 1980), by Tang Xianxu (1550–1617), based on the annotated editions by Xu Shuofang (Shanghai: Shanghai Guji, 1958) and Yang Xiaomei (Beijing: Zhonghua, 1963).

24. For an analysis of Bao-qin's riddles and the figure of Bao-qin as a woman historian, see Haun Saussy, "Women's Writing Before and Within the *Hong lou meng*," in Widmer and Chang, *Writing Women in Late Imperial China*, 295–301.

25. *SS* I, Introduction, 20; *HLM* I.1.1. For the debate on the proper place of women in literary culture, see Robyn Hamilton, "The Pursuit of Fame: Luo Qilan (1775–1813?) and the Debates About Women and Talent in Eighteenth-Century Jiangnan," *Late Imperial China* 18.1 (June 1997): 39–71.

26. James Hightower, *The Poetry of T'ao Ch'ien* (Oxford: Clarendon Press, 1970), 254–258. For a comparison of two formative poems on this theme, by Tao Qian and Wang Wei, see Levy, *Chinese Narrative Poetry*, 10–15.

27. On the notion of transforming archetypes, see Dore J. Levy, "Transforming Archetypes in Chinese Poetry and Painting: The Case of Ts'ai Yen," *Asia Major*, 3d series, 6.2 (1993), 147–168.

28. Cf. *SS* II.31.118, *HLM* I.31.315, where Bao-chai describes Xiang-yun's fondness for dressing in boy's clothes, and how Grandmother Jia actually mistook her for Bao-yu.

29. On the conventions of linked verse composition in late imperial China, see Pollack, *Linked-Verse Poetry in China*, 295–325.

30. While some schools of thought held that women were best kept ignorant, there was also an explicit ideology favoring women's education to enable them to perform their household duties well, as the domestic spheres of men and women were interdependent. See Bettina Birge, "Chu Hsi and Women's Education," in Wm. Theodore de Bary and John W. Chafee, eds., *Neo-Confucian Education: The Formative Stage* (Berkeley: University of California Press, 1989), 325–367. For a study of the role of women's education, especially writing, in Qing China, see Ko, *Teachers of the Inner Chambers*, 143–179; and Mann, *Precious Records*, 76–120.

31. Plaks, *Archetype and Allegory*, 60–70.

32. For studies and translations of the original works, see James R. Hightower, "Yüan Chen and 'The Story of Ying-ying,' " *HJAS* 33 (1973): 90–123. For a comprehensive study of the evolution of the heroine, see Lorraine Dong, "The Creation and Life of Cui Ying-ying," 2 vols. (Ph.D. dissertation, University of Washington, 1978). Timothy Wong has made a study of the original Ying-ying in terms of the conflict of social convention and romantic fulfillment. See his "Self and Society in T'ang Dynasty Love Tales," *Journal of the American Oriental Society* 99.1 (1979): 95–100.

33. On the phenomenon of transforming archetypes, including Cui Ying-ying, see Levy, "Transforming Archetypes in Chinese Poetry and Painting," 152; Lorraine Dong, "The Many Faces of Cui Ying-ying," in Richard W. Guisso and Stanley Johannesen, eds., *Women in China: Current*

Directions in Historical Scholarship (Youngstown, NY: Philo Press, 1981), 71–98; Waltner, "On Not Becoming a Heroine," 61–78.

34. Attributed to the Yuan dynasty playwright Yu Tianxi (fl. 1251–1260). In the *Gudian xiju cunmu huigao*, 3 vols.(Shanghai: Shanghai guji, 1982), vol. 1, 218, Zhuang Yifu lists the title *Qiuye Ruizhu gong* (Autumn Night in the Palace of Pearls) as one of 15 plays written by Yu, but declares that "the plot is unknown" *(benshi weixiang)* and the play does not survive. The *Xiqu cidian* (Taipei: Taiwan Zhonghua) has an entry for the title *Ruizhu ji* and identifies it as *Qiuye ruizhu gong*.

Chieh-fang Ou Lee recognizes the verse from *kunqu* repertory, but I have been unable to locate a text. Considering the custom of dramatic troupes performing selected scenes in private engagements, the longevity of a favorite set piece apart from its original context is not surprising. I am also grateful to Siu-leung Li for his help with this puzzle.

35. See Liu, *The Interlingual Critic*, 33; Stephen Owen, *The Poetry of the Early T'ang* (New Haven: Yale University Press, 1977), 11, 281–293; Pauline Yu, *The Reading of Imagery in the Chinese Poetic Tradition* (Princeton: Princeton University Press, 1987), 169–170.

36. Red Inkstone explicitly notes the significance of these metaphors in his comments on chapter 22. See Chen Qinghao, *Xinbian "Shitou ji" Zhiyan zhai pingyu jijiao* (Taipei: Lianjing, 1986), 429. Haun Saussy has considered the riddle of the riddles in two studies: "Reading and Folly in the *Dream of the Red Chamber*," *CLEAR* 9 (1987), 36–37, and "Women's Writing Before and Within the *Hong lou meng*," in Widmer and Chang, *Writing Women in Late Imperial China*, 288–293.

37. The fact that the mirror is a key Buddhist symbol of the "original mind" (the mind free from time and space) is just one of the levels on which Bao-yu's riddle operates, sounding the pervasive theme of the boy's final escape to religion. See Demiéville, "Le miroir spirituel." On the symbol of the mirror in *The Story of the Stone*, see Plaks, *Archetype and Allegory*, 65; Li, *Enchantment and Disenchantment*, 226.

38. On the distinction between explicit and implicit texts, see Levy, "Transforming Archetypes," 153.

39. Arthur Waley, *The Book of Songs* (London: George Allen and Unwin, 1937), poem 14, 28–29; Chinese text: Yang Jialuo, ed., *Maoshi zhushu ji buzheng* (Taipei: Shijie, 1963), 31.

40. Although today the *shaoyao* (herbaceous peony, *paeonia officinalis*) and *mudan* (tree peony, *paeonia suffruticosa*) are regarded as two different plants, both words also refer to the same flower, the Chinese tree peony. According to Tao Jiheng, the *shaoyao* began to be known as *mudan* during the reign of the Tang emperor Xuanzong (r. 715–755), who had planted them in

his palace gardens. See Tao Jiheng, ed., *Shi jing tonglun* (Shanghai: Zhonghua, 1958), 113. Yang Jialuo identifies this exchange as a betrothal ritual (*Mao shi zhushu ji buzheng*, vol. 1, 31). Waley comments: "The peony has, of course, a great reputation for medicinal and magical powers, both in the west and in China. . . . It was probably the root rather than the flower that first interested the Chinese; for the second element in the name (*shao-yao*) means "medicinal herb," and it is the root of the peony that has always been used in medicine. It probably figured in courtship first as a love-philtre, and later (as in this poem) as a symbol of lasting affection" (*The Book of Songs*, 28–29). On the peony in Chinese garden and medical culture, see Joseph Needham with Lu Gwei-djen and a special contribution from Huang Hsing-tsung, *Science and Civilization in China*, vol. 6, part I, *Botany* (Cambridge: Cambridge University Press, 1986), 394–408.

41. For commentary on the "Elegy to the Spirit of the Hibiscus" (*Furong lei*), see Cai Yijiang, "*Honglou meng*" shici qufu pingzhu, 332.

5. THE CHIMING OF THE VOID
Poetry as a Vehicle to Enlightenment

1. Luis O. Gomez, "Purifying Gold: The Metaphor of Effort and Intuition in Buddhist Thought and Practice," in Gregory, ed., *Sudden and Gradual*, 67–165. See also Fauré, *The Rhetoric of Immediacy*, 32–53; and Thomas P. Kasulis, Roger T. Ames, and Winal Dassanayake, eds., *Zen Action, Zen Person* (Honolulu: University of Hawaii Press, 1981), part I, "The Context of Nothingness," 3–52, esp. 16–19, 21–22.

2. For the relationship between Chan Buddhism and classical Chinese poetry and poetics, see Du Songbo, *Chanxue yu Tang Song shixue* (Taipei: Liming wenhua, 1976), esp. chap. 5 (365–406) for a discussion of the similarities of the experience of Chan and poetry. I am grateful to Charles Hartman for guiding me to this book. For a detailed study of poetic theory as it participates in the vocabulary and process of enlightenment, see Richard John Lynn, "The Sudden and the Gradual in Chinese Poetry Criticism," in Gregory, ed., *Sudden and Gradual*, 381–427. See also Paul Demiéville, "Le Tch'an et la poésie chinoise," *Hermès* 7 (1970): 123–136; reprinted in his *Choix d'études bouddhiques*, 456–469: 457; and Iriye Yoshitaka, "Chinese Poetry and Zen," *Eastern Buddhist* 6.1 (May 1973): 54–67.

3. Reading *miaowu* as "arational illumination." See Yan Yu, Guo Shaoyu, ed., *Cang Lang shihua jiaoshi* (Beijing: Renmin, 1962), I.5. On Yan Yu's literary aesthetics and influence, see Lynn, "The Sudden and Gradual in Chinese Poetry Criticism," 402–409; idem, "The Talent-Learning Polari-

ty in Chinese Poetics: Yen Yü and the Later Tradition," *CLEAR* 5 (1983): 157–184. For a discussion of the role of Buddhism in Chinese literary life, see Kenneth K. S. Ch'en, *The Chinese Transformation of Buddhism* (Princeton: Princeton University Press, 1973), 179–239. Ch'en's analysis concentrates on Bo Juyi (772–846) as an exemplar of the relationship between Buddhism and literary output. For a more nuanced discussion of the influence of Buddhist, particularly Chan, thought on an individual poet's literary and intellectual development, see Charles Hartman, *Han Yü and the T'ang Search for Unity* (Princeton: Princeton University Press, 1986), chap. 3 ("The Oneness of the Sage"), 173–210.

4. O'Flaherty, *Dreams, Illusions and Other Realities*, 225–227.

5. According to the commentary by Red Inkstone in the Jiaxu edition of *Shitou ji* (1754), "Only one who understood the secret message of this book *could* have the hot and bitter tears with which to finish it" (*SS* I, Introduction, 35; Chen Qinghao, *Xinbian "Shitou ji" Zhiyan zhai pingyu jijiao*, 12). As noted above, *The Story of the Stone* is regarded as drawing extensively on the life and experiences of the author. The comment, therefore, reflects the admittedly subjective understanding and sympathy of one of his closest associates: that those who had the experience and insight to respond to the author's most intimate feelings would be few indeed.

6. The physiological basis of Bao-yu's eccentricity and unusual sense of self is discussed in chapter 3.

7. The last two lines can be translated more literally as: "Though outwardly of handsome appearance / Inside, he was just a tangled mess."

8. On Dai-yu's affiliation with the attributes of the wood element and its association with spring, see Plaks, *Archetype and Allegory*, 62–65.

9. On the expressive function and poetic genealogy of the *qin*, see Ronald Egan, "The Controversy over Music and 'Sadness' and Changing Conceptions of the *Qin* in Middle Period China," *HJAS* 57.1 (June 1997): 5–66.

10. Egan renders *zhiyin* as "knowing listeners"; see ibid., 19.

11. Owen, *Readings in Chinese Literary Thought*, 181.

12. As per "The Great Preface": "Poetry is the fulfillment of intent; what dwells in the mind is intent, what comes forth in words is poetry." See note 8.

13. Chen Qinghao, *Xinbian "Shitou ji" Zhiyan zhai pingyu jijiao*, 33.

14. On the affectation of reincarnation in the present life as a sign of spiritual liberation, see chapter 3 in this volume, 98.

15. A more literal translation of the line would be: "The caltrop flower in vain reflects melting snow." The caltrop is a water plant with freshsmelling flowers that produces an edible tuber of distinctive curved shape. The flowers are often used in the decoration of the backs of mirrors. In

chapter 57, Bao-yu asks Dai-yu's maid, Nightingale, to give him one from her vanity-box ("Why don't you give me that little [mirror] with the pattern of caltrops on it as a keepsake?" [SS III.57.101, HLM II.57.612]). Hawkes's translation reflects the allusion in Chinese, in which "caltrop flower" would be a synecdoche for a mirror decorated with that motif. The word for "snow" (xue) is a pun on Xue Pan's surname.

16. This ironically evokes Confucian notions of self-realization. See Wei-ming Tu, "Embodying the Universe: A Note on Confucian Self-Realization," in Roger T. Ames, ed. (with Wimal Dissanayake and Thomas P. Kasulis), Self as Person in Asian Theory and Practice (Albany: State University of New York Press, 1994), 177–186.

17. On the nature of sudden enlightenment, see Gregory, Sudden and Gradual, Introduction, 3–6.

GLOSSARY

Aojing guan　凹晶館　(Concave Pavilion)

baihaitang　白海堂　(white Crab-flower)

baiyu zaoni xian　白玉遭泥陷　(a "jade sunk in the mud," a beauty despoiled)

bao-yu　寶玉　("precious jade")

bian　辮　(queue)

Bo Juyi　白居易　(772–846)

bu shi yuanjia bu jutou　不是冤家不聚頭　(an aphorism, "'tis fate brings foes and lovers together")

Caomu tu　草木圖　(Qing botanical encyclopedia)

Cao Xueqin　曹雪芹　(1715?–1763)

Cao Zhi　曹植　(192–232)

Chang E　嫦娥　(the moon goddess)

Changhen ge　長恨歌　("Song of Everlasting Sorrow" or, "Song of Enduring Grief")

Cheng Weiyuan　程偉元　(1747?–?)

chiqing　癡情　(obsessive longing)

chu　處　(place)

chujia　出家　(literally, "to leave the family" [to become a Buddhist monk])

ci　詞　(song lyrics)

daguan　大觀　(total vision, literally, "grand view")

Daguan yuan　大觀園　(Garden of Total Vision)

Daoxiang cun　稻香村　(Sweet-Rice Village)

duodong zonghe zheng　多動綜合症　(hyperactivity syndrome, now known as Attention Deficit Disorder)

Fang-guan　芳官　(Parfumée, one of the members of the Jia family's private theatrical troupe)

fengliu biezhi　風流別致　(elegance and originality)

Feng Menglong　馮夢龍　(1574–1646)

fengqing yuezhai 風情月債 (debts of passion)

fengyue baojian 風月寶鑑 (Mirror for the Romantic)

fu 賦 (rhymeprose)

furong hua 芙蓉花 (hibiscus)

ganlu 甘露 (sweet dew)

Gao E 高鶚 (1740–1815?)

gong 公 (duke)

Guan Yin 觀音 (Bodhisattva of Mercy)

guobei 過悲 (terribly sad)

Haitang shishe 海堂詩社 (Crab-Flower Club)

hanxu hunhou 含蓄渾厚 (character and depth)

"*Heng-heng yun*" 哼哼韻 ("Hum-bum Song")

Hengwu jun 蘅蕪君 (Lady All-spice, Bao-chai's pen name)

Hengwu yuan 蘅蕪院 (All-spice Court)

hongchen shi 紅塵世 ("world of the red dust," i.e., the mundane world, especially the mortal realm of human affairs)

Honglou meng 紅樓夢 (*The Dream of the Red Chamber*, also translated as "The Dream of Golden Days")

huashen 花神 (flower spirit)

Huo-qi 霍啟 (Calamity, a servant of Zhen Shi-yin)

huanlei 還淚 (debt of tears)

Jihu sou 畸笏叟 (Odd Tablet)

Jiqiu 箕裘 alludes to *shao jiqiu* 紹箕裘 ("continuing the family trade," an aphorism from *The Book of Rites*)

jia 假 (false)

Jia 賈

Jia Bao-yu 賈寶玉

Jia Dai-ru 賈代儒 (master of the Jia clan school)

Jia Gui 賈桂 (son of Bao-yu and Bao-chai)

Jia Huan 賈環 (Bao-yu's half-brother, son of Jia Zheng and Aunt Zhao)

Jia Jing 賈敬 (father of Jia Zhen, abdicated head of the Ning-guo House)

Jia Lian 賈璉 (son of Jia She, husband of Wang Xi-feng)

Jiamu 賈母 (Grandmother Jia)

Jia Rui 賈瑞 (grandson of the schoolmaster Jia Dai-ru)

Jia She 賈赦 (elder son of Grandmother Jia, nominal head of the Rong-guo House)

Jia Yu-cun 賈雨村 (pun on *Jiayu cun* 假語存 ["false discourse"])

Jia Zhen　賈珍　(head of the Ning-guo House)

Jia Zheng　賈政　(second son of Grandmother Jia, father of Bao-yu)

Jia Zhu　賈珠　(eldest son of Jia Zheng, deceased husband of Li Wan)

jiazhang　家長　(head of family)

Jian-mei　兼美　("Two-in-one," or "two beauties united"; also called Ke-qing　可卿, a pun on *keqin*　可親 ["lovable, desirable"])

Jiangzhu xiancao　絳珠仙草　(Crimson Pearl Flower)

Jiao Da　焦大　("Big Jiao")

Jiang Yu-han　蔣玉函　(actor/manager, friend of Bao-yu and husband of Aroma, stage name "Bijou" [*Qi-guan-er*　琪官兒])

Jin-chuan-er　金釧兒　(Golden; literally, "Gold Bracelet")

jinyu yinyuan　金玉姻緣　(affinity of gold and jade, also called *jinyu yuan* 金玉緣)

Jinghuan xiangu　警幻仙姑　(the fairy Disenchantment)

Jiushi tongju　九世同居　(*Nine Generations of Family Togetherness*)

keqin　可親　(lovable, desirable)

Kongkong daoren　空空道人　(the Taoist adept Vanitas)

laihama xiang chi tian'e rou　癩蛤蟆想吃天鵝肉　("the toad on the ground wanting to eat the goose in the sky")

laonian　老年　(old age, elder)

laozheng　癆症　or *laoqie zhi zheng*　癆怯之症　(tuberculosis [*mycobacterium tuberculosis*], or "consumption")

Leng Zi-xing　冷子興　(friend of Jia Yu-cun, husband of Zhou Rui's daughter)

Li Wan　李紈　(widow of Jia Zheng's eldest son, Jia Zhu; mother of Jia Lan)

Lin Dai-yu　林黛玉

ludu　祿蠹　("career worms")

lüshi　律詩　(regulated verse)

maili　脈理　(pulse)

Mangmang dashi　茫茫大士　(the lame Taoist Mysterioso)

milu　迷津　(Ford of Error)

Miaomiao zhenren　渺渺真人　(the scabby-headed Buddhist monk Impervioso)

miaowu　妙悟　(arational illumination)

Miao-yu　妙玉　(Adamantina, the unshorn nun who takes up residence in the Green Bower Hermitage in the Garden of Total Vision)

"Ming sheng"　冥昇　("The Transfiguration," a scene from a play called

Ruizhu gong 蕊珠宮 [*The Palace of Pearls*])

mudan 牡丹 (peony, titled "Empress of the Garden" [*yanguan qunfang* 艷冠群芳])

mushi yinyuan 木石姻緣 (affinity of stone and flower)

naoshi tiao 腦失調 (minimal brain dysfunction)

neishi, neiwu 內室，內務 (inside; here, the women's realm of house-hold management)

Ning-guo House 寧國府

Ou-guan 藕官 (Nenuphar, one of the actresses in the Jia family's private theatrical troupe)

qi 氣 (breath)

qizhongwei 其中味 ("secret message"; literally, innermost flavor, essence)

Qiao-jie 巧姐兒 (daughter of Wang Xi-feng and Jia Lian)

qin 親 (kin, including marriage kin)

Qin Ke-qing 秦可卿 (wife of Jia Rong, Jia Zhen's daughter-in-law, also known as Qin-shi 秦氏)

Qing 清 dynasty (1644–1911)

qing 情 (attachment)

qinggen 情根 (root of [emotional] attachment)

Qinggeng feng 青埂峰 (Greensickness Peak)

qingke 清客 (literary gentlemen; literally, "pure guests")

Qing seng 情僧 (Brother Amor, "the Passionate [Buddhist] Monk")

Qing-wen 晴雯 (Skybright, one of Bao-yu's maids)

Qiushuang zhuzhai 秋爽書齋 or *Qiuyan shuzhai* 秋掩書齋 (Autumn Studio)

Qujing tongyou 曲徑通幽 (Pathway to Mysteries)

ren 忍 (forbearance)

renshen yangrong wan 人參養榮丸 ("Ginseng Tonic Pills")

Rong-guo House 榮國府

rumen 入門 or *jinmen* 進門 ("entering the gate," i.e. to embrace Buddhism and become a monk or nun)

Ruizhu gong 蕊珠宮 (*The Palace of Pearls*, also known as *Qiuye ruizhu gong* 秋夜蕊珠宮 [*Autumn Night in the Palace of Pearls*])

se 色 (sex, the object of sensual attraction)

shi 時 (time)

Shi da xu　（詩大序）　（Wei Hung's　〔衛宏〕　"Great Preface" to the *Shi jing*）

Shi ji　史記　（*Records of the Historian*）

shijiao　失教　（failure to instruct）

Shi Xiang-yun　史湘雲　（great-niece of Grandmother Jia, cousin of Bao-yu）

Shu jing　書經　（*The Classic of History*）

Sima Qian　司馬遷　（144–90 B.C.）

Taixu huanjing　太虛幻境　（Land of Illusion）

Tan-chun　探春　（daughter of Jia Zheng and Aunt Zhao, younger sister of Bao-yu）

Tang Gaozu　唐高祖　（r. 618–627）

Taohua she　桃花社　（Peach-Flower Club）

Taohua xing　桃花行　（"The Flower of the Peach"）

Taohua yuan　桃花源　（"Peach Blossom Spring"）

tianpei de yinyuan　天配的姻緣　（heaven-ordained affinity）

tianwang buxin dan　天王補心丹　（Deva-King Cardiac Elixir Pills）

Tianxian baojing　天仙寶境　（Precinct of the Celestial Visitant）

waitou　外頭　（outside; here, the men's realm of household management）

wanwu　玩物　（an object of amusement）

Wang furen　王夫人　（Lady Wang, Jia Zheng's principal wife, mother of Yuan-chun, Jia Zhu and Bao-yu）

Wang Xi-feng　王熙鳳　（wife of Jia Lian, niece of Lady Wang）

Wu-erh　五兒　（Fivey）

Wumei yin　五美吟　（"Songs for Five Fair Women"）

Wushi mang　無事忙　（"Busybody," a nickname for Bao-yu; literally, "busy to no purpose"）

wuzhi wujue　無知無覺　（"without knowledge or feeling"）

Xixiang ji　西廂記　（*Romance of the Western Chamber*）

Xiang-ling　香菱　（Caltrop, concubine of Xue Pan; actually Zhen Shi-yin's daughter, Ying-lian）

Xiaoxiang feizi　瀟湘妃子　（River Queen, Dai-yu's pen name）

Xiaoxiang guan　瀟湘館　（Naiad's house）

xinbing　心病　（lovesickness）

Xingqin bieshu　省親別墅　（Hall of Reunion）

Xing-shi　邢氏　（Lady Xing, Jia She's principal wife, mother of Jia Lian）

Xue Bao-chai　薛寶釵

Xue Pan　薛蟠　(Bao-chai's elder brother)

Yan Yu　嚴羽　(c. 1180–1235)

yanzhi　言志　(expressing individual intent)

yidu zhengdu, yihuo zhenghuo　以毒攻毒，以火攻火　("fight poison with poison and fire with fire")

Yihong gongzi　怡紅公子　(Green Boy; literally, "lord of the pleasures of youth")

Yihong yuan　怡紅院　(House of Green Delights)

yijue　宜絕　(a crime that destroys social bonds; literally, "to break [the bonds of] righteousness")

yiniang　姨娘　("Aunt," correct address of father's concubines)

yi se wukung　以色悟空　("awaken to the nature of emptiness by means of passion")

yi zhi shi shilu qi shi　亦只是實錄其事　("a true record of real events")

yiyin　意淫　(lustful, lust of the mind)

Yinjue qingchi　引覺情癡　("Awaken from Love's Folly")

yinren　淫人　(dissolute person)

Ying-lian　英蓮　(daughter of Zhen Shi-yin, later known as "Caltrop" [Xiang-ling　香菱])

Ying-ying zhuan　鶯鶯傳　("The Story of Ying-ying," by Yuan Zhen)

yongwu shi　詠物詩　(poems about objects)

You Er-jie　友二姐　(Jia Lian's secondary wife, married in secret)

Yu Tianxi　庾天錫　(fl. 1251–1260)

Yuxia ji　玉匣記　(*The Jade Casket*, almanac of folk wisdom)

Yuan-chun　元春　(the imperial concubine, daughter of Jia Zheng and Lady Wang, Bo-yu's older sister)

yuannie zhi zheng　冤孽之症　(retributory illness)

Yuan-yang　鴛鴦　(Faithful, Grandmother Jia's primary maid)

Yuan Zhen　元稹　(779–861)

yunpai xiazi　韻牌匣子　(rhyme cards)

zhanhua ming'er　佔花名兒　("Choosing the Flower," a drinking and fortune-telling game)

Zhang Gongyi　張公藝

zhang qi fu　杖期夫　("to lose the support of his wife," said of one whose wife has died)

Zhang Xinzhi　張新之　(fl. 1828–1850)

Zhang You-shi　張友士　(one of the Jia family's regular doctors)

Zhao Yiniang　趙姨娘　(Aunt Zhao, Jia Zheng's concubine, biological mother of Tan-chun and Jia Huan) *zhen* 真 (true)

Zhen Shi-yin 甄士隱 (pun on *zhenshi yin* 真事隱 ["true matters concealed"])

Zhenxia jiuyou 枕霞舊友 (Cloud Maiden)

Zhen Bao-yu 甄寶玉 (son of Zhen Ying-jia)

Zhen Ying-jia 甄應嘉 (head of the Zhen family, old friend and colleague of Jia Zheng)

zhenqing zhenshi 真情真事 (proper aspect)

Zhiyan zhai 脂硯齊 (Red Inkstone)

zhiyin 知音 (perfect listener)

zhufuren 竹夫人 ("bamboo wife")

zhu ge zhang 拄個杖 ("to support himself with a staff")

Zi-juan 紫鵑 (Nightingale)

Zuo zhuan 左傳 (the Zuo Commentary to the *Spring and Autumn Annals*)

CHINESE SOURCES

Cai Yijiang. "Cao Xueqin bixia di Lin Daiyu zhi si." *"Honglou meng" xuekan* 1 (1981): 39–74.

——. *"Honglou meng" shici qufu pingzhu.* Beijing: Xinhua, 1991.

Cao Xueqin. Wang Yunwu, ed. *Shitou ji.* Shanghai: Shangwu, 1931.

——. *Zhiyan zhai chongping "Shitou ji."* 2 vols. Beijing: Wenxue guji kanxingshe, 1955.

——. Zhang Xinzhi, Wang Xilian, and Yao Xie, comments. *"Honglou meng" sanjia pingben.* 4 vols. Shanghai: Shanghai guji, 1988.

——. Zhao Cong, ed. *Honglou meng.* 3 vols. Hong Kong: Youlian, 1960.

Chen Menglei, comp. "Caomu tu." In *Gujin tushu jicheng.* Beijing, ca. 1728. Reprint, Taipei: Wenxing, 1964.

Chen Qinghao, ed. *Xinbian "Shitou ji" Zhiyan zhai pingyu jijiao.* Taipei: Lianjing, 1986.

Chen Yupi and Liu Shide, eds. *"Honglou meng" luncong.* 2 vols. Shanghai: Guji, 1977.

Du Songbo. *Chanxue yu Tang Song shixue.* Taipei: Liming wenhua, 1976.

Feng Qiyong. *Cao Xueqin jiashi xinkao.* Shanghai: Guji, 1980.

——. *"Honglou meng" jiaozhu.* Shanghai: Shanghai wenyi, 1978.

Feng Qiyong et al., comp. *"Honglou meng" daguan: Guoji "Honglou meng" yantaohui lunwenji.* Hong Kong: Baixing banyuekan, 1987.

Feng Menglong. Zhang Fugao, ed. *Qingshi leilue.* 2 vols. Shenyang: Chunfeng wenyi, 1986.

Fu Shan, attrib. *Nüke xianfang,* in *Zhongguo yixue dacheng xubian.* Reprint of 1827 ed. Beijing: Zhongyi guji, 1990.

Hu Shi. *Baihua wenxue shi.* Shanghai: Shangwu, 1928.

Huo Guoling and Huo Jiping. *Honglou jiemeng.* 2 vols. Beijing: Yanshan, 1995.

Jiang Shunyi. "Du *Honglou meng* zaji." In *"Honglou meng" juan.* Taipei: Qihai, 1981.

Li, Xuerong. "Duodong zonghe zheng" (Hyperactivity Syndrome). In Li, ed., *Ertongzhong de zhengchang yu fanchang xingwei,* 15–44.

Li Xuerong, ed. *Ertongzhong de zhengchang yu fanchang xingwei* (Normal and

Abnormal Behavior in Children). Changsha: Human Science and Technology Press, 1983.

Liao Hsien-hao. "Shiyueyuan de jia wei zhen: *Honglou meng* zhong hou she lunjian." *Lianhe wenxue* 12.6 (1996): 127–140.

Liu Caonan. "Shixi Miaoyu de shenshi." *"Honglou meng" xuekan* 4 (1981): 57–70.

Liu Xu, ed. *Jiu Tang shu*. 16 vols. Beijing: Zhonghua, 1975.

Mai Huiting. *Zhongguo jiating gaizao wenti*. Shanghai: Commercial Press, 1930.

Pan Zhonggui. "*Honglou meng* faduan." *"Honglou meng" yanjiu jikan* 9 (1971): 367–382.

Shekim, W. O., Y. F. Wang, and L. Yang. "Ruozhi zheng." *Zhongguo shenjing yu jingshen bing xuebao* (Chinese Journal of Neurology and Psychiatry) 18 (1985): 29–32.

Shi Changlun. "Taocheng gaoben qian bashi hui dui Jia Baoyu xingxiang di xugao." *"Honglou meng" yanjiu jikan* 2 (March 1980): 121–146.

Sun Shuyu. "*Honglou meng* de chuantong yishu ganxing." In Hu Wenbin and Zhou Lei, eds., *Hongxue shijie*. Beijing: Beijing chubanshe, 1984.

Tang Xianzu. Xu Shuofang and Yang Xiaomei, eds. and annots. *Mudan ting huanhun ji*. Beijing: Renmin wenxue, 1978.

Tao Jiheng, ed. *Shi jing tonglun*. Shanghai: Zhonghua, 1958.

Wu Kun. *Yi fang kao*. Fascimile of 1584 ed. Beijing: Renmin weisheng, 1990.

Wu Xinlei. *Cao Xueqin Jiangnan jia shigao*. Fuzhou: Renmin, 1983.

——. "Lun Lin Daiyu xingxiang de meixue jingjie ji qi wenxue yuanyuan." *"Honglou meng" yanjiu jikan* 14 (1989): 210–228.

Xu Fuming. *"Honglou meng" yu xiqu bijiao yanjiu*. Shanghai: Shanghai Guji, 1984.

Xu Shen. "Shuowen jiezi." In Ding Fubao, ed., *Shuowen jiezi gulin*. 12 vols. Taipei: Shangwu, 1966.

Xu Xiurong, ed. *"Honglou meng" zhuan*. Taipei: Qihai, 1981.

Xu Zhenjun. *Xinzeng buhui tuxuan ze wanbao Yuxia ji quanshu*. Facsimile of 1684 ed. n.p., n.d.

Yan Yu. Guo Shaoyu, ed. *Cang Lang shihua jiaoshi*. Beijing: Renmin, 1962.

Yang Bojun, ed. *Liezi jishi*. Hong Kong: Taiping, 1954.

——. *Mengzi yizhu*. Beijing: Zhonghua, 1963.

Yang Jialuo, ed. *Maoshi zhushu ji buzheng*. Taipei: Shijie, 1963.

Yi Su (pseud.). *"Honglou meng" zhuan*. Shanghai: Shanghai guji, 1981.

Yu Pingbo. *"Honglou meng" yanjiu*. Shanghai: Changfeng, 1953.

——. *Zhiyan zhai "Honglou meng" jiping*. Shanghai: Zhongguo gudai shenhua, 1957.

Yü Ying-shih. "Cao Xueqin de fan chuantong sixiang." *"Honglou meng" yanjiu jikan* 5 (1980): 153–170.

——. *"Honglou meng" de liangge shijie.* Taipei: Lianjing, 1978.

Zeng Yanghua. *Manbu Daguan yuan.* Taipei: Yuanliu, 1989.

Zhang, Y. I.; W. Z. Sang; and H. G. Cui. "Ertong xinli teyan yu jiating zhi-jian de guanxi" (The Relation Between the Psychological Assessment of Children and Their Family). *Xinlixue nianjian* 18 (1986): 371–375.

Zhu, S. L., L. Y. Su et al., "Ertongzhong de duodong zhonghe zheng: 814 lie linchuang yu xinli yanjiu" (Hyperactivity Syndrome in Children: A Clinical and Psychological Study of 814 Cases). *Zhongguo shenjing yu jingshen bing xuebao* (Chinese Journal of Neurology and Psychiatry) 18 (1985): 382–385.

Zhao Gang. *"Honglou meng" lunji.* Taipei: Zhiwen, 1975.

——. *Mantan "Honglou meng."* Taipei: Jingshi, 1981.

Zhao Gang and Chen Zhongyi. *"Honglou meng" xintan.* 2 vols. Hong Kong: Wenyi, 1970.

Zhou Ruchang. *"Honglou meng" xinzheng.* 2 vols. Rev. ed. Beijing: Renmin, 1976.

——. *"Honglou meng" yu Zhonghua wenhua.* Beijing: Renmin, 1989.

WESTERN SOURCES

Adshead, S.A.M. *Material Culture in Europe and China, 1400–1800: The Rise of Consumerism.* New York: Macmillan, 1997.

Alexander, Edwin. "China's 'Three Ways' as Reflected in *Dream of the Red Chamber*." *Chinese Culture* 17 (1976): 145–157.

American Psychological Association. *Diagnostic and Statistical Manual of Mental Disorders.* 3d ed., rev. Washington, DC: American Psychiatric Association, 1980.

Ames, Roger T., with Winal Dassanayake and Thomas P. Kasulis, eds. *Self as Person in Asian Theory and Practice.* Albany: State University of New York Press, 1994.

Baker, Hugh D. *Chinese Family and Kinship.* London: Macmillan, 1979.

Baker, Hugh D., and Stephen Feuchtwang, eds. *An Old State in New Settings: Studies in the Social Anthropology of China in Memory of Maurice Freedman.* Oxford: Oxford University Press, 1991.

Barkley, Russell. *Attention Deficit Hyperactivity Disorder: A Handbook for Diagnosis and Treatment.* New York: Guilford, 1990.

Belsey, Catherine. *Desire: Love Stories in Western Culture.* Oxford: Blackwell, 1994.

Birch, Cyril, trans. *The Peony Pavilion*, by Tang Xianzu. Bloomington: Indiana University Press, 1980.

——. *Scenes for Mandarins: The Elite Theatre of the Ming.* New York: Columbia University Press, 1995.

Birge, Bettina. "Chu Hsi and Women's Education." In William Theodore de Bary and John W. Chafee, eds., *Neo-Confucian Education: The Formative Stage.* Berkeley: University of California Press, 1989, 325–367.

Bol, Peter K. "Chu Hsi's Redefinition of Literati Learning." In de Bary and Chafee, eds., *Neo-Confucian Education*, 151–185.

Botton, Alan de. *How Proust Can Change Your Life.* London: Picador, 1997.

Bourdieu, Pierre. *In Other Words: Studies Towards a Reflexive Sociology.* Stanford: Stanford University Press, 1990.

Bowersock, Glen. *Fiction as History, Nero to Julian.* Berkeley: University of California Press, 1994.

Bradley, Charles. "The Behavior of Children Receiving Benzadrine." *American Journal of Psychiatry* 94 (1937): 577–585.

——. "Benzadrine and Dexadrine in the Treatment of Children's Behavior Disorders." *Pediatrics* 5 (1950): 24–36.

Brandauer, Frederick P. "Some Philosophical Implications of the *Hung-lou Meng.*" *Ching Feng* 9.3 (1966): 14–23.

Braswell, Lauren, and Michael L. Bloomquist. *Cognitive-Behavioral Therapy with A.D.H.D. Children: Child, Family and School Interventions.* New York: Guilford, 1991.

Bray, Francesca. *Technology and Gender: Fabrics of Power in Late Imperial China.* Berkeley: University of California Press, 1997.

Brown, Carolyn T., ed. *Psycho-Sinology: The Universe of Dreams in Chinese Culture.* Lanham and London: University Press of America, 1988.

Brumberg, J. J. "Chlorotic Girls, 1870–1920: A Historical Perspective on Female Adolescence." *Child Development* 53 (1982): 1468–1477.

Chan, Bing C. *The Authorship of "The Dream of the Red Chamber": Based on a Computerized Statistical Study of Its Vocabulary.* Hong Kong: Joint Publishing, 1986.

——. "A Computerized Stylostatistical Approach to the Disputed Authorship of *The Dream of the Red Chamber.*" *Tamkang Review* 16.3 (1986): 247–278.

Chan, Ping-leung. "Myth and Psyche in *Hung-lou Meng.*" In Yang and Atkins, eds., *Critical Essays on Chinese Fiction*, 165–179.

Chang, Hao. "Confucian Cosmological Myth and Neo-Confucian Transcendence." In Smith and Kwok, eds., *Cosmology, Ontology and Human Efficacy*, 11–33.

Ch'en, Kenneth. *Buddhism in China: A Historical Survey.* Princeton: Princeton University Press, 1964.

——. *The Chinese Transformation of Buddhism.* Princeton: Princeton University Press, 1973.

Ch'en, Li-li, trans. *Master Tung's Western Chamber Romance (Tung Hsi-hsiang chu-kung-tiao): A Chinese Chantfable.* Cambridge: Cambridge University Press, 1976.

Cheng, Weijun. "The Politics of the Queue." In Alf Hiltbeitel and Barbara D. Miller, eds., *Hair: Its Power and Meaning in Asian Cultures.* Albany: State University of New York Press, 1998.

Chess, Stella. "Diagnosis and Treatment of the Hyperactive Child." *New York Journal of Medicine* 60 (1959): 2379–2385.

Chin, Ai-li S. "Family Relations in Modern Chinese Fiction." In Freedman, ed., *Family and Kinship in Chinese Society,* 87–120.

Chow Tze-tsung. "The Early History of the Chinese Word *Shih* (Poetry)." In Chow, ed., *Wen-lin: Studies in the Chinese Humanities.* Madison: University of Wisconsin Press, 1968, 151–210.

Chü, Tung-tsu. *Law and Society in Imperial China.* Paris: Mouton, 1961.

Clunas, Craig. *Fruitful Sites: Garden Culture in Ming Dynasty China.* Durham: Duke University Press, 1996.

——. *Superfluous Things: Material Culture and Social Status in Early Modern China.* Cambridge: Polity Press, 1991.

Cohen, Robert. *Giraudoux: Three Faces of Destiny.* Chicago: University of Chicago Press, 1968.

Collier, Jane F., and Sylvia J. Yanagisako, eds. *Gender and Kinship: Essays Toward a Unified Analysis.* Stanford: Stanford University Press, 1987.

Cooper, Eugene, and Meng Zhang. "Patterns of Cousin Marriage in Rural Zhejiang and in *The Dream of the Red Chamber.*" *Journal of Asian Studies* 52.1 (1993): 90–106.

Daniels, Marvin. "The Dynamics of Morbid Envy in the Etiology and Treatment of Chronic Learning Disabilities." *Psychoanalytic Review* 51 (1964): 45–57.

Demiéville, Paul. "Le miroir spirituel." *Sinologica* 1 (1948): 112–137 (reprinted in his *Choix d'études bouddhiques* [Leiden: Brill, 1973], 131–156).

——. "The Mirror of the Mind." Neal Donner, trans. In Gregory, ed., *Sudden and Gradual,* 13–40.

——. "Le Tch'an et la poésie chinoise." *Hermès* 7 (1970): 123–136 (reprinted in his *Choix d'études bouddhiques,* 456–469).

Dikötter, Frank, ed. *Sex, Culture and Modernity in China: Medical Science and the Construction of Sexual Identities in the Early Republican Period.* London: Hurst, 1995.

Dong, Lorraine. "The Creation and Life of Cui Ying-ying." 2 vols. Ph.D. dissertation, University of Washington, 1978.

——. "The Many Faces of Cui Ying-ying." In Richard W. Guisso and Stanley Johannesen, eds., *Women in China: Current Directions in Historical Scholarship*. Youngstown, NY: Philo Press, 1981, 71–98.

Eberhard, Wolfram. *Guilt and Sin in Traditional China*. Berkeley: University of California Press, 1967.

Ebrey, Patricia Buckley. *Confucianism and Family Rituals in Imperial China: A Social History of Writing about Rites*. Princeton: Princeton University Press, 1991.

——. *The Inner Quarters: Marriage and the Lives of Chinese Women in the Sung Period*. Berkeley: University of California Press, 1993.

——. "Women, Marriage and the Family in Chinese History." In Paul S. Ropp, ed., *Heritage of China: Contemporary Perspectives on Chinese Civilization*. Berkeley: University of California Press, 1990.

Ebrey, Patricia Buckley, and James Watson, eds. *Kinship Organization in Late Imperial China*. Berkeley: University of California Press, 1986.

Edwards, Louise P. *Men and Women in Qing China: Gender in the Red Chamber Dream*. Leiden: Sinica Leidensica [Brill], 1994.

Egan, Ronald. "The Controversy over Music and 'Sadness' and Changing Conceptions of the *Qin* in Middle Period China." *Harvard Journal of Asian Studies (HJAS)* 57.1 (June 1997): 5–66.

Elman, Benjamin A. *Classicism, Politics and Kinship: The Ch'ang-chou School of New Text Confucianism in Late Imperial China*. Berkeley: University of California Press, 1990.

Elman, Benjamin A., and Alexander Woodside, eds. *Education and Society in Late Imperial China 1600–1900*. Berkeley: University of California Press, 1994.

Farquhar, Judith. "Multiplicity, Point of View and Responsibility in Traditional Chinese Healing." In Dikötter, ed., *Sex, Culture and Modernity in China*, 78–99.

——. *Knowing Practice: The Clinical Encounter in Chinese Medicine*. Boulder: Westview Press, 1994.

Fauré, Bernard. *Chan Insights and Oversights: An Epistomological Critique of the Chan Tradition*. Princeton: Princeton University Press, 1993.

——. *The Rhetoric of Immediacy: A Cultural Critique of Chan/Zen Buddhism*. Princeton: Princeton University Press, 1991.

Fêng, Han-yi. "The Chinese Kinship System." *HJAS* 2 (1937): 141–275.

Freedman, Maurice. *Lineage Organization in Southeastern China*. London: Athalone Press, 1958; rev. ed. 1965.

——. *The Study of Chinese Society: Essays of Maurice Freedman*. Stanford: Stanford University Press, 1979.

Freedman, Maurice, ed. *Family and Kinship in Chinese Society*. Stanford: Stanford University Press, 1970.

——. *Social Organizations: Essays Presented to Raymond Firth*. London: Cass, 1967.

French, Herbert. *French's Index of Differential Diagnosis*. 12th ed., ed. F. Dudley Hart. Bristol: Wright, 1985.

Furth, Charlotte. "Blood, Body and Gender: Medical Images of the Female Condition in China 1600–1850." *Chinese Science* 7 (1986): 43–66.

——. "The Patriarch's Legacy: Household Instructions and the Transmission of Orthodox Values." In Liu Kwang-ching, ed., *Orthodoxy in Late Imperial China*. Berkeley: University of California Press, 1990, 187–211.

Gallin, Bernard. "Cousin Marriage in China." *Ethnology* 2 (1963): 104–108.

Giraudoux, Jean. *La Guerre de Troie n'aura pas lieu*. Paris: L'Illustration, 1935.

Gracey, Douglas R., and Whitney W. Addington. *Discussions in Patient Management: Tuberculosis*. Garden City, NY: Medical Examination Publishing Company, 1979.

Graham, A.C. *The Book of Lieh-tzu*. New York: Columbia University Press, 1960.

Gregory, Peter, ed. *Sudden and Gradual: Approaches to Enlightenment in Chinese Thought*. Honolulu: University Press of Hawaii, 1987.

Guy, R. Kent. *The Emperor's Four Treasuries: Scholars and the State in the Late Ch'ien-lung Era*. Cambridge: Council on East Asian Studies, Harvard University, 1987.

Hallowell, Edward M., and John J. Ratey. *Driven to Distraction: Coping with Attention Deficit Disorder from Childhood Through Adulthood*. New York: Pantheon, 1994.

Hamilton, Robyn. "The Pursuit of Fame: Luo Qilan (1775–1813?) and the Debates About Women and Talent in Eighteenth Century Jiangnan." *Late Imperial China* 18.1 (June 1997): 39–71.

Han, Pao-teh. *External Forms and Internal Visions: The Story of Chinese Landscape Design*. Carl Shen, trans. Taipei: Youth Cultural Enterprise, 1992.

Hanan, Patrick, trans. *The Carnal Prayer Mat*, by Li Yü. New York: Ballantine, 1990.

——. *The Chinese Vernacular Story*. Cambridge: Harvard University Press, 1981.

Hartman, Charles. *Han Yü and the T'ang Search for Unity*. Princeton: Princeton University Press, 1986.

Hawkes, David, ed. and trans. *The Story of the Stone*: vol. 1, *The Golden Days* (London: Penguin, 1973); vol. 2, *The Crab-Flower Club* (London: Penguin, 1977); vol. 3, *The Warning Voice* (London: Penguin, 1980).

——. "*The Story of the Stone*: A Symbolist Novel." *Renditions* 25 (spring 1986): 6–17.

Hegel, Robert E. *The Novel in Seventeenth Century China*. New York: Columbia University Press, 1981.

Hegel, Robert E., and Richard C. Hessney, eds. *Expressions of Self in Chinese Literature.* New York: Columbia University Press, 1985.

Hightower, James. *The Poetry of T'ao Ch'ien.* Oxford: Clarendon Press, 1970.

——. "Yüan Chen and 'The Story of Ying-ying,' " *HJAS* 33 (1973): 90–123.

Hsia, C. T. *The Classic Chinese Novel: A Critical Introduction.* New York: Columbia University Press, 1968.

——. "Love and Compassion in *The Dream of the Red Chamber.*" *Criticism* 5 (summer 1963): 261–271.

Hsieh, Andrew C. T., and Jonathan Spence. "Suicide and the Family in Pre-Modern Chinese Society." In Kleinman and Lin, eds., *Normal and Abnormal Behavior in Chinese Culture,* 29–47.

Hsiung Ping-chen. "Constructed Emotions: The Bond Between Mothers and Sons in Late Imperial China." *Late Imperial China* 15.1 (1994): 87–117.

Hsu, Francis L. K. "The Myth of Chinese Family Size." *American Journal of Sociology* 48.5 (March 1943): 555–562.

——. "Observations on Cross-Cousin Marriage in China." *American Anthropologist* 47.1 (1945): 83–103.

Huang, Martin W. "The Dilemma of Chinese Lyricism and the Qing Literati Novel." Ph.D. dissertation, Stanford University, 1991.

——. *Literati and Self-Re/Presentation: Autobiographical Sensibility in the Eighteenth Century Chinese Novel.* Stanford: Stanford University Press, 1995.

——. "Notes Towards a Poetics of Characterization in the Traditional Chinese Novel: *Hung-lou Meng* as Paradigm." *Tamkang Review* 21.1 (autumn 1990): 1–27.

Hume, Edward H. *The Chinese Way in Medicine.* Baltimore: Johns Hopkins University Press, 1940.

Hyatt, Richard. *Chinese Herbal Medicine: Ancient Art and Modern Science.* New York: Schocken Books, 1978.

Isshu, Miura, and Ruth Fuller Sasaki. *The Zen Koan: The History of the Koan and Koan Study in Rinzai (Lin-chi) Zen.* New York: Harcourt Brace and World, 1967.

Jaschok, Maria. *Concubines and Bondservants: The Social History of a Chinese Custom.* London: Zed Press, 1988.

Johnson, David; Andrew J. Nathan; and Evelyn S. Rawski, eds. *Popular Culture in Late Imperial China.* Berkeley: University of California Press, 1985.

Johnston, Joseph A., M.D. *Nutritional Studies in Adolescent Girls and Their Relation to Tuberculosis.* Springfield, IL: Charles C. Thomas, 1953.

Kahn, Harold. *Monarchy in the Emperor's Eyes: Image and Reality in the Ch'ien-lung Reign.* Cambridge: Harvard University Press, 1971.

Kao, Yu-kung. "The Aesthetics of Regulated Verse." In Lin and Owen, eds., *The Vitality of the Lyric Voice*, 332–385.

——. "Lyric Vision in the Chinese Narrative Tradition: A Reading of *Hung-lou Meng* and *Ju-lin Wai-shih*." In Plaks, ed., *Chinese Narrative*, 227–243.

Kasulis, Thomas P.; Roger T. Ames; and Winal Dassanayake, eds. *Self as Body in Asian Theory and Practice*. Albany: State University of New York Press, 1993.

——. *Zen Action, Zen Person*. Honolulu: University Press of Hawaii, 1981.

Keswick, Maggie. *The Chinese Garden: History, Art and Architecture*. New York: Rizzoli, 1978.

Keys, John D. *Chinese Herbs: Their Botany, Chemistry and Pharmacodynamics*. Rutland, VT: Charles E. Tuttle, 1976.

King, Helen. "Green Sickness: Hippocrates, Galen and the Origins of the 'Disease of Virgins.' " *International Journal of the Classical Tradition* 2.3 (winter 1996): 372–387.

Kleinman, Arthur, ed. *Culture and Healing in Asian Societies: Anthropological, Psychiatric and Public Health Studies*. Cambridge, MA: Schenkman, 1978.

Kleinman, Arthur, and Lin Tsung-yi, eds. *Normal and Abnormal Behavior in Chinese Culture*. Dordrecht, Netherlands: D. Reidel, 1981.

Knoerle, Jeanne. *"The Dream of the Red Chamber": A Critical Study*. Bloomington: Indiana University Press, 1972.

Ko, Dorothy. *Teachings of the Inner Chambers: Women and Culture in Seventeenth Century China*. Stanford: Stanford University Press, 1994.

Lang, Olga. *Chinese Family and Society*. New Haven: Yale University Press, 1946.

Lee, Peter H. *Celebration of Continuity: Themes in Classic East Asian Poetry*. Cambridge: Harvard University Press, 1979.

Legge, James. *The Chinese Classics*, vol. 5, *The Ch'un Ts'ew with the Tso Chuen*. Rev. ed., Shanghai: Mer Sang Press, 1935.

Levy, Dore J. "The Chiming of the Void: Poetry and Liberation in *The Story of the Stone*." *Common Knowledge* 6.3 (winter 1997): 99–114.

——. *Chinese Narrative Poetry: The Late Han Through T'ang Dynasties*. Durham: Duke University Press, 1988.

——. "Transforming Archetypes in Chinese Poetry and Painting: The Case of Ts'ai Yen." *Asia Major*, 3d series, 6.2 (1993): 147–168.

——. "Why Bao-yu Can't Concentrate: Attention Deficit Disorder in *The Story of the Stone*." *Literature and Medicine* 13.2 (fall 1994): 255–273.

Levy, Marion J., Jr. "Some Aspects of the Analysis of Family Structure." In Ansley J. Coale, Lloyd A. Fallers, Marion J. Levy, Jr., David M. Schneider, and Silvan Tompkins, eds., *Aspects of the Analysis of Family Structure*. Princeton: Princeton University Press, 1965.

——. *The Family Revolution in Modern China*. Cambridge: Harvard University Press, 1949.

——. *Modernization and the Structure of Societies*. Princeton: Princeton University Press, 1966; repr., New Brunswick: Transaction Publishers, 1996.

——. *The Structure of Society*. Princeton: Princeton University Press, 1952.

Li, San-pao. "Ch'ing Cosmology and Popular Precepts." In Smith and Kwok, eds., *Cosmology, Ontology, and Human Efficacy*, 113–139.

Li, Wai-yee. *Enchantment and Disenchantment: Love and Illusion in Chinese Literature*. Princeton: Princeton University Press, 1993.

——. "The Rhetoric of Spontaneity in Late Ming Literature." *Ming Studies* 35 (August 1995): 32–52.

Li, Xuerong, Lin-yan Su, Brenda D. Townes, and Christopher K. Varley. "Diagnosis of Attention Deficit Disorder with Hyperactivity in Chinese Boys." *Journal of the American Academy of Child and Adolescent Psychiatry* 28.4 (1989): 497–500.

Lin, Keh-ming. "Traditional Chinese Medical Beliefs and Their Relevance for Mental Illness and Psychiatry." In Kleinman and Lin, *Normal and Abnormal Behavior in Chinese Culture*, 95–111.

Lin, Shuen-fu. "Chia Pao-yu's First Visit to the Land of Illusion: An Analysis of a Literary Dream in an Interdisciplinary Perspective." *CLEAR* 14 (1991): 77–106.

Lin, Shuen-fu and Stephen Owen, eds. *The Vitality of the Lyric Voice: Shih Poetry from the Late Han to the T'ang*. Princeton: Princeton University Press, 1986.

Lin, Yueh-hua. *The Golden Wing: A Sociological Study of Chinese Familism*. New York: Oxford University Press, 1947.

Liu, Hui-chen Wang. *The Traditional Chinese Clan Rules*. Glückstadt: J. J. Augustin for the Association of Asian Studies, 1959.

Liu, James J. Y. *Chinese Theories of Literature*. Chicago: University of Chicago Press, 1975.

——. *The Interlingual Critic*. Bloomington: Indiana University Press, 1982.

Lynn, Richard John. "The Sudden and the Gradual in Chinese Poetry Criticism." In Gregory, ed., *Sudden and Gradual*, 381–427.

——. "The Talent-Learning Polarity in Chinese Poetics: Yen Yü and the Later Tradition," *CLEAR* 5 (1983): 157–184.

Macioccia, Giovanni. *The Foundations of Chinese Medicine: a Comprehensive Text for Acupuncturists and Herbalists*. Edinburgh and London: Churchill Livingstone, 1989.

Mann, Susan. "Grooming a Daughter for Marriage: Brides and Wives in the Mid-Ch'ing Period." In Watson and Ebrey, eds., *Marriage and Inequality in Chinese Society*, 204–230.

——. *Precious Records: Women in China's Long Eighteenth Century.* Stanford: Stanford University Press, 1997.

McKnight, Brian E. *The Quality of Mercy: Amnesties and Traditional Chinese Justice.* Honolulu: University Press of Hawaii, 1981.

——. *Law and Order in Sung China.* Cambridge: Cambridge University Press, 1992.

McMahon, R. K. *Causality and Containment in Seventeenth Century Chinese Fiction.* Leiden: Brill, 1987.

——. "The Classic 'Beauty-Scholar' Romance and the Superiority of the Talented Woman." In Zito and Barlow, eds., *Body, Subject and Power in China,* 227–252.

——. "Eroticism in Late Ming and Early Qing Fiction: The Beauteous Realm and the Sexual Battlefield." *T'oung Pao* 73 (1987): 217–264.

——. *Misers, Shrews and Polygamists: Sexuality and Male-Female Relations in Eighteenth Century Chinese Fiction.* Durham: Duke University Press, 1995.

Merton, Robert K. *On Theoretical Sociology: Five Essays, Old and New.* New York: Free Press, 1949.

——. *Social Theory and Social Structure.* Glencoe, IL: Free Press 1957. Revised and enlarged ed., New York: Free Press, 1961.

Miller, Lucien M. *Masks of Fiction in Dream of the Red Chamber: Myth, Mimesis, and Persona.* Tuscon: University of Arizona Press, 1975.

Minford, John. "The Last Forty Chapters of The Story of the Stone: A Literary Appraisal." Ph.D. dissertation, Australian National University, 1980.

Minford, John, ed. and trans. *The Story of the Stone*: vol. 4, *The Debt of Tears* (Harmondsworth: Penguin, 1982); vol. 5, *The Dreamer Wakes* (Harmondsworth: Penguin, 1986).

Mote, F. W. *The Poet Kao Ch'i.* Princeton: Princeton University Press, 1962.

Motsch, Monika. "The Mirror and Chinese Aesthetics: A Study of the *Honglou meng.*" *Ming Qing yanjiu* (1996): 117–136.

Naquin, Susan, and Evelyn S. Rawski. *Chinese Society in the Eighteenth Century.* New Haven: Yale University Press, 1987.

Needham, Joseph, with Lu Gwei-djen and a special contribution from Huang Hsing-tsung. *Science and Civilization in China.* Vol. 6, part 1, *Botany.* Cambridge: Cambridge University Press, 1986.

Newman, C. Janet, Cynthia Fox Dember, and Othilda Krug. " 'He Can But He Won't': A Psychodynamic Study of So-Called 'Gifted Underachievers,'" *Psychoanalytic Study of the Child* 28 (1973): 83–129.

Ng, Vivien W. *Madness in Late Imperial China: From Illness to Deviance.* Norman: University of Oklahoma Press, 1990.

Ocko, Jonathan. "Hierarchy and Harmony: Family Conflict as Seen in Ch'ing Legal Cases." In Liu, ed., *Orthodoxy in Late Imperial China*, 212–230.

O'Flaherty, Wendy Doniger. *Dreams, Illusions and Other Realities*. Chicago: University of Chicago Press, 1984.

Oliviero, Annemarie, and Pat Lauderdale. "Therapeutic States and Attention Deficits: Differential Cross-Cultural Diagnostics and Treatments." *International Journal of Politics, Culture and Society* 10.2 (winter 1996): 355–373.

Owen, Stephen. *The Poetry of the Early T'ang*. New Haven: Yale University Press, 1977.

——. *Readings in Chinese Literary Thought*. Cambridge: Council on East Asian Studies, Harvard University, 1992.

——. *Traditional Chinese Poetry and Poetics: Omen of the World*. Madison: University of Wisconsin Press, 1985.

Perot, Michelle, ed. Georges Duby and Philippe Ariès, gen. eds. *A History of Private Life*: vol. 4, *From the Fires of Revolution to the Great War*. Cambridge: Belknap Press of Harvard University Press, 1987.

Plaks, Andrew H. *Archetype and Allegory in the "Dream of the Red Chamber."* Princeton: Princeton University Press, 1976.

——. "Towards a Critical Theory of Chinese Narrative." In Plaks, ed., *Chinese Narrative*, 309–352.

Plaks, Andrew H., ed. *Chinese Narrative: Critical and Theoretical Essays*. Princeton: Princeton University Press, 1977.

Pollack, David. "Linked-verse Poetry in China: A Study of Associative Linking in *Lien-chü* Poetry with Emphasis on the Poems of Han Yü and His Circle." Ph.D. dissertation, University of California at Berkeley, 1976.

Porkert, Manfred. *The Theoretical Foundations of Traditional Chinese Medicine: Systems of Correspondence*. Cambridge: MIT Press, 1974.

——. With Dr. Christian Ullmann. Translated and adapted by Mark Jowson. *Chinese Medicine*. New York: William Morrow, 1982.

Praz, Mario. *La carne, la morte et il diavolo nella letteratura romantica*. Milan and Rome: La Cultura, 1930; trans. Angus Davidson as *The Romantic Agony*. London: Oxford University Press, 1970.

Rawski, Evelyn; David Johnson; and Andrew Nathan, eds. *Popular Culture in Late Imperial China*. Berkeley: University of California Press, 1985.

Rolston, David, ed. *How to Read the Chinese Novel*. Princeton: Princeton University Press, 1990.

Ropp, Paul S. "A Confucian View of Women in the Ch'ing Period—Literati Laments for Women in the *Ch'ing Shi tuo*." *Chinese Studies* 10.2 (1992): 399–435.

——. "Love, Literacy, and Laments: Themes of Women Writers in Late Imperial China." *Women's History Review* 2.1 (1993): 107–141.

——. "The Seeds of Change: Reflections on the Condition of Women in the Early and Mid Ch'ing," *Signs* 2.1 (1976): 5–23.

Ruey-Shuang, Francis. *Ling shu jing: The "Silent" Art of Ancient China: Historical Analysis of the Intellectual and Philosophical Influences of the Earliest Medical Corpus, Ling Shu Jing.* Taipei: Linking, 1985.

Sacks, Oliver. *An Anthropologist on Mars: Seven Paradoxical Tales.* New York: Knopf, 1995.

——. *The Island of the Colorblind.* New York: Knopf, 1996.

——. *The Man Who Mistook His Wife for a Hat and Other Clinical Tales.* New York: Summit Books, 1988.

Saussy, Haun. "Reading and Folly in the *Dream of the Red Chamber.*" *CLEAR* 9 (1987): 25–48.

——. "Women's Writing Before and Within the *Hong lou meng.*" In Widmer and Chang, eds., *Writing Women in Late Imperial China,* 285–305.

Scott, Mary. "The Image of the Garden in *Jin Ping Mei* and *Honglou meng.*" *CLEAR* 8 (1986): 83–94.

Simon, Harvey B. *Scientific American Medicine,* vol. 3. New York: Scientific American, 1980.

Sivin, Nathan. "Emotional Counter-Therapy." In Sivin, ed., *Medicine, Philosophy and Religion in Ancient China: Researches and Reflections.* 2 vols. Aldershot, UK, and Brookfield, VT: Variorum, 1995, vol. 2, 1–19.

——. *Science in Ancient China: Researches and Reflections.* Ann Arbor: Science Medicine and Technology in the East Series, Center for Chinese Studies, 1987.

——. *Traditional Medicine in Contemporary China.* Ann Arbor: Science Medicine and Technology in the East Series, Center for Chinese Studies 1987.

Smith, Frederick Porter. *Chinese Materia Medica: Vegetable Kingdom.* 2d ed. edited by Daven Wei. Taipei: Ku-ting, 1969.

——. *Contributions Towards the Materia Medica and Natural History of Chinese: For the Use of Medical Missionaries and Native Medical Students.* Shanghai: American Presbyterian Mission Press, 1871.

Smith, Richard J., and D.W.Y. Kwok, eds. *Cosmology, Ontology, and Human Efficacy: Essays in Chinese Thought.* Honolulu: University Press of Hawaii, 1993.

Sontag, Susan. *Illness as Metaphor.* New York: Farrar, Straus and Giroux, 1978.

Spence, Jonathan. *Ts'ao Yin and the K'ang-hsi Emperor: Bondservant and Master.* New Haven: Yale University Press, 1966.

Stead, W. W. "Pathogenesis of the Sporadic Case of Tuberculosis." *New England Journal of Medicine* 277 (1967): 1005–1016.

Stead, W. W., and J. H. Bates. "Evidence of a 'Silent' Bacillema in Primary Tuberculosis." *Annals of Internal Medicine* 74 (1971): 552–569.

Still, George F. "Some Abnormal Psychical Conditions in Children." *Lancet* (April 1902): 1008–1012, 1077–1082, 1163—1168.

Stone, Lawrence. *Family and Fortune: Studies in Aristocratic Finance in the Sixteenth and Seventeenth Centuries.* Oxford: Clarendon Press, 1973.

Traditional Chinese Medicine and Pharmacology. CD-ROM. Hopkins, MN: Hopkins Technology, 1996.

Trilling, James. "Medieval Interlace Ornament: The Making of a Cross-Cultural Idiom." *Arte Medievale*, 2d series, 9.2 (1995): 59–86.

Tu, Wei-ming. "Embodying the Universe: A Note on Confucian Self-Realization." In Ames et al., eds., *Self as Person in Asian Theory and Practice*, 177–186.

Unschuld, Paul U. *Medicine in China: A History of Ideas.* Berkeley: University of California Press, 1985.

——. *Medicine in China: A History of Pharmaceuticals.* Berkeley: University of California Press, 1986.

——. *Nan ching. A Classic of Difficult Issues.* Berkeley: University of California Press, 1986.

Vila, Anne C. *Enlightenment and Pathology: Sensibility in the Literature and Medicine of Eighteenth-Century France.* Baltimore: Johns Hopkins University Press, 1998.

Visvader, John, and William C. Doub. "The Problem of Desire and Emotions in Taoism and Ch'an." In Whalen Lai and Lewis R. Lancaster, eds., *Early Ch'an in China and Tibet.* Berkeley: Berkeley Buddhist Studies Series, 1983, 281–297.

Vitiello, Giovanni. "The Fantastic Journey of an Ugly Boy: Homosexuality and Salvation in Late Ming Pornography." *positions: east asia cultures critique* 4.2 (fall 1996): 291–320.

Vrettos, Athena. *Somatic Fictions: Imagining Illness in Victorian Culture.* Stanford: Stanford University Press, 1995.

Wakeman, Frederick, Jr., and Carol Grant, eds. *Conflict and Control in Late Imperial China.* Berkeley: University of California Press, 1970.

——. *The Great Enterprise: The Manchu Reconstruction of Imperial Order in Seventeenth Century China.* Berkeley: University of California Press, 1985.

Waley, Arthur. *The Book of Songs.* London: George Allen and Unwin, 1937.

——. *Yuan Mei: Eighteenth Century Chinese Poet.* London: George Allen and Unwin, 1956.

Waltner, Ann. "Breaking the Law: Family Violence, Gender and Hierarchy in the Legal Code of the Ming Dynasty." *Ming Studies* 36 (1996): 29–43.

——. "Early Chinese Narrative: The *Tso-chuan* as Example." In Plaks, ed., *Chinese Narrative*, 3–20.

——. "On Not Becoming a Heroine: Lin Dai-yu and Cui Ying-ying." *Signs* 15 (1989): 61–78.

Wang, Jing. *The Story of Stone: Ancient Chinese Stone Lore and the Stone Symbolism of "Dream of the Red Chamber," "Water Margin," and "The Journey to the West."* Durham: Duke University Press, 1992.

Wang, John C. Y. "The Chih-yen-chai Commentary and *Dream of the Red Chamber*: A Literary Study." In Adele Rickett, ed., *Chinese Approaches to Literature from Confucius to Liang Ch'i-ch'ao.* Princeton: Princeton University Press, 1978, 189–220.

Watson, James L. "Chinese Kinship Reconsidered: Anthropological Perspectives on Historical Research." *China Quarterly*, no. 92 (1982): 589–622.

Watson, Rubie S., and Patricia Buckley Ebrey, eds. *Marriage and Inequality in Chinese Society.* Berkeley: University of California Press, 1991.

Wender, Paul H. *The Hyperactive Child, Adolescent, and Adult.* New York and London: Oxford University Press, 1987.

——. *Minimal Brain Dysfunction in Children.* New York: John Wiley and Sons, 1971.

West, Stephen H., and Wilt L. Idema, eds. and trans. *Wang Shifu: The Moon and the Zither: The Story of the Western Wing, With a Study of Its Woodblock Illustration by Yao Daijun.* Berkeley: University of California Press, 1991.

Whalen, Carol K. "Attention Deficit and Hyperactivity Disorders." In T. H. Ollendick and M. Hersen, eds., *Handbook of Child Psychopathology.* New York: Plenum, 1989, 131–169.

Widmer, Ellen, and Kang-i Sun Chang, eds. *Writing Women in Late Imperial China.* Stanford: Stanford University Press, 1997.

Wolf, Arthur P., and Chien-shan Huang. *Marriage and Adoption in China, 1845–1945.* Stanford: Stanford University Press, 1980.

Wolf, Margery, and Roxanne Witke, eds. *Women in Chinese Society.* Stanford: Stanford University Press, 1975.

Wong, Chun-kit Joseph. *The Changing Chinese Family Pattern in Taiwan.* Taipei: Southern Materials Center, 1981.

Wong, Kam-ming. "Point of View and Feminism: Images of Women in *Honglou meng.*" In Anna Gerstlacher et al., eds., *Women and Literature in China.* Bochum: Brockmeyer, 1985, 29–97.

——. "Point of View, Norms, and Structure: *Hung-lou Meng* and Lyrical Fiction." In Plaks, ed., *Chinese Narrative*, 203–226.

Wong, Timothy. "Self and Society in T'ang Dynasty Love Tales." *Journal of the American Oriental Society* 99.1 (1979): 95–100.

Wright, Arthur F. *Buddhism in Chinese History*. Stanford: Stanford University Press, 1959.

Wu, Hung. "Beyond Stereotypes: The Twelve Beauties in Qing Court Art and the *Dream of the Red Chamber*." In Widmer and Chang, eds., *Writing Women in Late Imperial China*, 306–365.

Wu, Shih-Ch'ang. *On the Red Chamber Dream*. Oxford: Clarendon Press, 1961.

Yang, Winston L. Y., and Curtis P. Atkins. *Critical Essays on Chinese Fiction*. Hong Kong: Chinese University Press, 1980.

Yee, Angelina. "Counterpoise in *Honglou meng*." *HJAS* 50.2 (December 1990): 613–650.

——. "Self, Sexuality and Writing in *Honglou meng*." *HJAS* 55.2 (December 1995): 373–407.

Yoshitaka, Iriye. "Chinese Poetry and Zen." *Eastern Buddhist* 6.1 (May 1973): 54–67.

Yu, Anthony C. "Heroic Verse and Heroic Mission: Dimensions of the Epic in *HYC*." *Journal of Asian Studies* (JAS) 31 (1972): 879–897.

——. "Narrative Structure and the Problem of Ch. 9 in *HYC*." *JAS* 37 (1975): 295–311.

——. "The Quest of Brother Amor: Buddhist Intimations in *The Story of the Stone*." *HJAS* 49.1 (June 1989): 55–92.

——. *Rereading the Stone: Desire and the Making of Fiction in "Dream of the Red Chamber."* Princeton: Princeton University Press, 1997.

——. "Self and Family in the *Hung-lou Meng*: A New Look at Lin Tai-yü as Tragic Heroine." *CLEAR* 2 (1980): 199–201.

——. "The Stone of Fiction and the Fiction of Stone: Reflexivity and Religious Symbolism in *Hung-lou meng*." *Studies in Language and Literature* 4 (1990): 1–30.

Yu, Pauline. *The Reading of Imagery in the Chinese Poetic Tradition*. Princeton: Princeton University Press, 1987.

Yü, Ying-shih. "The Two Worlds of *Hung-lou Meng*." Diana Yü, trans. *Renditions* 2 (spring 1974): 5–21.

Zito, Angela, and Tani E. Barlow, eds. *Body, Subject and Power in China*. Chicago: University of Chicago Press, 1994.

actual patterns. *See* ideal and actual patterns

Adamantina (Miao-yu, resident nun in the Garden of Total Vision), 125–126, 145–147, 167–168n44

affinity of gold and jade (*jinyu yinyuan*), 14, 40–41, 51, 53, 64–65, 91, 147

affinity of wood and stone (*mushi yinyuan*), 41, 50, 64–65, 92–94, 96, 147

Allspice Court (*Hengwu yuan*, Bao-chai's residence), 109, 111

amenorrhea, 67, 72; *see also* illness

Aroma (Xi-ren, Bao-yu's principal maid), 51, 54, 81, 89, 92

attachment (*qing*), 9–12, 15, 19–22, 27, 104, 106, 139

attention deficit disorder: clinical description, 86–87; and hyper-activity, 86–88; as afflicting Jia Bao-yu, 86–99; as afflicting the author, 99–101

Aunt Zhao (Jia Zheng's concubine, mother of Tan-chun and Jia Huan), 47, 164–165n19

Bao-chai. *See* Xue Bao-chai

Bao-yu. *See* Jia Bao-yu

Big Jiao (Jiao Da, old Ning-guo family retainer), 30, 45

Bijoux. *See* Jiang Yu-han

Bo Juyi (772–846), 136

Book of Songs (*Shi jing*), 134–135

bondservants, 9; *see also* Jia family

Brother Amor (*Qing seng*), 11–12, 139–141; *see also* Vanitas

Buddhism: and spiritual transcendence, 2–4, 108, 155–156; and personal liberation, 9–10, 96–101; forms of practice, 125–126; poetry as vehicle, 126–128, 139–156 *passim; see also* Chan Buddhism

Calamity (Huo-qi, servant of Zhen Shi-yin), 150

Caltrop (Xue Pan's concubine, Zhen Shi-yin's daughter Ying-lian), 79, 120, 150, 153, 180–181n15

Cao Xue-qin (1715?–1763): as author, 1, 99–101, 103, 140–141, 155–156, 158n1; relation to Bao-yu, 86, 100–101, artistic purpose, 12, 104, 120–123, 140–141, 155–156; medical knowledge, 67–68

Cao Zhi (192–232), 105

causality, 14

Celestial Registers, 21, 44, 57, 61–62, 71, 96, 105, 137, 139, 142

Chan Buddhism, 139–141, 154–155, 179n2

Chang E (Goddess of the Moon), 132

Chapter 5, 4, 21–23, 43–45, 71, 105–106, 134, 142, 167–168n44

Cheng Weiyuan (1747?–?), 7
chlorosis. *See* greensickness
chrysanthemum poems, 116–118
civil service (examination system),
   20, 32
Cloud Maiden (*Zhenxia jiuyou*). *See*
   Shi Xiang-yun
concubines, 36–37, 47, 64, 164–
   165n19, 167–168n35
confiscation, 48–49, 58, 168n45–46
Confucianism, 3, 8–9, 18–19, 28, 65,
   151–153, 181–182n16
Confucius, 28, 119
consumption (*laozheng* or *laoqi zhi
   zheng*). *See* tuberculosis
Crab-Flower Club (*Haitang she*),
   113–123 *passim*
Crimson Pearl Flower (*Jiangzhu
   xiancao*), 10, 13–14, 40, 80, 85, 118,
   122–123, 132, 140, 147–149; *see also*
   Lin Dai-yu

Dai-yu. *See* Lin Dai-yu
Daguan yuan. See Garden of Total
   Vision
Dante, 4
Daoism. *See* Taoism
debt of tears (*huanlei*), 10, 40–42,
   80, 84, 148–149
debts of passion (*fengqing yuezhai*),
   73
Disenchantment (*Jinghuan xiangu*),
   21–22, 27, 40, 71–73, 89, 105, 137
Doctor Wang (Jia family physician), 84–85
Doctor Zhang. *See* Zhang You-shi
doubles, 23–24, 97–98, 123–125, 135,
   145
doctors, 67, 69–70, 81–85
drama, 118–119, 126–132; *see also*
   theatrical entertainments

"Dream of Golden Days" (*Honglou
   meng*), 21–23, 27, 105–106
dreams, 21–23, 25, 41, 50, 52, 105–106,
   161n32

Edwards, Louise, 167–8n45, 170n15
Embroidered Jackets, 58

femmes d'histoire (fatal beauties), 44,
   121
Fairy Disenchantment. *See*
   Disenchantment
Faithful (Yuan-yang, Grandmother
   Jia's personal maid), 45, 73,
   165n19
Feng Yuan (Ying-lian's betrothed),
   78–79
fengyue baojian. See Mirror for the
   Romantic
filial piety, 31, 33–34, 37–38
Fivey (Wu-er, one of Bao-yu's
   maids), 80
flowers, 113–117, 121–122, 134–136
fu (rhymeprose, rhapsody), 105

Galenic medicine, 70
Gao E (1740–1815?), 7
Garden of Total Vision (*Daguan
   yuan*, also called Prospect
   Garden): as microcosm, 4–5, 92,
   97, 103, 137; poetry inscriptions,
   106–112; as environment for
   romantic release, 112–113
Golden (Jin-chuan-er, Lady Wang's
   maid), 35–36, 49, 90
Goddess of the River Lo, 105
Gone with the Wind (Margaret
   Mitchell), 1
Grannie Liu (Liu Laolao), 69, 117–
   119, 129
Grandmother Jia (Jiamu), 30–39,

42–43, 47, 51–54, 58–60, 62–63, 83–84, 90–91, 96, 111, 115–117, 164–165n19, 165n22

Green Bower Hermitage, 125

Green Boy (*Yihong gongzi*). See Jia Bao-yu

greensickness (chlorosis), 10, 67–68

Greensickness Peak (*Qinggeng feng*), 10–11, 27, 32, 67, 95

gynecological disorders, 71–73; *see also* illness

Hall of Reunion (*Xingqin bieshu*), 109, 111, 122

Hawkes, David, 10, 21–22, 86, 110, 157n1, 159n14, 163n3, 174n1

Hippocratic medicine, 70

homosexuality, 74, 77–79

Honglou meng (*Dream of the Red Chamber*). See *The Story of the Stone*

hongxue ("Dream of the Red Chamber studies"), 4

House of Green Delights (*Yihong yuan*), 109, 111–112

"Hum-bum Song" (*Hengheng yun*), 153–155

hyperactivity. *See* attention deficit disorder

hyperactivity syndrome (*duodong zonghe zheng*), 87; *see also* attention deficit disorder

ideal and actual patterns, 4–5, 16–20, 27, 24, 28ff

illness: as allegory and metaphor, 67; and medical practice, 68–70; retributory, 69–71, 73–74, 79ff, 94–97; different kinds, including amenorrhea, 67, 72; gynocological disorders, 71–73; kidney

failure, 74; pneumonia, 74; *see also* attention deficit disorder, tuberculosis

illusion, 15, 19, 68, 137, 152

Impervioso (*Miaomiao zhenren*, Buddhist immortal), 2, 11, 15, 40–41, 61, 79, 81, 95, 125, 137, 139, 141, 149–151

incest, 44–46, 71–73, 166n31

incest taboo, 39, 44–46

intent (*zhi*), 103–104

Jade Casket (*Yuxia ji*), 69

Jia / *jia* (fiction, false), 14–16, 23

Jia Bao-yu: meaning of his name, 13; and the author, 86, 99–101; and his jade, 20–21, 32, 34, 54, 61–62, 136–137; affinity of gold and jade, 14, 40–41, 91–92; affinity of wood and stone, 92–94, 96; personal liberation, 1–2, 18, 23–24, 50, 61–65, 105–106; as incarnation of the Stone, 11–14, 24–26, 40–42, 139, 147; sexual initiation, 21–23, 43–44; as a double, 23–24, 97–98, 123–124 (*see also* Shi Xiang-yun, Zhen Bao-yu); attention deficit disorder, 86–101 *passim*; and poetry, 106–115, 117–118, 120, 122–123, 126–128, 134–136, 142–147; and his father, 34–39, 63, 82, 92–94, 96–97, and Bao-chai, 25–26, 50, 62–63, 91–92, 95–96, 126–128; and Dai-yu, 25–26, 40–43, 50–58, 79–95 *passim*, 131–132, 141–149, 111, 113, 123, 127–129, 136–137, 143–149

Jia family, 18–20, 53; origins, 8–9; downfall, 28, 58–61, 152

Jia Dai-ru (schoolmaster, grandfather of Jia Rui), 74, 77–78

Jia Huan (son of Jia Zheng and Aunt Zhao), 31, 35–36, 47, 164–165n19

Jia Jing (abdicated head of the Ning-guo House, father of Jia Zhen), 27, 29

Jia Lan (son of Li Wan, grandson of Jia Zheng), 31, 65

Jia Lian (son of Jia She, husband of Wang Xi-feng), 31, 47, 58, 71, 75, 87

Jia Qiang (foster brother of Jia Lian), 75

Jia Rong (son of Jia Zhen, husband of Qin Ke-qing), 31, 44–46, 70, 72–75

Jia Rui (grandson of Jia Dai-ru), 74–78, 82

Jia She (eldest son of Grandmother Jia, nominal head of the Rong-guo House), 58, 60–61, 65, 87–88, 164–165n19

Jia Yu-cun ("false discourse," distant kinsman of the Jia family), 14–15, 28, 34, 98

Jia Zhen (head of the Ning-guo House, father of Jia Rong), 31, 37, 44–46, 58, 60, 65, 71, 73, 87–88

Jia Zheng (second son of Grandmother Jia, father of Jia Bao-yu), 28, 31, 33–39, 47, 53–54, 56, 58–61, 63–64, 92–94, 96, 106–111, 133–134, 164–165n19

Jia Zhu (deceased first son of Jia Zheng), 31, 47

Jiamu. See Grandmother Jia

Jiang Yu-han (stage name, "Bijoux"), 36, 164n17

jiazhang (head of household), 28, 38–39, 61

Jihusou. See Odd Tablet

Kao, Yu-kung, 157n3–4

karma, 14, 41, 69–70, 74, 77, 111, 146–147, 149, 160n19

Ke-qing (Disenchantment's sister), 22; see also Qin Ke-qing

Lady Allspice (Hengwu jun). See Xue Bao-chai

Lady Wang (Wang Furen, mother of Bao-yu), 36–38, 47, 49, 51, 80, 93, 135

Lady Xing (wife of Jia She), 47–49

Land of Illusion (Taizu huanjing), 1, 4, 15, 21–23, 40, 80, 85, 89, 97, 137, 140–143, 147, 149

laonian (elder), 31

Leng Zi-xing (colleague of Jia Yu-cun), 28–29, 34

Levy, Marion J. Jr., 16–18, 161n26

Li, Wai-yee, 159n10, 159n12, 175n7

Li Wan (mother of Jia Lan), 47–48, 66, 112–115, 118–119

Lin Dai-yu: as Crimson Pearl Flower, 13–14, 25–26, 56, 80, 85, 118, 122, 132; affinity of wood and stone, 41, 50, 64–65, 92–94, 96; dreams, 50, 52, 83; garden inscriptions, 113; crab-flower poems, 113–115; chrysanthemum poems, 117–118; "Flower of the Peach," 121–123; linked verse, 123–126; burial mound for flowers, 143–145; poem suite for qin, 145–147; handkerchief poems, 82, 148–149; illness, 79–85; death, 55–56, 64, 66, 105, 111, 113, 149; and Bao-chai, 25–26, 40–41, 55–56, 82–83, 115, 119, 122, 129–131; and Bao-yu, 25–26, 40–43, 50–58, 79–95 passim, 127–129, 131–132, 141–149

Liu Laolao. *See* Grannie Liu

lovesickness (*xinbing*), 54, 67, 84; *see also* greensickness

lust of the mind (*yiyin*) 22, 40, 89

lyric aesthetics, 1–2

Manchus, 1, 8–9, 28

materia medica, 67*ff*

medicine: Chinese traditional practice and methods of diagnosis, 69*ff*, pharmacopia, 72–76, 81; prescriptions, 83, 85; *see also* illness

Mencius, 114, 120

Minford, John, 158*n*2, 174*n*1

Mirror for the Romantic (*fengyue baojian*), 77–78, 170*n*18

mirrors, 23, 77–78, 82, 98, 111, 134

Mudanting (*The Peony Pavilion*). *See* Return of the Soul

Mysterioso (*Mangmang dashi*, Taoist immortal), 2, 9, 15, 76–78, 141, 149–153

Naiad's House (*Xiaoxiang guan*), 112

names, 113

Nenuphar (Ou-guan, member of the Jias' acting troop), 132–133

Nightingale (Zi-juan, Dai-yu's maid), 52–53, 56–57, 129, 180–181*n*15

Ning-guo House, 8–9, 28–30, 47, 58–59, 74, 87, 163*n*3

obsessive longing (*chiqing*), 89

Odd Tablet, 7, 99–100, 113

omens, 54, 63–64

Palace of Pearls (*Zhurei ji*), 132

Pathway to Mysteries (*Qujing tongyou*), 109

Peach Blossom Spring (*Taohua yuan*), 121–122

Peach-Flower Club (*Taohua she*), 123

peony, 134–135, 178*n*40

Peony Pavilion (*Mudan ting*). *See* Return of the Soul

perfect listener (*zhiyin*), 104, 115, 143–147, 175*n*4

pharmacopia. *See* medicine

Plaks, Andrew H., 8, 89, 108, 158*n*3, 175*n*11

poetry: as social practice for public career, 103–111; garden inscriptions, 106–111, and Chan Buddhism, 139–141; as vehicle for enlightenment, 21–22, 126–128, 139–156 *passim*; *see also* Crab-Flower Club, Peach-Flower club, Jia Bao-yu, Lin Dai-yu, Xue Bao-chai

Precinct of the Celestial Visitant (*Tianxian baojing*). *See* Hall of Reunion

prescriptions. *See* medicine

Prospect Garden. *See* Garden of Total Vision

Qin Ke-qing (Qin-shi), 43–47, 53, 58, 71–73, 105, 121

qing. *See* attachment

Qing dynasty (1644–1911), 1, 8–9

Qiao-jie (daughter of Xi-feng), 63

reading the pulse (*maili*), 71–72

real (*you*) and not-real (*wu*), 14, 16–19, 78, 155

Red Inkstone (*Zhiyan zhai*), 7, 99–100, 113, 180*n*5

reincarnation, 70

retributory illness (*yuannie zhi zheng*), 5, 69–70

Return of the Soul (*Huanhun ji*), 118–119, 128–129, 131

River Queen (*Xiaoxiang feizi*). *See* Lin Dai-yu

Romance of the Western Chamber (*Xixiang ji*), 92, 118–119, 128–131

Rong-guo House, 8–9, 28–30, 47, 58, 74, 87

rhyme cards (*yunpai xiazi*), 114

samsara (cycle of rebirth), 10

se (material form), 10, 22

sexual passion, 72, 78, 161n32

sexual segregation, 33

Shakespeare, 1, 4

Shi Xiang-yun (Grandmother Jia's great-niece), 55, 66, 81, 92, 105, 115–118, 123–127, 176n16

Sima Qian (145–90 B.C.E.), 7

Skybright (Qing-wen), 80, 135–136, 148

Spence, Jonathan, 168n45

Still, George F., 86, 171–172n29, 172n31

Stone: as narrator, 11, 15, 19, 27, 64, 139, 155; as jade, 15, 139; under Greensickness Peak, 95; *see also* Jia Bao-yu

Story of the Stone (*Shitou ji*, also known as *Honglou meng*): authorship and textual history, 1, 7, 103; as cultural compendium, 7–9, 109; as roman à clef, 1, 86, 99–101, 114; as allegory, 3–5, 104; as social novel, 7, 27, 103–104; as autobiography, 7, 99–101, 120–121; as vehicle to enlightenment, 18–19, 139–141, 155–156; translation by Hawkes and Minford, 157n1

"Story of Ying-ying" (*Ying-ying zhuan*), 132

suicide, 44–46, 73, 168n45

Sweet-rice Village (*Daoxiang cun*), 109–110, 112

Taixu huanjing. *See* Land of Illusion

Tan-chun (daughter of Jia Zheng), 47–49, 90–91, 112–117, 164–165n19, 167–168n35

Taoism, 2–3, 12, 154–155

Tealeaf (Bao-yu's page), 90

theatrical entertainments, 42–43, 126–134

tuberculosis, 79–85, 105, 135–136

Two-in-one (Jian-mei). *See* Ke-qing

Ulysses (James Joyce), 1

Vanitas (*Kongkong daoren*, also known as Brother Amor), 11–12, 19, 43, 64–65, 139–141

vignettism, 2–4

Wang Furen. *See* Lady Wang

Wang Xi-feng (wife of Jia Lian), 30, 46–49, 53, 55, 58–59, 74–78, 118

"Won-done Song" (*Haoliao ge*), 149–154

world of the red dust (*hongchen shi*), 11, 16

Wu Zetian, 44

Xi-chun (sister of Jia Zhen), 57, 167–168n44

Xi-feng. *See* Wang Xi-feng

Xi Shi, 44, 121

Xixiang ji. *See* Romance of the Western Chamber

Xue Bao-chai: affinity of gold and jade, 14, 40–41, 147; as guardian of the Garden, 47–49, 167n36; and poetry, 104, 113–121, 126–128,

130–131, 144–145; and Bao-yu, 25–
26, 52–56, 62–66, 105; and Dai-
yu, 25–26, 40–41, 55–56, 82–83,
115, 119, 122, 129–131
Xue Bao-qin (cousin of Xue Bao-
chai), 118–119, 123
Xue Pan (brother of Xue Bao-chai),
78–79, 120, 153–155

Yan Yu (c. 1180–1235), 140
Yang Guifei, 44, 115
yin and *yang*, 72, 76
Ying-chun (daughter of Jia She),
49–50, 54–55, 90, 105, 114
Ying-ying zhuan. See "Story of Ying-
ying"
You Er-jie (Jia Lian's secondary
wife), 58, 71
You-shi (wife of Jia Zhen), 45–47, 58
Yu, Anthony C., 9, 158n2
Yü Ying-shih, 16

Yuan-chun (the imperial concu-
bine), 31–32, 63, 106–109, 111, 133
Yuan Zhen (779–861), 132
Yuxia ji. See Jade Casket

Zen Buddhism. *See* Chan Buddhism
Zhang Gongyi, 60–61, 169n49
Zhang Xinzhi (fl. 1828–1850), 27,
162n38, 162n1
Zhang You-shi (doctor), 71–73
Zhen/*zhen* (true), 14–16, 23
Zhen Bao-yu, 23–24, 97–98, 161n35
Zhen family, 4, 23, 48–49
Zhen Shi-yin ("true matters con-
cealed"), 14–16, 23, 98, 149–155
Zhen Ying-jia (father of Zhen Bao-
yu), 24
"Zhi-shen at the Monastery Gate,"
126–127
Zhiyan zhai. *See* Red Inkstone
zhiyin. See perfect listener